DOGEN'S GENJO KOAN

Dogen's Genjo Koan

THREE COMMENTARIES

Eihei Dogen Zenji

Translations and commentaries by Nishiari Bokusan,
Shohaku Okamura, Shunryu Suzuki, Kosho Uchiyama,
Sojun Mel Weitsman, Kazuaki Tanahashi,
and Dairyu Michael Wenger

COUNTERPOINT · BERKELEY

Cover design by Gopa & Ted2, Inc
Interior design by Gopa & Ted2, Inc
Printed in the United States of America

COUNTERPOINT
1919 Fifth Street
Berkeley, CA 94710
www.counterpointpress.com

Distributed by Publishers Group West

10 9 8 7 6 5 4 3 2 1

Library of Congress
Cataloging-in-Publication Data

Dogen, 1200-1253.
[Shobo genzo. Genjo koan. English]
Dogen Zenji's Shobogenzo Genjo-koan :
three commentaries / Eihei Dogen Zenji ;
with commentary by Kosho Uchiyama
Roshi ; translated by Shohaku Okumura.
    p. cm.
ISBN 978-1-58243-743-9 (hardback)
1. Dogen, 1200-1253. Shobo genzo. Genjo
koan. 2. Sotoshu—Doctrines. I. Uchiyama,
Kosho, 1912- II. Okumura, Shohaku, 1948-
III. Title.
BQ9449.D654S53213 2011
294.3'85—dc22
2011011248

CONTENTS

INTRODUCTION:

Three commentaries on Dogen's *Genjo koan*

DOGEN AND THE *GENJO KOAN*

ZEN MASTER EIHEI DOGEN (1200–1253), a man of many talents—poet, monk, thinker, and creative essayist—brought Soto Zen from China to Japan. Though he lived but a short time his writings and his enduring presence have had a large and lasting effect, which, if anything, has grown through the years. His collection of essays the *Shobo genzo* (the treasury of the true dharma eye) is currently the most extensively studied East Asian buddhist work in the Western world. Dogen placed the *Genjo koan* as the first essay in the *Shobo genzo*. It has a broad scope, and yet it is full of specific images. It evokes a life dedicated to practice.

The title *Genjo koan* has been translated in many ways: the question of everyday life, actualizing the fundamental point, the matter at hand, the realized law of the universe, manifesting absolute reality, the actualization of enlightenment, manifesting suchness, living what is, according with the truth.

The essay was written in Japanese rather than the more formal classical Chinese and was dedicated to a lay supporter of Dogen's. Its focus on practice in everyday life is what attracts us to it today. How to manifest who we are and who we are becoming is practice.

Genjo koan seeks to address two modalities simultaneously. The first: Don't just do something, sit there; the second: Don't just sit there, do something: being and doing as one.

Dogen's rhetorical writing style is a unique one. He will state something and then either partially or totally contradict it with his next assertion. It's the trajectory of the statements, not any one statement alone, that expresses his understanding. It operates in much the same way that *koan* study does, below the surface of our ordinary discursive mind.

The difficulty of Dogen's writing may be one reason why it was kept in manuscript form in the Soto monasteries (not as a working text, but as a symbolic talisman of transmission) and not circulated outside of Sotoshu circles. It wasn't until 1811 that the *Genjo koan* and the entire *Shobo genzo* were available in print.

The celebrated poet Ryokan (1758–1841), lamenting the unavailability of Dogen's writings, wrote: "For five hundred years it's been covered with dust just because no one has had an eye for recognizing dharma. For whom was all his eloquence expounded? Longing for ancient times and grieving for the present, my heart is exhausted."

THREE MODERN COMMENTARIES ON *GENJO KOAN*

Nishiari Bokusan (1821–1910) was the most prominent Dogen scholar of the Meiji period. A teacher of Oka Sotan and Kishizawa Ian, the author of *Shobo genzo Keiteki*, the opening way of the *Shobo genzo*, he eventually became abbot of Sojiji temple and the head of Soto-Shu. His commentary is the first in this collection. In fact, all of the other commentaries in this volume are in his lineage.

Bokusan said of the *Genjo koan*, "Dogen's . . . entire teaching begins and ends with this essay . . . the other essays are just offshoots of this one." Nishiari Bokusan's importance in modern Japanese study of Dogen led to this translation by Kazuaki Tanahashi and Sojun Weitsman. They translate this work because it is both a traditional commentary and at the same time the focal point of a renewed interest in Japan in Dogen's writings.

Shunryu Suzuki (1904–1971) studied with two teachers who studied with Bokusan: Kishizawa Ian (1865–1955), his textual teacher, and Gyokujin So-on (1877–1934), his transmission teacher. He gave his talks in English. He gave six series of talks to his American students on *Genjo koan* in 1965, 1966, 1967, 1969, 1970, and 1971. Unfortunately, while we have some talks from each series, no series is complete; so they were edited together in order to make a complete commentary. Jeffrey Schneider and I compiled the series into one document, and Sojun Weitsman and I did the final editing of the lectures together. Sojun was ordained by Shunryu Suzuki and received dharma transmission from his son Hoitsu Suzuki. I received dharma transmission from Sojun.

Uchiyama Kosho (1912–1998) received transmission from Sawaki Kodo (1880–1965), who studied with Bokusan). Uchiyama's commentary was written in Japanese and translated by Shohaku Okumura, Uchiyama's disciple.

In the 20th century, the work of Sartre and Heidegger, coupled with a thirst for religious practice, triggered a Western interest in Zen Buddhism and particularly Dogen's writings. Shunryu Suzuki and Uchiyama Kosen are not only respected in Japan but have also been important teachers in spreading Zen practice to the West.

When Sojun, Shohaku, and I realized that we had three unpublished commentaries on a seminal text from these three exemplars of Dogen studies, we felt this book could help introduce the twenty-first century to Eihei Dogen's insight.

Please open your hearts to these great teachers of Soto Zen. May Dogen's and their wisdom and compassion help us in these troubled times.

Dairyu Michael Wenger
Beginners Mind Temple

I.

COMMENTARY BY NISHIARI BOKUSAN

Translated by Sojun Mel Weitsman
and Kazuaki Tanahashi

Translator's Introduction

Nishiari Bokusan, who was also called Kin'ei Nishiari, was born in 1821. He is regarded as an outstanding mainstream Soto Zen scholar of Dogen's *Shobo genzo* from the last half of the nineteenth century. He was active at a time when Soto Zen scholars and practitioners were beginning to study and make generally available Dogen Zenji's *Shobo genzo* after an interval of about 500 years. He was considered one of the leading Dogen scholars of his time and had outstanding disciples, such as Kichizawa Ian, who carried on his work. At that time, translating Dogen into modern Japanese was not an easy task, because thirteenth-century Japanese is to present-day Japanese what Chaucer is to present-day English, with the added difficulty of dealing with Dogen's unique use of the language. Bokusan's student Soei Toyama transcribed his lectures on over sixty fascicles of *Shobo genzo,* but passed away in 1929. In 1965, Kodo Kurabayashi, a student of Soei's, edited his transcripts of Bokusan's lectures on twenty-nine fascicles and published the text as *Shobo genzo Keiteki* (*Shobo Genzo: Right to the Point*), in three volumes, from Daihorin-kaku, Tokyo. *Genjo koan* is one of the fascicles included in *Keiteki.*

The young Shunryu Suzuki, who was born six years before Nishiari's death in 1910, attended lectures on Dogen's *Shobo genzo* given by Nishiari's disciple and Suzuki's second teacher, Kichizawa Ian, whose temple is close to Suzuki Roshi's temple, Rinso-in, in Yaizu, Shizuoka prefecture.

When we read or recall Suzuki Roshi's talks and his teaching, Nishiari's influence becomes apparent in tracing his understanding, style, and presentation from Nishiari through Kichizawa. Suzuki Roshi is just one example of the influence Nishiari had on his generation of practitioners who were interested in understanding Dogen's work.

Nishiari seems to have had a good sense of humor and playfulness, with a down-to-earth, non-dualistic approach, as when he talks about the well-known "firewood and ash" passage. He says, "Go where there is ash and ask, 'Right now you have a very fluffy body. But you used to be called firewood, which was very solid and flammable when put into a fire. You were burned little by little and got yourself to where you are now.' Do you think the ash will agree with this? It will surely reply, 'Nonsense! I have never met anyone called firewood.'" And this: "The principal of thoroughly experiencing one dharma can be understood through the example of beans and tofu. Beans become tofu. From the tofu maker's point of view, beans are boiled and turned into tofu. It appears that beans are before and tofu after. But this is a perspective from outside. If you say to tofu, 'Your former body was a hard material called beans which I boiled, ground, strained, and hardened with nigiri, and now you have a soft body with a rectangular face, so different from your former body,' then tofu would say, 'This is nonsense.' Tofu can never meet beans again. Beans are beans, tofu is tofu. It is not that 'this' turns into 'that,' but there is only one direction at one time; there is only one undivided activity at one time."

Although he was a scholar of Dogen, his understanding emerged from his many years of zazen, strict practice, and deep intuition, working all together in the cauldron of an opened mind. Nishiari seems to have written this commentary when he was 80 years old, as he mentions that people might wonder why an 80-year-old man would still be training monks.

His family name was Sasimoto, which he changed to Nishiari, possibly when he became an acolyte when he was twelve, under Kinryu of the Choryu temple. At nineteen he became the attendant monk to Ten'o Etsuon. At twenty-one he was at the Kichijo Monastery in Edo, and in 1842, he became a dharma heir of Anso Taisen of Honnen Monastery. At thirty he joined Gettan Zenryu at Kaizo Monastery. One day, hearing Gettan lecture on the Surangama Sutra and discussing the phrase "Seeing does not depend on seeing," Bokusan suddenly experienced realization. After that, he had a long, distinguished career as head of many temples, too numerous to mention here. In 1891 he became abbot of the Sojiji Monastery Head Temple. The next year he was made head of the Soto School. He was given the title Jikishin Jokoku by the

Emperor. Every year he alternated this position with Daikyu Doyu, the abbot of Eiheiji Monastery Head Temple. I believe this custom still prevails. He retired in 1905 to Yokohama and died in 1910.

Sojun Mel Weitsman
Abbot, Berkeley Zen Center

AUTHOR'S INTRODUCTION
by Nishiari Bokusan

THIS FASCICLE, *Genjo koan,* is the most difficult of the entire *Shobo genzo (Treasury of the True Dharma Eye).* Even the teachers of old made mistakes and developed distorted views. All of you should open the great vital eye and penetrate Dogen Zenji's words without sparing body or life.

This fascicle is the skin, flesh, bones, and marrow of Dogen. The fundamental teaching of Dogen's lifetime is expounded in this fascicle. The *Buddha dharma* of his entire life is revealed in this work. The ninety-five fascicles of *Shobo genzo* are the offshoots of this fascicle.

In general, when the old teachers presented their essential teaching, they each had one phrase that none of their predecessors had chosen, and on which they based their teaching. With this phrase they penetrated a whole lifetime. Teachers in the past did not have two phrases. Therefore, that one phrase expressed their Dharmakaya. For example, the "One Bright Jewel" of Xuansha, the "Cypress Tree" of Zhaozou, and "This very mind is Buddha" of Mazu are all words of iron never spoken by anyone before. With one phrase they thrust forward the suchness of the cosmos, and set in motion the same wheel of dharma as the Buddha.

The same thing can be said of Dogen. He sees straight through the world of the ten directions as *Genjo koan,* which are his words of iron. When this phrase is cracked, the ninety-five fascicles appear here and there as branches of it. For that reason, the lifetime teaching of Dogen is all in the one phrase, *Genjo koan.* So, this fascicle is placed first in the seventy-five–fascicle version of *Shobo genzo,* edited by Zen Master Ejo. It was done under the supervision of Dogen, who had the vision for the basic teaching of the school.

Bendowa (On the Endeavor of the Way), on the other hand, is placed first in the ninety-five–fascicle version, which is most commonly read now. This version is arranged according to the dates when the fascicles were first expounded. We can see why Dogen expounded *Bendowa* first when we think about this compassionate heart that raised the teaching of correctly transmitted samadhi in Japan, where Zen was not yet spread. However, it is in *Genjo koan* that Dogen opened up his body and mind and presented the foundation of the Buddha's lifetime dharma.

Thus Dogen Zenji concentrated his mind wholeheartedly on this fascicle, dividing it into fourteen sections, explaining it in detail. Both the style and the teaching are exquisitely profound and subtle. Therefore you who are his dharma descendants should read this fascicle day and night with respect and make it the root of your practice, birth after birth, world after world.

Then what in the world is *"Genjo koan"*? First of all, you should get it right down in your *hara*. This cannot be done solely by thinking. On the other hand, you cannot grasp it without knowing the basic principle. So first I will explain it for the moment in an analytical fashion.

Genjo koan is the original self-nature of the universal dharma realm as it is. This dharma realm is immeasurable and limitless. It contains past and present, the three worlds, the ten directions, delusions, enlightenment, all buddhas, sentient beings, birth, and death. It also contains all other things. Each and every dharma element turns into being, emptiness, liberation, and ultimate reality.

Being is *Genjo koan* as being. Emptiness is *Genjo koan* as emptiness. Nirvana is *Genjo koan* as nirvana.

In brief, concerning delusion and enlightenment, ordinary people try to get to enlightenment by sweeping away delusion. They may think delusion is false existence and enlightenment is true existence. The *Genjo koan* that is meant here is otherwise. Among all beings, there is not a single existence that is a mistake. Delusion is the *Genjo koan* of delusion. It is not that we have enlightenment by excluding delusion. Enlightenment is the *Genjo koan* of enlightenment. It is not that we slip out of enlightenment and fall into delusion.

Generally speaking, in all directions the big cannot contain the small. The long cannot contain the short. Each and every dharma element is itself ultimate reality. Even a single particle is immovable and does not admit the slightest slippage. The entire world, as it is, is what is called *Genjo koan*.

Therefore, *Genjo koan* is the dharma road for the entire world. Discrimination and non-discrimination are both *Genjo koan*. To say "non-discrimination" is *Genjo koan*, because it is the dharma realm of non-duality, and the world of discrimination is not, because it is the mind of measuring thought is not *Genjo koan*.

Each and every element of the discriminated world is itself *Genjo koan*. The discriminated has a thousand types and ten thousand kinds. For those who are enlightened it is not sufficient to call enlightenment the whole body of the dharma realm. To those who are deluded it is delusion all the way to the bottom of the Avici Hell. When we see with the discriminating mind, the distance between enlightenment and delusion appears to be like that between heaven and deep water. So we exhaust ourselves in oscillating between the true and the false.

The *Genjo koan* here is such that we do not exclude false views, nor do we seek the true. Those who are deluded are deluded within *Genjo koan*. In all dharmas there is no lack; they cannot be broken, obtained, or thrown away. The original face, the original nature as it is, is called *Genjo koan*.

Therefore, "All dharmas are ultimate reality," as spoken by Shakyamuni Buddha and "One Bright Pearl," as spoken by Xuansha, are like this. The conclusion of the Shobo's lifetime teaching is "All dharmas are ultimate reality." The *Genjo koan* spoken here is the expression of the meaning of this ultimate reality as spoken by the Shobo.

Now, in what sense is *Genjo koan* the dharma road of the entire world? I will now talk about each separate ideogram of the words *Genjo koan*.

As for *gen*, it usually refers to an appearance that has been hidden as in *genzen* (surface appearance) or *genzai* (present being). But that is not how it is meant here in *Genjo koan*. The *gen* spoken of here is not the *gen* that is related to hiding or appearing, remaining or perishing. There is neither hiding nor appearing in the true genjo. When we say that a hidden thing appears, it usually refers to the appearance or gen that is relative to hiding. In this dualistic sense, it is the phenomenon of birth and death. But actually, in the realm of the true genjo, there is no hiding. Thus there is no appearing.

The "eyes horizontal and nose vertical" of every person is bright and clear. There is nothing to hide, so there is nothing to reveal. The genjo that is meant here is like this. A great secret is greatly apparent. What is greatly apparent is a great secret. What can be merely hidden or revealed is not true genjo. When we say there is no hiding or appearing, it means that there is no arising or perishing, no increasing or decreasing. The dharma realm of heaven and earth, as it is, extends from the Kashyapa Buddha in the past to Maitreya Buddha in the future, unceasingly through past, present, and future, regardless of the creation or destruction of the world. This is *gen*.

Next, "*jo*" means completion. Usually when something is given its form, we call it completion. But that is not what is meant here. That which is not confined to integration and disintegration is called complete here. That which is immediately present is itself completion. The reason is that all dharmas that appear and fulfill themselves are essentially beyond birth and death, or coming and going.

In the *Heart Sutra* it says, "There is no birth, no death, no defilement, no purity . . ." No dharmas have been created by buddhas, devas, human beings, or asuras. All dharmas are complete of themselves in the original face. They are free from integration or disintegration.

Ko means impartiality and fairness. Large is not small. Long is not short. A plateau is high and flat. A plain is low and flat. All dharmas dwell in their dharma positions. They do not hinder one another; things are as they are and their original nature is nirvana. This is "*ko*."

The three characters *gen*, *jo*, and *ko*, although their meanings are different, refer to one thing. Because of *genjo*, things are originally complete; because they are originally complete they are level and equal.

An means to hold, or to bear the three qualities—*gen*, *jo*, and *ko*—without losing them.

This is the meaning of these characters, but among them *koan* means law or government. A nation has a government, as does a region or a village. Where there is government, there is law. When the law is established it cannot be reversed. No one can change it. This is *koan*.

It is important that it cannot be moved or changed. Then what is koan? The *dharmadhatu* has nothing to do with large or small, superior or inferior. Even a single particle of dust cannot be removed. Why not? Because the *dharmadhatu* is as it is. Since it is as it is, it never moves. Think of a mountain; a mountain cannot be moved. Think of an ocean;

an ocean cannot be moved. All dharmas are like this. They can never be changed. This is called *koan*.

Upon hearing this, you might say, "No, you can change a mountain if you crumble it; an ocean can be a plain if you fill it with earth; a fool can become a wise person and a wise person can become a fool." But that's foolish; however you crumble a mountain, it will never move. A mountain is like a long piece of iron and cannot be moved. However you fill an ocean, it can never be moved. An ocean is an ocean, which is a long piece of iron. Not only a mountain or an ocean but everything is like this.

Those who are deluded are deluded and those who are enlightened are enlightened. This is *koan*. To turn delusion into enlightenment is not *koan*. If we go along the road of delusion, we will certainly be deluded. This is *Genjo koan*. If we go along the road of enlightenment, we will certainly be enlightened. This is *Genjo koan*.

There are ways for us to be deluded today. We cannot say that it is not so. For that reason, delusion and enlightenment are natural things that we can never change. There is only the fact that those who are deluded are deluded and those who are enlightened are enlightened. This is *Genjo koan*.

Not only delusion and enlightenment but appearance and reality as well as essence and form are like this. To hold the dharmas of genjo as genjo, without contriving, without causing increase or decrease, throughout past, present, and future, without changing or turning, is *Genjo koan*. It is nothing but "All dharmas themselves are ultimate reality."

Priest Honko says about *Genjo koan*, "Study with your hands in shashu[1] over your chest." Honko was an outstanding person in the ancestral Soto lineage, a person with complete practice and comprehension. He summarized the essence in this way. The fact is that *Genjo koan* is not something speech can reach. It is just shashu upon your chest, just this total activity. There is no other way but to understand it as it is and accept it as it is.

Speech and reasoning promote discrimination; where there is

---

1 Shashu is the right hand wrapped around the left hand at chest level with the forearms haeld parallel to the floor when doing walking meditation or standing in the zendo.

discrimination, there are picking and discarding. What is confined by picking up and discarding is in the realm of construction. It is not *koan*. Nonconstruction is *Genjo koan*. In order to accept [things as they are], within the realm of nonconstruction, there is no other way than shashu upon your chest. Honko was a master indeed.

If we knead it like this, *Genjo koan* reveals all things as ultimate reality. And all things as ultimate reality are shashu upon your chest. It is, "Stop asking for discourse. My dharma is wondrous and impossible to think about." If we examine the right aspects of all dharmas, they are all like that.

If we raise the thought of a hungry ghost, we take the path of the hungry ghosts. If we raise the thought of an ashura, we take the path of the fighting spirits. It is not that the Buddha handmade the path of the hungry ghosts or fighting spirits. It is not that hell was created by King Yama in his court. You put yourself on trial and send yourself to where you choose to go. Water goes down and fire goes up. When you are deluded you become an ordinary person, and when you are enlightened you become a buddha. This is *Genjo koan*.

A mountain is high from the beginning, and there is no construction. Likewise, *Genjo koan* cannot be constructed. It is hot in summer and cold in winter. When the conditions are right, there is birth. When the conditions are spent, there is death. This is *Genjo koan*. A wholesome cause brings forth a wholesome effect, and an unwholesome cause brings forth an unwholesome effect. This is *Genjo koan*. This is an elevated point of view.

It's a big mistake to try to construct enlightenment with your own hands. This cannot be understood unless you have a penetrating eye, free from delusion and enlightenment. Regardless of delusion or enlightenment, the actual aspect of all dharmas is *Genjo koan*. Even though at present you may be deluded, you should make an effort to step outside of delusion and enlightenment and see straight forward.

Now it is a shame that so many people view the essential teaching of Dogen Zenji with small eyes. Be more expansive! Be like the roof covering the monks' hall! Look up there! It doesn't concern itself about whether you are a deluded person, an enlightened person, a sleeping monk, or a great priest. It glares at you with baggy eyes. Your every day should be like the state of that roof. If you are stuck on your desire to be enlightened, you will never get to the essential teaching of Dogen Zenji.

Let me add a few words on the major commentaries of *Shobo genzo* by Dogen's dharma descendants. They are:

Shobo genzo Gosho by Sen'e, 1303–1308

Shobo genzo Monge by Menzan, 1760s

Shobo genzo Shiki by Zokai, c.1779

Shobo genzo Sanchu (Kyakutai Ichijisan) by Honko, 1793

Among these, *Gosho* (*Selected Commentaries*) is an old one, and the three others came later. *Gosho* is precious as it is based on Sen'e's direct hearing of Dogen Zenji's teisho. It is special.

Next is *Monge* (*Hearing and Understanding*), which gives a painstaking, detailed explanation. But there are points where sermonizing takes over and strays from the essential teaching. Besides this, there are statements in his commentary that we can't agree with. I am afraid that Master Menzan, with his grandmotherly solicitude, sometimes focused too much on the literal meaning, which seems to be a shortcoming of his book. However, it is an essential commentary that should not be missed as a guide for beginners.

Master Honko being a scholar, his commentary *Sanchu* (*Study Notes*), written in Chinese, has a more sophisticated approach. Zokai corrected mistakes in Honko's *Sanchu* and made it more accessible in a book called *Shiki* (*Personal Comments*). Since *Shiki* is more recent, it is more complete. Though it is faultless in outlining the essential teaching, it is not so helpful in interpreting specific sentences. The explanation is sometimes overextended and loses touch with the original meaning. To put it strongly, it has a tendency to insist on the commentator's own teaching apart from *Shobo genzo*. Therefore, although it is of high quality in its explanation of the essential teaching, it is distressing for beginners.

There are the individual characteristics of the three major commentaries of the Edo Period—*Monge*, *Shiki*, and *Sanchu*. When you read *Shobo genzo,* you should put these three commentaries side by side and compare.

Besides these commentaries, there is *Benchu* (*Critical Notes*) by Master Tenkei, 1730. His commentary is the most controversial. With his exceptional views, independent of all the earlier commentaries, Tenkei speaks in a never-ending torrent of crushing force, attending to every doubtful point and anticipating every problem. This is a characteristic of *Benchu* that is absent from other commentaries. However, his views are so extreme that they seem destructive. His commentary on the fascicles of "Menju" and "Shisho" of *Shobo genzo* is undoubtedly heretical, for which Master Otsudo attacked him severely in *Zokugen Kogi* (*One Continuous Thread*), 1731, with which I concur. Although Master Tenkei certainly read extensively, he did not know much about this aspect of teaching. On the other hand, Master Otsudo was an outstanding student of the famous Hotan and was well versed in the essential teaching. He was able to point out and criticize every part of *Benchu* that was not consistent with the teaching or was not one with the Buddha's mind.

These are some things you should be aware of. An extraordinary and assertive figure, Tenkei is still condemned nowadays by many people. In spite of the fact that he produced extensive writings, he is regarded as a heretic by those with discerning eyes in the Soto School. Why is that so? Because his abusive style is so vigorous. It is meant to slander and defame others. By doing so your virtue is lost. It is better to directly present what you have clarified out of the desire to benefit and give joy to sentient beings. Tenkei gave no essential teaching concerning actual practice in his lifetime. He has only his unscrupulous, abusive style. That is why he is not read today.

On the other hand, Menzan is thorough and detailed. There is no one to compare with him in his thoroughgoing attitude that "Manners themselves are the essential teaching." So in connection with the instruction for our day, Menzan is irreplaceable. However, it is Honko who went beyond him to explain the complete unity of actual and principle. It means not falling into the actual aspect and not falling into the theoretical aspect. His teaching contains no perverted views and no hindrances; the essential teaching is straight and true. He is unique in both past and present.

Tenkei is said to be a great person but not a gracious person. This should be carefully noted. Only a person who explains the essential teaching through the complete unity of actual and principle can be called a real master of the school. There are various other commentaries, but these three—*Monge*, *Shiki*, and *Sanchu*—are the only ones that cover all the ninety-five fascicles.

Prologue

When all dharmas are Buddha dharma, *there are delusion, realization, practice, birth and death, buddhas and sentient beings.*

When the myriad dharmas are without a self, there is no delusion, no realization, no buddha, no sentient being, no birth and death.

The Buddha Way, basically, is leaping clear of abundance and lack; thus there are birth and death, delusion and realization, sentient beings and buddhas. Yet in attachment blossoms just fall, and in aversion weeds just spread. (Sections 1–3)

P AY ATTENTION to this opening statement, which embodies the essence of the entire *Genjo koan*. When this is opened up, the fourteen-section *Genjo koan* is actualized. People in the past broke their bones working on this.

The first thing you should notice is that this section consists of three segments. The first segment is, "When all dharmas are *Buddha dharma* . . . ," the second section, "When the myriad dharmas are without self . . . ," and the third section, "The Buddha Way, basically, is leaping clear of abundance and lack. . ." This is the Dharma Gate of three steps.

Regarding these three steps, what should not be forgotten is the title *Genjo koan*. Dogen Zenji presented these steps with the idea that each of the three steps is *Genjo koan*. So if we elaborate his writing by interpreting his intention, it will be like: "When all dharmas are *Buddha dharma* . . . this is *Genjo koan*." "When the myriad dharmas are without self . . . this is *Genjo koan*." "The Buddha Way, in essence, is leaping clear . . . this too is *Genjo koan*."

Since his writing develops from "When all dharmas are *Buddha dharma*" to "leaping clear of abundance and lack," it might appear through superficial understanding that the earlier line is shallow, and the later line is deeper. It might appear that the first step is ephemeral and the last step is real.

For the time being, if we regard the first step as the characterization of existence and the second step as the characterization of emptiness, then it could appear that existence and nonexistence are both ephemeral, which is not discussed in *Buddha dharma*, and the third step, which is transcendence of existence and nonexistence, is the settling place of *Buddha dharma*.

However, that is not so. In terms of *Genjo koan*, existence-nonexistence, and transcending existence and nonexistence, are eight ryo and half a kin (weight measures) and are equally *Genjo koan*. This nonexistence is not nonexistence that is separate from existence. It is nonexistence that is itself *Genjo koan*. The same can be said about existence. It is not existence that is separate from nonexistence. So it is existence no other than *Genjo koan*.

In this way, when we say transcending existence and nonexistence, it is not transcendence outside of existence and nonexistence. The totality of existence and nonexistence is called transcendence of existence and nonexistence. Therefore, Dogen Zenji's understanding is that at the time of being, it is the entire *dharmadhatu* of being that is the *Genjo koan*. At the time of transcendence, it is the entire *dharmadhatu*, which is *Genjo koan*.

Within *Genjo koan* there is an aspect that is seen as being, there is an aspect that is seen as non-being, and there is an aspect that appears as transcendence of being and non-being. In other words, we see *dharmadhatu* from the back, from the front, and see them together as one. All these are aspects of *Genjo koan*.

As a guide, to illuminate these aspects of *Genjo koan*, this part is divided and presented in three steps. Therefore being, non-being, and transcendence are each the entire world and *Genjo koan*. It is the same as "All dharmas are themselves the true mark." It is "the form of unconditioned nature," or it is "the dharma of one vehicle is neither two nor three" as said in the *Lotus Sutra*.

The bull's-eye of *Genjo koan*, which misses nothing in seeing through the past and present of the entire world at a glance, is explained in the three sections. Therefore, shallow, deep, high, or low are not discussed in these three steps. Being and non-being are being and non-being within *Genjo koan*. Therefore, delusion, enlightenment, sentient beings, and buddhas are also within *Genjo koan*. They are not delusion, enlightenment, sentient beings, and buddhas as they are usually understood. For that reason, you should not miss that the settling point of each of the three steps is *Genjo koan*, without making distinctions between shallow and deep.

ACTUALIZING THE FUNDAMENTAL POINT

Genjo Koan

1

When all dharmas are Buddha dharma, there are delusion, realization, practice, birth and death, buddhas and sentient beings.

2

When the myriad dharmas are without a self, there is no delusion, no realization, no Buddha, no sentient being, no birth and death.

3

The Buddha Way, basically, is leaping clear of abundance and lack; thus there are birth and death, delusion and realization, sentient beings and buddhas. Yet in attachment blossoms just fall, and in aversion weeds just spread.

4

To carry the self forward and illuminate myriad dharmas is delusion. That myriad dharmas come forth and illuminate the self is enlightenment.

5

Those who have great realization of delusion are buddhas; those who are greatly deluded about realization are sentient beings. Further, there are those who continue realizing beyond realization, who are in delusion through delusion.

6

When buddhas are truly buddhas, they do not necessarily notice that they are buddhas. However, they are actualized buddhas, who go on actualizing Buddha.

7

When you see forms or hear sounds fully engaging body-and-mind, you intuit dharmas intimately. Unlike things and their reflections in the mirror, and unlike the moon and its reflection in the water, when one side is illuminated, the other side is dark.

8

To study the Buddha Way is to study the self. To study the self is to forget the self. To forget the self is to be actualized by myriad things. When actualized by myriad things, your body and mind as well as the bodies and minds of others drop away. No trace of enlightenment remains, and this no-trace continues endlessly.

9

When you first seek dharma, you imagine you are far away from its environs. At the moment when dharma is correctly transmitted, you are immediately your original self.

10

When you ride in a boat and watch the shore, you might assume that the shore is moving. But when you keep your eyes closely on the boat, you can see that the boat moves. Similarly, if you examine myriad things with a confused body and mind you might suppose that your mind and nature are permanent. When you practice intimately and return to where you are, it will be clear that nothing at all has unchanging self.

10B

Firewood becomes ash, and it does not become firewood again. Yet, do not suppose that the ash is after and the firewood before. You should understand that firewood abides in the phenomenal expression of firewood, which fully includes before and after and is independent of before and after. Ash abides in the phenomenal expression of ash, which fully includes before and after. Just as firewood does not become firewood again after it is ash, you do not return to birth after death.

This being so, it is an established way in *Buddha dharma* to deny that birth turns into death. Accordingly, birth is understood as no-birth. It is an unshakable teaching in Buddha's discourse that death does not turn into birth. Accordingly, death is understood as no-death.

Birth is an expression complete this moment. Death is an expression complete this moment. They are like winter and spring. You do not call winter the beginning of spring, nor summer the end of spring.

11

Enlightenment is like the moon reflected on the water. The moon does not get wet, nor is the water broken. Although its light is wide and great, the moon is reflected even in a puddle an inch wide. The whole moon and the entire sky are reflected in dewdrops on the grass, or even in one drop of water.

Enlightenment does not divide you, just as the moon does not break the water. You cannot hinder enlightenment, just as a drop of water does not hinder the moon in the sky.

The depth of the drop is the height of the moon. Each reflection, however long or short its duration, manifests the vastness of the dewdrop, and realizes the limitlessness of the moonlight in the sky.

12

When dharma does not fill your whole body and mind, you may assume it is already sufficient. When dharma fills your body and mind, you understand that something is missing.

For example, when you sail out in a boat to the middle of an ocean where no land is in sight, and view the four directions, the ocean looks circular, and does not look any other way. But the ocean is neither round nor square; its features are infinite in variety. It is like a palace. It is like a jewel. It only looks circular as far as you can see at that time. All things are like this.

Though there are many features in the dusty world and the world beyond conditions, you see and understand only what your eye of practice can reach. In order to learn the nature of the myriad things, you must know that although they may look round or square, the other features of oceans and mountains are infinite in variety; whole worlds are there. It is so not only around you, but also directly beneath your feet, or in a drop of water.

13

A fish swims in the ocean, and no matter how far it swims there is no end to the water. A bird flies in the sky, and no mater how far it flies there is no end to the sky. However, the fish and the bird have never left their elements. When their activity is large their field is large. When their need is small their field is small. Thus, each of them totally covers its full range, and each of them totally experiences its realm. If the bird leaves the air it will die at once. If the fish leaves the water it will die at once.

Know that water is life and air is life. The bird is life and the fish is life. Life must be the bird and life must be the fish.

Besides this, further steps can be taken. Thus there are practice and enlightenment, which encompass both eternal life and limited life.

Now if a bird or a fish tries to reach the end of its element before moving in it, this bird or this fish will not find its way or its place. When you find your place where you are, practice occurs, actualizing the fundamental point; for the place, the Way, is neither large nor small, neither yours nor others'. The place, the Way, has not carried over from the past, and it is not merely arising now.

Accordingly, in the practice-enlightenment of the Buddha Way, to attain one dharma is to penetrate one dharma, to meet one practice is to sustain one practice.

Here is the place; here the Way unfolds. The boundary of realization is not distinct, for the realization comes forth simultaneously with the mastery of *Buddha dharma*.

14

Do not suppose that what you attain becomes your knowledge and is grasped by your consciousness. Although actualized immediately, the inconceivable may not be apparent. Its appearance is beyond your knowledge.

Zen Master Baoche of Mount Mayu was fanning himself. A monk approached and said, "Master, the nature of wind is permanent and there is no place it does not reach. Why, then, do you fan yourself?"

"Although you understand that the nature of the wind is permanent," Baoche replied, "you do not understand the meaning of its reaching everywhere."

"What is the meaning of its reaching everywhere?" asked the monk again. The master just kept fanning himself. The monk bowed deeply.

The actualization of the *Buddha dharma,* the vital path of its correct transmission, is like this. If you say that you do not need to fan yourself because the nature of wind is permanent and can have wind without fanning, you will understand neither permanence nor the nature of wind. The nature of wind is permanent; because of that, the wind of Buddha's house brings forth the gold of the earth and makes fragrant the cream of the long river.

Written in mid-autumn, the first year of Tempuku [1233], and given to my lay student Koshju Yo of Kyushu Island. [Revised in] the fourth year of Kencho [1252].

Text translated by Robert Aitken and Kazuaki Tanahashi
Revised at San Francisco Zen Center

COMMENTARY ON THE *GENJO KOAN*

SECTION 1

When all dharmas are Buddha dharma, there are delusion, realization, practice, birth and death, buddhas and sentient beings.

YOU MAY THINK, "What a funny thing! If all dharmas are the *Buddha dharma*, there should not be birth or death or delusion or enlightenment." You may think, "It is funny to say, there is. . . ," but it is not so.

Because this is a time when all buddhas in the *Buddha dharma* are *Buddha dharma*, invariably it is *Genjo koan*. There is not a single dharma that is extra when all dharmas are *Buddha dharma*. For that reason, you should fully experience that when all dharmas are *Buddha dharma*, "all dharmas are *Buddha dharma*."

When you try to figure out "At the time when all dharmas are *Genjo koan*," you already fall into interpretation. It does not reach to your *hara* (belly). The reason is that you are holding something there that is not helpful for the practice of the Way. You should first clean it up and make it empty in order to be receptive. Don't think that you can brew sake without squeezing water out of the steamed rice.

Think deeply. As all dharmas are *Buddha dharma*, there are delusion and enlightenment. It is a common view to presume that there is no delusion or enlightenment "at the time" of *Buddha dharma*. However, just because delusion and enlightenment are within the *Buddha dharma*, it is said that "at the time when all dharmas are *Buddha dharma*, there are delusion and enlightenment, practice. . ."

How about it? Maintain a broad view that includes sentient beings and buddhas—delusion and enlightenment. The entire *dharmadhatu*, including heaven and earth, is "at the time" of *Buddha dharma*. *Buddha dharma* is not so small-minded that it would say, "I don't like such and such a thing," and retire to a house on a back street.

There are birth and death, and there are delusion and enlightenment. You see heaven and earth as heaven and earth, and all dharmas as all dharmas. That is *Genjo koan* that includes delusion, enlightenment, and practice. Where there is delusion there is practice. Where there are sentient beings there are buddhas. Where there is birth there is death. It is the place where there is no "I." It is the place where you see each and every thing as *Buddha dharma*.

SECTION 2

When the myriad dharmas are without a self, there is no delusion, no realization, no buddha, no sentient being, no birth and death.

The myriad dharmas or myriad dharmas that are mentioned here are the same as all dharmas as mentioned in the beginning. It is a general term for the entire *dharmadhatu*.

The "self" mentioned here is not our "self" as we usually conceive of it. It is a self of the myriad dharmas. Then what are the selves of the myriad dharmas? We say pines or bamboo or mountains or rivers. They are all selves. Why are they selves? A mountain is the self of a mountain; you cannot call a mountain a "river." A river is the self of a river; you cannot call a river a "mountain." Each of the myriad dharmas has a self.

But now it is said, "At the time when myriad dharmas are without self." Here the principle of the myriad dharmas as having no self is expounded. Study carefully this no-self of the myriad dharmas. This is truly the *Genjo koan*. In whatever you see there is no self.

To say "you" or "I" is relative. When we say, "the *dharmadhatu* is just one person" there is no you and no I. We say pines and bamboo, mountains and rivers. Although there is originally no self-nature, we call something standing steadfastly high a "mountain." And we call someplace where water flows abundantly in a long way a "river." In this way a name is what we use for convenience, and it is, of course, arbitrary.

All names are arbitrary names, and all dharmas are arbitrary dharmas. They are only a compound of conditions. We say "you" in relation to "I." When we say "I," it is nothing but "I," however much we try to make of it. There appears to be a substantial being that is called "I," but it is merely a compound of conditions. "You" are also merely a compound of various conditions. The Buddha explained this as "all beings are without self."

Truly all beings have no aspect of "self." If we examine the actual bodies of the myriad dharmas, none of them has a self-nature. A mountain is liberated from a mountain. If we take away earth, rocks, and pebbles, there is no mountain. An ocean is liberated from an ocean. If we take away fish, shells, plants, boats, and oars, there is no ocean.

When we say "the empire of Japan," it sounds great. But it is only the assemblage of the four classes of people. If we take the people away, there is no Japan. If we remove the unbroken line of emperors, or the Japanese spirit, there is no such thing as Japan. It doesn't matter if Western people come and settle here. Mount Fuji will not go somewhere else, disliking Western people. Or if Mount Fuji goes to Formosa, Formosa won't get angry and step aside.

The reason is that the myriad dharmas are conjoined with various conditions, and have no aspect of self. Just as the myriad dharmas are of no self-nature, people are of no self-nature. Just as people are of no self-nature, those who have infinite life and those who have finite life are also of no self-nature. After all, the entire *dharmadhatu* is of no self-nature and ungraspable. This principle of unconditioned no self-nature is explained as "when myriad dharmas are without self."

This is what is called "Self always has the mark of Nirvana" in the *Lotus Sutra*. The myriad forms and appearances stand side by side, immeasurable and without limit. No single set of antlers is especially distinguished. The essential nature of all things is the actualization of emptiness in Nirvana.

At this time there is no delusion or enlightenment, and there are no sentient beings and buddhas, no birth and death. They exist, but they exist completely. There is not one thing that is not nirvana. This is true of sentient beings and buddhas, delusion and enlightenment. It is true of eternity and the present moment, ascending and descending. In this regard the teachers of old say, "The dojo of the moon on water," or, "attaining the fruit of buddhahood in a dream." Nanyue said, "What is it that comes in this way?" Those who have attained can express it in any way they like.

Then why are the parts of being and emptiness—sections 1 and 2—shown in parallel? The reason is that just this is truly *Genjo koan*. Being and non-being, form and emptiness are both just as they are. There is an aspect of "being" and there is an aspect of "emptiness" in the context of *Genjo koan*. This is a matter of dharmas just as they are, and this is a koan without self. It appears to be a substantial form if we look at it from the front side, and it appears to be in the form of absolute stillness if we look at it from the back side. Things actualize openly and clearly as Nirvana. All dharmas are actualization.

All bottoms are dropped. This is truly the place of myriad dharmas where there is no self, just this without tipping the scale. For that reason, in *Genjo koan* there is a principle of form and emptiness and being and non-being. However, we don't regard the view of form and emptiness, or being and non-being, as *Genjo koan*. As this is the face of the *Buddha dharma,* thusness of the *dharmadhatu,* Dogen Zenji clearly put form and emptiness in order and demonstrated them to us.

Now these three sections are actually the bone and marrow of the *Buddha dharma*. Buddha's lifetime discourse does not go beyond the heart of these three sections. We must grasp the meaning of the *Buddha dharma* around this point. If you don't get this point, you'll misunderstand and take it as an ordinary view of negation versus affirmation. At this point, we can say these two sections bring forth being and non-being, or sentient beings and buddhas, in the context of *Genjo koan*.

SECTION 3

The Buddha Way, basically, is leaping clear of abundance and lack; thus there are birth and death, delusion and realization, sentient beings and buddhas. Yet in attachment blossoms just fall, and in aversion weeds just spread.

As being and emptiness were expounded in the last sections, transcendence of being and non-being are expounded in this section. But as I said before, it looks as if the approach is from shallow to deep. But it is not so.

For Dogen Zenji, transcendence is not apart from being and non-being. Rather, being and non-being are directly called transcendence.

But if we only say being and non-being, the meaning of this transcendence is not heard. For that reason he says "leaping clear of abundance and lack." But in fact being and non-being are all transcendent. This is a point that is very different from ordinary being and non-being, or annihilation and permanence. This is Buddha's intention and Buddha's road.

In the *Lotus Sutra,* Shakyamuni Buddha said, "All dharmas bear the true mark of reality" or "the mark of nirvana." Or "there is only one vehicle of dharma, not two, not three." These three sections of *Genjo koan* by Dogen Zenji are not a bit different from this buddha-road. Here is the koan that does not decay for a thousand years. So keep this well in your mind, and study the words.

Now "the Buddha Way" is nothing but *Genjo koan*. *Genjo koan* is nothing but the entire world. After all, no matter how we describe it, these words point to the entire world. When we talk about the Buddha Way, all dharmas, and myriad dharmas, they are the same. "Abundance and lack" are being and non-being, or form and emptiness. Abundance means that there are many dharmas, which is the gate of accumulation. Lack means scarcity. That is, to crush dharmas or decrease them, which is the gate of sweeping away or wiping out. Thus, being and non-being, or form and emptiness, are summarized with two words: "abundance and lack." However, the *Genjo koan* now comes off and jumps through the realm of being and non-being, form and emptiness, fullness and scarcity, without stagnating anywhere. This is the bones and marrow of Buddha's Way. This is the realm where "there are birth and death, delusion and realization."

Now here is where thorough study is necessary. In the Tendai School it is said, "The middle road of mutual shade and mutual illumination," but it is not enough to say this. You must actually practice it.

Form, emptiness, being, and non-being are *Genjo koan*, and are the great dynamic function of the universe. Both sentient and nonsentient beings receive it, grow, and develop. Not only is it not a bad thing, it is a necessary thing. The Buddha Way does not fall into form, and does not fall into emptiness. There is a point at which you jump off both form and emptiness, and do not abide there. You must see through this. That is practice.

Form-and-emptiness are necessary. But if we abide in either, it is not "the Buddha Way." The Buddha Way does not stay on the side of form or emptiness, being or non-being. For that reason, we say, "transcendence." So in transcendence, there is definitely form and emptiness. This is *Genjo koan*.

When we talk about transcending being and non-being, we might think that we go outside of being and non-being. When we say, "leaving the three worlds," we might think that our mind will find ease when we get outside. But it is not so. It is living within the three worlds as they are. It is transcendence within being and non-being just as they are.

At the time when we see all dharmas as all dharmas, we will not fall into being and non-being. The reason is that being is free from being, and emptiness is free from emptiness. As being is free from being, it is a real being. As emptiness is free from emptiness, it is true emptiness. Thus, all dharmas have the face and eyes of going beyond as dharmas suchness.

"Form is itself emptiness" in the *Heart Sutra* hits the point. Ordinarily people fall into a view of being, followers of the Two Vehicles sink into a view of emptiness, and people outside the Way stagnate in ideas of annihilation and permanence. Holding such views, dharmas never becomes dharmas. On the other hand, Buddha Way is transcendence of being and non-being.

The word "empty" is used in various contexts in the *Heart Sutra*. First it says, "The five skandhas are all empty." You may think then that it is only the five skandhas that are empty. Next it is explained by bundling form together with emptiness, that "form is not different from emptiness." Still, form and emptiness look like two separate dharmas. So it is explained that form is itself emptiness. This should be enough. But still there are the words "form" and "emptiness," and we are somehow attracted to that.

Then, in the fascicle of *Mahaprajnaparamita* of *Shobo genzo*, Dogen Zenji says, "Form is emptiness. So are one hundred grasses, myriad forms."

Now we need to go beyond this point by all means. Ordinarily a person will try to determine the entire *dharmadhatu* from the perspective of either being or non-being. But that falls short. In general the *dharmadhatu* is neither being nor non-being. Because it is neither, being manifests as being, and non-being manifests as non-being. This is clearly the principle that being and non-being are liberated from being and non-being, and the essential characteristic of being and non-being is going beyond.

At this point, let's look at the *dharmadhatu* as one pillar. This pillar is neither being nor non-being, but it is a pillar that goes beyond being and non-being. There is no way to find fault with this. But those who see, hear, and conceptualize tend to see being and non-being separately, and form and emptiness separately. Then two pillars emerge. These two pillars are obviously the two views of annihilation and permanence. That is not *Genjo koan*. That is not the whole mark of dharmas.

When we see through, that form is itself emptiness, there emerge the face and eyes of going beyond that do not stay within being or non-being of all dharmas. At this time, the *dharmadhatu* is just one pillar. The *Heart Sutra* says, "No hindrance . . . no hindrance." In this way, *Mahaprajnaparamita* uses being and non-being, freely going beyond being and non-being. This understanding is what we need today. In one sentence there is included practice, enlightenment, freedom, and the liberated body.

The words of High Ancestor Dogen are like this. Although being and non-being are *Genjo koan*, and being and non-being are originally going beyond, he talks about the further going beyond of being and non-being. This point is the entirety of the *Buddha dharma*. All of us need to find the power to penetrate here.

"The Buddha Way is, basically, leaping clear of abundance and lack; thus there are birth and death, delusion and realization, sentient beings and buddhas."

Dogen Zenji attained great liberation with the phrase "body and mind dropped off." "Leaping clear of abundance and lack" is Dogen Zenji's body and mind dropped off. "No hindrance" is Dogen Zenji's body and mind dropped off.

To attain this freedom is the pivotal point here. You may think, though, that the distinction between sentient beings and buddhas, delusion and enlightenment, and the coming and going of birth and death has ceased for a time, because *Buddha dharma* is beyond being and non-being. Then what about "there are . . . delusion and realization, sentient beings and buddhas"?

It is all right to understand in this way, because in going beyond, there are such dharmas. As I mentioned before, because being goes beyond being, it is true being, and because emptiness goes beyond emptiness, it is true emptiness. Because of going beyond, all dharmas are true dharmas.

The reason lotus flowers are not stained with mud is that they are free within mud. If they remove themselves from mud and go to a field, they will become dried out. But what would happen if the lotus flowers are stuck in the mud? Then they cannot give forth their fragrance. Now look! Being separate is not good. Being attached is not good. Not being separate and not being attached is called going beyond.

Buddha dharma is like this. As being, non-being, form, and emptiness go beyond being and non-being, form and emptiness, there are distinctly being, non-being, form, and emptiness. Sentient beings, buddhas, delusion, and enlightenment are all like this. All buddhas go beyond all buddhas, so they turn the dharma wheel and bring across sentient beings. Sentient beings go beyond sentient beings. Because of this they turn into wondrous causal conditions of the six paths. What we are hearing now is all buddhas going beyond and all sentient beings going beyond.

This is something that can be understood only by those who have departed from all views and attained true liberation. It cannot be seen with the eyes of those who are eager to be enlightened. *Genjo koan* comes forth where this eagerness is removed. What happens at the place where you go beyond being and non-being? Only after going beyond do the three realms come together and sentient beings come together. This is *Genjo koan*.

To tell you the truth, even when we are deluded we are within the three realms. Even when we are enlightened we are within the three realms. The three realms do not get riled up at the time of delusion. The three realms do not get crushed at the time of enlightenment.

Enlightenment does not heat water. Delusion does not lower mountains. Because abundance and lack are gone beyond, delusion, enlightenment, sentient beings, and buddhas are clearly there. This is *Buddha dharma*.

A common way of thinking is that something novel may appear at the time of enlightenment. You may think that you can eat five bowls of rice and have a luxurious time on top of the altar where flowers are offered.

However, even if you get enlightened, you would be criticized if you did something wrong, and you wouldn't be able to eat if you are too laid-back.

You may think, "Hmm! It might not be so enjoyable to get enlightened." Then you are way off. You should know that there are delusion and enlightenment even within enlightenment. There are delusion and enlightenment even when we are deluded.

To be free within this dynamic mechanism of going beyond— pow!—in the midst of delusion and enlightenment—this is practice.

In the *Genjo koan* there is no discriminatory thinking. Being and non-being are dropped off as they are. Going beyond abundance and lack is itself *Genjo koan*. To see the *dharmadhatu* beyond the dualistic view of delusion and enlightenment is the fundamental eye. Investigate thoroughly.

"Yet in attachment blossoms just fall, and in aversion weeds just spread." This "yet" means "therefore" in Dogen Zenji's common rhetoric.

Now *Genjo koan*, just as it is, is right on the mark of the scale. It does not sort out or choose delusion, enlightenment, ordinary or sacred. It is just that those who are deluded are deluded and those who are enlightened are enlightened.

At the time of delusion, flowers are flowers. At the time of enlightenment, weeds are weeds. At the time of delusion, three bowls of rice and two bowls of soup. It is the same at the time of enlightenment.

Then what's the difference between delusion and enlightenment? It's just that in attachment flowers fall, in aversion weeds spread.

Now this is fun. For what reasons do flowers fall? Ordinarily when we have love and attachment we say, "Oh! Beautiful. I want to keep them in bloom forever." Then flowers fall. How do weeds spread? They spread from the feeling of aversion. We say, "Ugh! That's disturbing. Here they come again." In this way, falling and blooming arise from love and hate.

Originally there is no falling or blooming. You say that you dislike weeds, but farmers use them for fertilizer. They wish for more and more weeds. For them, weeds are not weeds. Men, women, young and old, go on a spree after viewing cherry blossoms at Ueno, or at

Mukojima. But dogs lie underneath the trees every day thinking nothing of it. They are busy looking for leftovers under the trees. Look now. For those who do not fall into the duality of love and hate, there is no blooming or falling.

For grasshoppers, weeds are their world. When weeds spread they feel comfortable having a new living room. When the frost in the desolate winter season kills the grass, the grasshoppers think that their Buddha Hall is destroyed, and they think, "This Buddha Hall is crushed and needs to be restored." Look at this. Insects do not think that weeds are in the way. For those who like it "spreading" is not a problem.

Everything is like this. What is called blooming and what is called falling are based on ordinary views. The fact is, falling and blooming are all *Genjo koan*, and there is not a bit of self. By looking with correct eyes, falling and blooming are true marks of flowers and weeds.

For now, let us regard weeds as delusion and flowers as enlightenment. If we regard weeds as "sentient beings," flowers are buddhas. Ordinarily people dislike the false and go for the true, thinking that defilement is disgusting and nirvana is favorable. This view of grasping and rejecting creates a kind of false reality that runs after you the more you try to discard it.

The more you seek for Bodhi, the further away it goes. On the other hand, if you are not bound by hate and love it gets bright and clear. If there is no construction on your side, the other side will by itself drop off. There are no defilements for myriad *kalpas* to bind you. There is no enlightenment for myriad *kalpas* that will depart from you.

In this way, while there is a distinction between delusion and enlightenment, from the viewpoint of construction on your side, the other side is always dropping off. This is *Genjo koan*.

Think well. There is birth and death for those who keep on saying birth and death is terrible. However, there is no birth and death for those who see birth and death as the life of the buddha.

The matter of birth and death becomes a problem for those who ignore birth and are panicked by death. But there is no birth and death for those who welcome birth and are settled in death.

Things just happen in the realm of emotion and thought, such as love and hate, agreeing and not agreeing. Even though there is a distinction between sentient beings and buddhas, between delusion and enlightenment, and between birth-death and nirvana in the ordinary mind, we shouldn't be stuck with it. In the *Genjo koan* that goes beyond abundance and lack, flowers are the true mark of falling, weeds are the true mark of growing. Nothing is discriminated here.

This is what Dogen Zenji has made us aware of through these two lines. This "just" of "just falling" and "just spreading" makes the statement very emphatic. Because of our dualistic view of grasping and rejecting, love and hate, we separate delusion from enlightenment. But there is no path at all for delusion, nor is there any dharma at all to be enlightened with.

Every one of you is eager to be enlightened. How then do you get enlightened? Where do you arrive after enlightenment? You may say you don't want delusion. But after all, what are you deluded about? Or, where do you get settled if you are deluded about delusion? Or what gets in the way if you are deluded?

Think well. Upon hearing, "When all dharmas are *Buddha dharma*," what are you deluded about? What are you enlightened with? Where do you go in delusion? There is no place to go. Where do you go with enlightenment? There is no place to go. So we know that there is nothing to boast about, even if you are enlightened. There is nothing to have a headache about, even if you are deluded.

Autumn insects admire grass. Birds pick off blossoms without hesitation and they do not worry. Look now! In the end, where do falling and blooming take place? However beautifully flowers bloom, birds do not think about it. They are probably more concerned about grabbing crumbs from your cake if you are not alert. They act straightforwardly, as they are not bound by love and hate.

To selflessly see the inside and outside of the world together as one is *Genjo koan*. Here, there is no yardstick with which to measure delusion and enlightenment. When we look into ourselves, we see that all the common notions—delusion and enlightenment, the rising and sinking of suffering and pleasure, auspicious and inauspicious, tribulation and good fortune—exist only within the realm of love and hate, grasping and rejecting. If we look, free from dualistic views, all things are *Genjo koan* without any hindrance.

It is a monk's practice to be free from these dualistic views and lead a life with nothing extra.

SECTION 4

*To carry the self forward and illuminate myriad dharmas is delu-
sion. That myriad dharmas come forth and illuminate the self is
enlightenment.*

This needs to be seen thoroughly through practice. First you need
to see the outline. This is where Dogen Zenji tentatively presents a
picture of delusion and enlightenment as the *Genjo koan* of the entire
dharmadhatu.

What is called delusion and enlightenment here is different from
the delusion and enlightenment that are commonly spoken about. The
distinction between delusion and enlightenment is shown for the time
being in the interaction between self and myriad dharmas.

Self here does not mean the human self. The myriad dharmas here
are not objects opposed to self. The myriad dharmas are the myriad
dharmas of the self. This self is the self of myriad dharmas. For this
reason, dropping off self is called myriad dharmas, and myriad dharmas without self are called self. Here, the principle of the one thusness
of self and others, and the equality of delusion and enlightenment is
demonstrated.

Why does he present delusion and enlightenment in this way, while
the entire world is outlined as *Genjo koan*?

If you say, "Cheeks are soft, therefore soft things are cheeks," imply-
ing that all things are one and the same, it will be a bad equation that
has no meaning. So Dogen Zenji is making this statement in order to
explain that there are clearly delusion and enlightenment even in the
realm of *Genjo koan*.

Now, "to carry the self forward and illuminate myriad dharmas is
delusion" is a very difficult point; the old commentators broke their
bones in their great effort. They took hold of the essential vehicle freely
with their grappling hook and presented their teaching. Their commentaries are not accessible to those who do not have understanding and are not yet ready to grasp it. The authors of *Sanchu* and *Shiki*
are like this. They made excellent presentations, but it is very hard to
understand them from the very beginning.

"To carry the self forward and illuminate myriad dharmas is delusion.

That myriad dharmas come forth and illuminate the self is enlightenment." Within these two sentences there are the words "delusion" and "enlightenment," but it is not good to jump from here to "one thusness of delusion and enlightenment" or "the equality of practice and enlightenment." The words "delusion" and "enlightenment" of "self" and "other" as used by Dogen Zenji are different from the way that we usually use them. I would like us to first follow the text intimately and then say whatever we want later.

Now, what is it "to carry the self forward and illuminate myriad dharmas"? This is to look for the dharma outside of the mind. The self stays on one side, while you let your mind run about in the myriad dharmas somewhere else, saying that you want to be enlightened, you want to be a scholar, and so forth, saying the self is looking outside. This is the domain of delusion.

This is a common way. A novice thinks of becoming an elder. An elder thinks of becoming head priest. Head priest wants to be head of the council. A council member thinks of becoming head of the sect. Because of the many legs of the self, we are not really settled. We carry ourselves forward and then run after the myriad dharmas. This is delusion.

This is also the case when we discuss the dharma gate. Intellectual interpretations such as buddha's view, dharma's view, equality and distinction, the duality of this and that, the hierarchy of Mahayana and Hinayana, are all deluded ways of looking for the dharma outside the mind. In this way, to carry the self forward is delusion. If we only read the text literally, this is how you may see it. But you should go beyond this.

"To carry the self forward" does not mean that self and dharmas are in opposition. The self here means the self of the entire world. At this point each of the myriad dharmas is the self, and there are no myriad dharmas outside the self. To practice/realize the self of the entire world is "to carry the self forward and practice/realize the myriad dharmas." Therefore, delusion here does not mean to be at a loss. Since it is delusion in the midst of all *Buddha dharma*, there is no enlightenment outside of delusion.

As for the "myriad dharmas come forth . . ." you should understand these two sentences in reference to what is said in *Bendowa*: "In stillness mind and object merge in realization and go beyond enlightenment; nevertheless, because you are in the state of self-fulfilling samadhi, without disturbing its quality or moving a particle you extend the Buddha's great activity, the incomparably profound and subtle teaching."

However, "One thusness of delusion and enlightenment" and "the non-duality of self and other" can be discussed later. Here we should see, just as in the text, that to carry the self forward is delusion and that myriad dharmas coming forth is enlightenment.

Now look at it from this angle. Any one of you may understand how the self is carried forward toward the myriad dharmas. But how do you understand the myriad dharmas advancing to illuminate the self? If we say that the myriad dharmas travel toward us, would it be like a grand exhibition? It doesn't seem to be the case.

"The myriad dharmas come forth . . ." is practice. People who don't practice don't understand it. This is not something that is known to those who don't practice. How about that? The self is carried forward in the self. Are there delusion and enlightenment in this realm? At what point can you distinguish delusion and enlightenment?

Whether the self carries forward or the myriad dharmas come forth, it appears to be the same. "To carry the self forward and illuminate myriad dharmas" is delusion. "Myriad dharmas come forth and illuminate the self" could also be delusion. Or if the myriad dharmas come forth and illuminate the self is enlightenment, then carrying the self forward and illuminating the myriad dharmas could be enlightenment.

Nevertheless, that delusion is delusion and enlightenment is enlightenment is clearly stated here. What's the difference? You should investigate this thoroughly. It means that there are clearly delusion and enlightenment within one sitting. Practice and enlightenment or coming and going are all within one sitting. Simply speaking, there is a distinction between effort and non-effort. We don't need many words. It is the realm of non-effort where the entire *dharma-dhatu* becomes the buddha's seal. Thus, myriad dharmas enter the self. Thinking and discriminating take place in the realm of effort. By means of thinking and discriminating, the self and illumination are lost. This point cannot be understood without actually practicing and investigating.

But in the beginning if you jump to saying that delusion and enlightenment are thusness or that self and others are not two, this would be a poisonous view and would not be of any help to practice. Some teachers of old made this mistake.

When you adopt a son through marriage and say to him, "My property will someday be all yours; these acres and fields and buildings for income," he might feel free to squander it. You should not say this to him when he is not ready to hear it. Likewise, the oneness of self and others will naturally be understood without explanation when you penetrate where the border lies between delusion and enlightenment.

If you clearly understand the border between delusion and enlightenment, you will naturally understand the *Genjo koan* of delusion and enlightenment. You will also understand delusion and enlightenment within the *Buddha dharma* of all dharmas.

Practice is not just limited to one form. Sometimes we need to go onto high peaks; sometimes we need to go into the deep ocean. It's no use to say, "Originally, there is no one thing," or "not obtainable," jumping before your feet are settled. On the other hand, it is also foolish to be stuck under the ladder for a lifetime by being bound by cause and effect and not knowing how to get through it.

So in practice we need to go to that place, look back at this place, go to the absolute, look back at the relative and continue taking years and years to examine by asking, "What? What?"

Now each of these pursuits in your practice will become integral to the self. There is no way to practice without the self. This is the guidepost for practice in our school. This is the point.

What is the actual taste of "myriad dharmas come forth and illuminate the self?" When the self does not have a speck of contrivance, myriad dharmas pour into the self without hindrance. When the self is completely the self, there is no self. When there is no self, there is no other. In this way, myriad dharmas come forward and realize the self. When we see from this realm it is not at all different from "the self comes forward and illuminates myriad dharmas." When the self is completely the self, the myriad dharmas are in the realm of the self. When you get to this place, whether you like it or not delusion and enlightenment are one thusness.

Although self and others, delusion and enlightenment, are distinguished in the text, they are after all one. Self and others are ultimately not two. The discrimination between delusion and enlightenment is just an interaction between the self and myriad dharmas.

Originally there are no solid blocks called delusion or enlightenment. Now at this point it is possible to say that delusion and enlightenment are one thusness. There are inevitably delusion and enlightenment within *Genjo koan*. However, they are originally one thusness. If we carry the self forward and move toward the myriad dharmas, it is delusion. That is fine. There is no dharma that should be excluded as delusion. If the myriad dharmas come forward and pour into the self it is enlightenment. That is also fine. There is nothing to take up or grasp as enlightenment. There is nothing to get rid of as enlightenment.

In this way the principle that the self and the myriad dharmas are one body and not two is naturally understood. Because they are one body and not two, nothing comes forward from the other side, and neither does the self come forward.

When we say "myriad dharmas," it is not that the self is outside of them. It is the self of the myriad dharmas. When we say the self, it is the realm of the entire self, the myriad dharmas of the self. Therefore if the myriad dharmas come forward, the self comes forward. If the self moves forward, the myriad dharmas move forward. It is known in this way that the myriad dharmas and the self are not two.

In this way, it is not that there are no delusion and enlightenment but that delusion and enlightenment are one thusness, which is *Genjo koan*. Look at this closely. When we say the "self" or "myriad dharmas," they are never two separate dharmas. It is the self within "all dharmas are *Buddha dharma*"; it is also the myriad dharmas within "all dharmas are *Buddha dharma*."

Practice always requires two separate dharmas, which are subject and object. But as long as there are dualistic views of subject and object, that is not *Buddha dharma*. When the subject and object disappear and have no affairs to attend to, the self is the self and myriad dharmas are myriad dharmas, and nothing gets in the way. We need this today. Being free from subject and object, when we meet people, even hundreds of thousands of people, we have no hindrance and have freedom within the self. Whether we meet people who are disturbing or attractive, it doesn't matter. When this is not practiced, it is difficult to enter the paths of various beings and save them.

Although there are the two names, "self" and "myriad dharmas," the self does not retain the self; the myriad dharmas do not stay at the place of the myriad dharmas. Indeed, how the self and myriad dharmas become one is described as "carrying forward" or "coming forth." Delusion and enlightenment are mentioned independently here, but both are *Genjo koan*.

This corresponds to "the self turning the dharma wheel." [In *Gakudo Yojinshu*, it says,] "The dharma turns the self, the self turns the dharma." ["When the self is capable for turning the dharma, the self is strong and the dharma is weak. When the dharma, on the other hand, turns the self, the dharma is strong and the self is weak. The *Buddha dharma* has had these two aspects."]

The self of "to carry the self forward" is not the self of ego, but is the self that "turns the dharma wheel." The myriad dharmas that advance, in this case, are not the myriad dharmas of attachment, but the dharmas that turn the self.

When there is not a single hair of *Buddha dharma*, the self is strong. When turned around by practice on top of realization, the dharma is strong. Also, when we thoroughly go beyond going beyond through practice, swiftly passing the crown of the head of Vairocana, the self is strong. When we do not take the self for the dharma body, the dharma is strong.

In the end, what is called the self and what is called the dharma are one body. This section of *Genjo koan* illustrates that there are two modes of dharma, and it is not discussing what is normally called ego or human self. This being so, "To carry the self forward and illuminate the myriad dharmas" means that the self completely becomes the myriad dharmas. "That the myriad dharmas come forth and illuminate the self" means that the myriad dharmas thoroughly become the self. When we get here, we understand that the explanation of *Sanchu* is thorough. Now this is the principle. About the actual aspect of this, each of you needs to investigate through *shikantaza*. If you only hear lectures and stop there, you are merely looking for a shadow. It does not become your own.

SECTION 5

Those who have great realization of delusion are buddhas; those who are greatly deluded about realization are sentient beings. Further, there are those who continue realizing beyond realization, who are in delusion through delusion.

In the previous section, the meaning of delusion and enlightenment was shown. Now, in this section, the vital use of delusion and enlightenment is presented. In the previous section, the "person" was not discussed, but here buddhas and sentient beings are discussed. Here, also, it is important that we should first interpret the text as it is, and then investigate the points that bring out the meaning of *Genjo koan*.

"Those who have great realization of delusion are buddhas." That is so. Those who clarify this single great mass are called buddhas, wise ones, or awakened ones. So without experiencing this single great matter, it is impossible to turn forth and illuminate the self.

"Those who are greatly deluded about realization are sentient beings." This means that although people originally are buddha-nature, they are deluded because of a few mistaken views, and are like destitute children in a foreign land. This is the realm of sentient beings. This is not a place in which you should remain. This is the realm of looking for the dharma outside the mind, which was mentioned in the previous section. However, if we see it from the perspective of *Genjo koan*, it is not something that you can fiddle with. You cannot erase it with your views. You cannot crush it by force. When you are deluded, you are a sentient being. When you are enlightened, you are invariably a buddha. This is *Genjo koan*.

"Further, there are those who continue realizing beyond realization." There is also this: It is said that to still be able to see the self at the time of the ultimate fruition, you need to be enlightened on top of being enlightened. Then what is this enlightenment? It is to annihilate all traces of enlightenment. As long as you say that you have enlightenment, it is not a true enlightenment. Because "at the time of attainment you go beyond mind"; when you are truly enlightened, you should not be holding onto enlightenment.

Nevertheless, we do need a place to enter at the beginning, where we have great realization of delusion. But if you stop there, you will have the disease of enlightenment, so whatever enlightenment you have, you should let go of all traces of that enlightenment.

Still, there will be stages such as the forty-two stages of practice. If we were finished after having been enlightened once, the great practice of bodhisattvas throughout these *asamkyaya-kalpas* would not be necessary. One small candle provides light, but its light is not completely illuminating. The great round mirror wisdom of the inconceivable awakening has to come after passing through the forty-two stages. This is attaining enlightenment on top of enlightenment. There are clearly such people, from the perspective of *Genjo koan*.

"There are those who are deluded within delusion." On the other hand, you go further into darkness. You pile up delusion on top of delusion. Because of the power of karma, which is like a diamond, there are ignorant sentient beings who cannot cease transmigration all the way to the infinite future. If enlightenment is boundless, delusion is also boundless.

In the *Genjo koan* of the entire *dharmadhatu*, there is no above higher than above, and there is no below lower than below. While the wise and the sage spend their time to accumulate virtue and make an endeavor for good, the ordinary and foolish spend their time making an effort for evil. If good is boundless, evil is also boundless. Those who enter delusion are called sentient beings, and those who go for enlightenment are called "all buddhas." There is such a distinction. This is *Genjo koan* that is immovable. If we interpret the text straightforwardly, we can say this much.

Although we talk about distinctions between delusion and enlightenment, or sentient beings and buddhas, sentient beings and buddhas are all thusness. Why so? When we look at the text it says, "those who have great realization of delusion." What is it that you realize? You realize delusion. Also it says, "greatly deluded about delusion." Look. When you are deluded, what are you deluded about? You are deluded about enlightenment. In this way, when you say "delusion," and when you say "enlightenment," in the end, it is a borderline between the self and myriad dharmas.

There is nothing that shakes the face and eyes of *Genjo koan*. Only that the head becomes a foot, and the foot takes the place of the head.

Delusion is *Genjo koan*. Enlightenment is also *Genjo koan*. It is not that different dharmas are seen as delusion or enlightenment, but that we are deluded about and enlightened about the same thing. So when we face delusion, we say "sentient beings." And when we face enlightenment, we say, "all buddhas." But ultimately they are the same thing.

To make a buddha out of one who has in essence become buddha, and to be deluded while carrying the self that has in essence become buddha, either way it is not stepping outside of the *koan*. In this way, although sentient beings and buddhas are discussed in the text for the time being by alternating delusion and enlightenment, ultimately sentient beings and buddhas are one thusness; delusion and enlightenment are not two. Because sentient beings and buddhas are one thusness, when sentient beings appear, that is *Genjo koan* of all sentient beings. And when all buddhas appear, that is *Genjo koan* of all buddhas. Therefore it is said, "All buddhas and sentient beings do not hinder each other. Mountains are high of themselves, and waters are deep of themselves."

When we say "attaining enlightenment above enlightenment and delusion within delusion," it is the activity of delusion and enlightenment. Those who are deluded are deluded thoroughly. When we say delusion and when we say enlightenment, it may appear that there are two paths that are separate, one in the east and one in the west. But even if they are separate, east and west, they never stray outside of the mountain of *Genjo koan*.

After all, delusion and enlightenment are one track. You realize enlightenment through delusion, and you are deluded through enlightenment. In this way, delusion and enlightenment are one track. If you are deluded through and through, you become one with an enlightened person. When you are enlightened through and through, you become one with a deluded person. "Great realization furthers delusion" or [Linji's] "four guests and hosts" do not go beyond this meaning.

In this way, a person who is greatly deluded and a person who is greatly enlightened are eight *ryo* versus half a *kin*. For example, neither a guide who is familiar with the place and walks ahead half asleep, nor someone who does not have a plan to go anywhere, can get lost. If you get lost (are deluded) all the way and penetrate your getting lost (your delusion), you are not lost (deluded) anymore. If you are enlightened all the way, going beyond the forty-two stages, there is no more enlightenment. If you are not sure, and wandering around from one mountain to another, you may happen to appear in the town right in front of the Kaga Castle. It is because delusion and enlightenment are originally inseparable.

What is called delusion is as it is and what is called enlightenment is as it is, on the scale of *Genjo koan*. Delusion should not be detested, and enlightenment does not need to be devoured. They are as they are, and they do not get in the way at all. As *Genjo koan* they are inseparable. This is what is reverberating behind these words. You should not overlook this.

SECTION 6

When buddhas are truly buddhas, they do not necessarily notice that they are buddhas. However, they are actualized buddhas, who go on actualizing buddha.

The "buddhas" mentioned here can be understood as the self. When the self has truly attained the buddha realm, it has completely become a buddha, so the self does not need to be aware of itself as buddha. This intimately explains a realized buddha. It's not that there is an extra self outside to recognize.

A true enlightenment is like this. When a buddha truly becomes a buddha, it is not necessary to say, "I am a buddha." If all buddhas recognize themselves as buddhas, there is a polarization of self and other. That is not enlightenment. The *Gakudo Yojinshu* says, "At the place of seeing, knowing perishes. At the time of attaining, mind is suppressed."

When the buddha is the self and the self is the buddha, both the self and the buddha have to be dropped off simultaneously. When not a speck of dust of what is like delusion, what is like the self, or what is like all buddhas is visible, it is true enlightenment and the true buddha. So it is said in the text. "When buddhas are truly buddhas, they do not necessarily notice that they are buddhas." This is the intimate understanding of realized buddhas.

"However, they are actualized buddhas, who go on actualizing buddha." This is to illustrate how practice-enlightenment should go beyond the view of the emptiness of enlightenment.

At the time of actualizing buddhas, there are no buddhas. You pass straight through all buddhas. In this way, those who realize and that which is realized are both empty and serene. Although this is true, there are, beyond doubt, actualizing buddhas.

It is not good to say, "Look, I am OK because I am enlightened," and to proclaim, as Linji said, "The entire canon is just old pieces of toilet paper." If you are enlightened to that extent, you don't need to use such dusty old crinkle paper for wiping. It's better to use soft paper for wiping. That is self-inflated enlightenment. It's far from actualizing buddha.

Although the realm of all buddhas is inconceivable, buddhas have to be actualized. Even if we exhaust going beyond buddha and rush through the head of Vairocana, we have to turn around and look. As it is said, "Do not mistake the self as the dharma-body." This is the point of looking.

Although there is no conception, actualized buddhas invariably exist. So it appears that there are subject and object. You may think that buddha and yourself are subject and object. But it is not so. When you have truly experienced great enlightenment, that which realizes and that which is realized are one. Look at this closely. Not a speck of dust gets in your way at the time of great enlightenment. And yet there have to be actualized buddhas.

Look at this closely. If you stay in a place where enlightenment is finalized and going beyond is finalized, that is a dead thing. As soon as you have insight, you should remove your body from there and be engaged in the practice where each movement has essential clarity.

People today often lack this mindful practice, so they become retainers of devils. When we say that there is no "out there" in the *dharmadhatu,* then we cannot help but return to today. There is no higher thing that is to be feared, and there is no lower thing that is to be belittled. When we seek for the self and realize that the self is originally empty and serene, we need to make today's activities just today's.

If we thrust through everything as empty, there is no attachment. So we do not get stuck at the present moment, nor are we stuck with the view of emptiness. So, today is today and we take a steady step with our daily activities. In this way, we are not stuck with the ascent of the real, and we are not stuck with the descent of the phenomenal. This is the middle way. This is the final rank, the mutual integration of *zheng* and *pian* [of the five ranks]. You should pinpoint this and understand the true returning of the practice.

SECTION 7

When you see forms or hear sounds fully engaging body-and-mind, you intuit dharmas intimately. Unlike things and their reflections in the mirror, and unlike the moon and its reflection in the water, when one side is illuminated, the other side is dark.

The first sentence here demonstrates the intimacy of intuitive illumination. We normally talk about enlightenment this and enlightenment that, but what do we actually regard as enlightenment? I want you to fully understand this point(the immovable principle of enlightenment). To regard one person's one-time experience of realization, or an insight leading to a prediction of the future, as enlightenment is absolutely demonic. When we have true enlightenment there is not even a speck of what you thought was enlightenment.

Look now. "When you see forms or hear sounds fully engaging body-and-mind . . ." This is usually understood as "seeing forms with bright mind, hearing sounds with enlightenment of the Way." Avalokitesvara is enlightened with sound, as it is said, "The root of the ear fully penetrates the root of the ear." Maitreya is enlightened through forms. Lingyun had realization when looking at peach blossoms; it is seeing forms with bright mind. Xiangyan had realization through the sound of a stone striking bamboo; it is hearing the sound and being enlightened with the Way. In this way it appears that the seeing and the hearing are accompanied with enlightenment. However, at the time of true enlightenment of the Way, there is no form and no sound. Only when the eyes are blinded and the ears are clogged up does true enlightenment occur.

The moment when the mind and object perish is enlightenment. There is no recognition at all such as "that is form" or "that is voice." When we see peach blossoms, the entire sky and ground become peach blossoms. Mind and objects (self and the realm outside) are crushed all at once. When the bamboo is hit with the stone, the single "crack" of sound knocks down the entire *dharmadhatu,* and the whole body completely becomes the sound. Only at this moment is there the total undivided self. In this way we say, "you see forms or hear sounds." But it is not to see with eyes or to hear with ears, but to hear with body-and-mind. This is presented as "fully engaging body-and-mind." The words "fully engaging" are emphasized. That is fully engaging body, fully engaging mind, and fully engaging unity.

Responding to the object of form, the eye consciousness functions. That is to see forms with fully engaged body and with fully engaged mind. Responding to the object of sound, the ear consciousness functions. That is to hear sounds fully engaging body and fully engaging mind. Intuiting occurs in this way.

"You intuit dharmas intimately." This is good. There is no dharma outside of the self, and there is no self outside of the dharma. Facing forms, the entire body becomes forms. Facing voice, the entire body becomes voice. The self and the object become not-two. At the time of "seeing peach blossoms," the entire world becomes peach blossoms. At the time of "hitting bamboo," the entire world is "crack!" That is the moment when the forms are truly seen and the voice is truly heard. At this moment you intimately intuit it.

How do you intuit it? With one hit, knowledge "perishes" and "directly arriving at this moment, there is no more doubt." Briefly speaking, this is great enlightenment that penetrates to the bottom. There is nothing anymore to doubt in the entire earth. Where the entire earth is covered with peach blossoms all over, and when the entire dharmadhatu becomes the "crack" of hitting bamboo, you penetrate through the self and the *dharmadhatu,* mind and object, and experience great emancipation. In this way it is truly "intimately intuited."

What is intimate? The self and myriad dharmas are not arrayed as two separate things. Rather, the self and myriad dharmas explode all at once, and mind and object are thus, body and mind are thusness. There is no second person directly where you are. There is nothing more intimate than this.

"You intuit dharmas." This intuiting is it. Intuiting is truly intuiting, clearly intuiting where there is no doubt. But it is not like a reflection in the mirror or like the moon reflecting on the water. A reflection in the mirror or the moon reflected on the water are two things relative to each other. This is rejected here. When you say, "intuit dharmas," there is also "not intuit dharmas." If there is someone who intuits it, there is something intuited. But now it is not subject and object that are relative to each other. Intuiting is just intuiting. At the moment of [seeing] peach blossoms, the entire world is peach blossoms. There is no seer or that which is seen. That is intuiting. Therefore this intuiting has no opposites. When there is great laughter, ha, ha, ha, there is nothing but peach blossoms. That is dropping off. There is no other side.

The "reflections in the mirror" or "the moon . . . in the water" are often used to indicate leaving no trace or having no hindrance. This is often used in a positive way. But here these images are used in a negative way to indicate the separation of two things, the opposition of subject and object. In other words, what is discouraged here is such opposition. This being so, "at the place of seeing, knowledge perishes. At the time of attaining, mind has gone beyond." This should not be attributed only to Xiangyan or Lingyun. We all encounter seeing forms and hearing sounds every day. But because we cannot perish the self and give up our dualism, everything becomes delusion and the dharma does not come to our hands. Investigate this closely.

"When one side is illuminated, the other side is dark." This is an intimate presentation. Indeed, when you realize on one side the other side is not visible. When you say *zhang, pian* (light, dark) is completely covered. When you carry on one practice, all other practices are unseen. In each activity, you thoroughly experience one dharma. By penetrating one direction in this way, you master the ten directions. If you go to the east ten miles, you also go to the west ten miles. When you go east, you just go east. But going east encompasses going west.

So Dogen Zenji says, later in the text, "to attain one dharma is to penetrate one dharma; to meet one practice is to sustain one practice." When you truly practice one activity, it means that you practice myriad activities. Therefore, those who neglect one activity neglect myriad activities. This is an understanding through words, but the real meaning is already explained in the text as "you intuit dharmas intimately."

When we intuit that the self and the outer realm(mind and object(are not two, but one, there is not a second person throughout heaven and earth. When we illuminate one side, the *dharmadhatu* becomes one side, the ten directions become dark and all collapse.

The ten directions are not standing anymore. This is the principle that one direction is no other than ten directions. You are enlightened with peach blossoms, you are enlightened with bamboo. Peach blossoms are one side and bamboo is one side. When you realize this one side and see that myriad dharmas are without self, then sound and form become dark and all at once are dropped, all dharmas attaining the Way simultaneously, as we grope. This is what is called *dark*.

Shobo genzo Shiki [by Zokai] interprets the term *dark* as all things merging in darkness. This is a good interpretation. All things merging in the dark means subtle comprehension. As one dharma is no other than myriad dharmas, whatever you realize embraces all the ten directions. In this way, to "intuit . . . intimately" is essential. When we intuit intimately, the ten directions drop off. This is called "a single bare body within myriad forms," "one bright pearl," or "a sramana's single eye in the entire great earth."

This one side merges with all dharmas in darkness and there is nothing left out. It is called *dark*. One dharma comprehends myriad dharmas in darkness. We don't say that Lingyun was enlightened with peach blossoms but couldn't have been enlightened with cherry blossoms. When you say "peach blossoms," the entire great earth becomes peach blossoms. When you say "cherry blossoms," the entire great earth becomes the world of cherry blossoms. What is intimate with one person is intimate with myriad people. This does not apply only to enlightenment; all dharmas are like this. But now the presentation is about *intimately intuiting*. You cannot call what is not broken through in this way "enlightenment."

Section 8

To study the Buddha Way is to study the self. To study the self is to forget the self. To forget the self is to be actualized by myriad things. When actualized by myriad things, your body and mind as well as the bodies and minds of others drop away. No trace of enlightenment remains, and this no-trace continues endlessly.

"To study the Buddha Way is to study the self." This is related to the previous line, "When one side is illuminated, the other side is dark." Dogen Zenji's intention is to demonstrate the daily course of practice-enlightenment. Here again there is the dynamic interplay between the self and the myriad dharmas.

In the fascicle "One Bright Pearl," it says, "Ceaselessly pursuing things and making them in the self, pursuing the self and making it things." In this way, to be enlightened is no other than fully experiencing the self and fully experiencing myriad dharmas. The self and myriad dharmas are originally one thusness. There is no self apart from the myriad dharmas. There are no myriad dharmas apart from the self. Therefore, when one dharma is actualized, the ten directions are comprehended.

It is essential in the practice to "fully experience one dharma." In whichever practice, it is good to solidly master one dharma. When we fully experience the self, it is not betrayed by myriad dharmas. When we fully experience myriad dharmas, the self drops off spontaneously.

However, ordinarily, the self and myriad dharmas are seen as subject and object, and dualistic views are employed. It is like the son of a wealthy man wandering in hardship in a foreign land. The practice does not become solid. Because of a lack of courage, investigation of myriad dharmas does not become thorough. It's like being on the edge of a rice field whose boundary is hard to discern. It doesn't work. You need to study thoroughly the all-inclusive one side with great urgency. That is "to study the self."

When you hear "to study the Buddha Way," you may think that it is to master the studies of the Tripitaka, to attain the three vidyas, to master the six powers and attain the eight types of liberation, or to go on a journey with the forty-two stages of a bodhisattva as a distant goal. This is not the case. That would be a practice where the self is on "this side" and you see the Buddha Way "over there." It is a dualistic mind.

"To study the Buddha Way" is not like that. It is to study the self. To study the self means the body-mind study of the Way; this entire body fully becomes *Buddha dharma*. What is this entire body fully becoming *Buddha dharma*? It is dropping off *Buddha dharma* and the self all at once.

The true practice of the Buddha Way is that there is no self outside of the *Buddha dharma*; there is no *Buddha dharma* outside of the self; the *Buddha dharma* is no other than the self. Dogen Zenji presents this as "to study the self." People study the Buddha Way but often don't study the self. If we don't study the self, it is not practice.

"To study the self is to forget the self." What does this mean? Look now. Practice while holding on to the self is not the Buddha Way. When we are young, we tend to misunderstand this. We may think that we have aspiration because we have the self. But this is not right. We should completely forget the self. It is all right to forget it. Only when we forget the self does the entire body become the *Buddha dharma*.

People say they cannot arouse the bodhi-seeking mind or that they can't hold the *Buddha dharma* in hand. That is because they have a certain view. If you want to pour sake into a sake bottle that is already filled with water, you can't pour it in, no matter how hard you try. Similarly, if you hold onto your old views (views of self) the dharma can't get in. If you surrender and throw your entire body into the Buddha's house, today's practice of walking, abiding, sitting, and lying down is done from the side of Buddha.

Only when you have not even a speck of the self do you match the *Buddha dharma*. "If you put even a little more weight on yourself than on the dharma, dharma is not transmitted, and the Way is not attained" [as said in "Bowing and Attaining the Marrow"]. Only when we make this body-mind a platform [for zazen] of *Buddha dharma* does dharma become our own. This being so, we should be bold enough to forget the self.

Of course we say "forgetting the self," but how do we do it? How do we picture this throwing off of the body? To be illuminated by myriad dharmas is the liver and bladder. To be illuminated by myriad dharmas is to thoroughly become myriad dharmas. *Shiki* comments: "To be illuminated by myriad dharmas means to stick the entire self to myriad dharmas." This is good. It is that the entire time and the entire place fully become Dharma, and not even a speck of self is recognized.

The intimacy of practice lies here. Only then does the self stand alone, at one. When having a meal, you thoroughly become a meal, forgetting yourself in the meal. At the time of zazen, you do zazen single-mindedly. This is to forget the self. Then the thought of before and the thought of after entirely become the self. During all hours of the day, you're guided by the dharma, without noticing the self.

Only when we practice each moment of time as the entire time and each dharma as the entire dharma do you know the intimacy of the self and myriad dharmas. At that time each thing becomes your dharma. In other words, "Where the mind arises, there is no place to abide." To abide at ease in the place of no abiding is to forget the self. In this way, to forget the self is to thoroughly become myriad dharmas. At this time, the self is the entire self, standing at one without conditions.

"When actualized by myriad things, your body and mind as well as the bodies and minds of others drop away." Now look, here is body-mind dropping away. The self is this body. "Others" means myriad dharmas. Whether self or other, they drop away all at once. This is called "being illuminated by myriad dharmas." If we look from this place, it is all right to say either "illuminated by myriad dharmas" or "illuminated by the self." The body-mind of the self and the body-mind of others both drop away at once.

If you are not attached to either the self or to myriad dharmas, what illuminates and that which is illuminated both drop away. "To allow all things to come forth in enlightenment and practice all-inclusiveness with non-attachment" [as said in "On the Endeavor of the Way"] (refers to dropping away.

This dropping away is essential. Dogen Zenji's point of settling mind was the phrase "body and mind dropped off." When body and mind are truly dropped off, it is the world of settling mind.

A naked doll cannot drop any clothes. People all suffer today because of attachment. Having attachment is called *naraka* (hell). There is no need to suffer by holding on to something. Deeply ponder. You might think that dropping off is suffering or a hardship, and that attachment is easier. This is called topsy-turvy thought.

Dropping off is not such a complicated thing. The mind that arises in the place of non-abiding is in the realm of dropping off. To take an everyday example, our love of Bonseki or plants is a form of attachment. But when a gardener plants a tree, that is dropping off, because he raises the mind without abiding. In this way, you do not rely on any one thing for all hours of the day, and everything your eyes touch is in the realm of emancipation.

In general, the attachment of ordinary people is small attachment. They don't have great attachment. Although we have the great fortune to have received a human body, which is very rare, most people do not aspire to make a vow and carry on a great practice. They are drowned in wine and sex, following desires, neglecting cause and effect, and indulging in petty pleasure. Even if they live for a hundred years, they are still ordinary people. What a pity.

Practice is to throw away these petty attachments and petty delusions, and arouse great attachment and great delusion. Great delusion is to vow not to receive the benefits of all the sages even if you are drowned for innumerable *kalpas*. Without this courage, practice is not possible. Therefore, you should always pursue this emancipation. It is worthless to worry about trifles. If you swallow this emancipation, you will find well-being within it. A hundred years' longevity is guaranteed. Longevity is not to die in death. Think about this.

"No trace of enlightenment remains, and this no-trace continues endlessly." This way there is continuous going beyond! Then what is the absence of any trace of enlightenment? Trace of enlightenment is the boundary of realization. You let it go. If you say that you are finally enlightened, the front door is locked with a golden chain. If you abide in the place where you are enlightened, going beyond is blocked. So it is taught that it should be let go of. It is a great disease if the dharmabody has a trace, or if enlightenment has a shadow. So it is said, "A cloudless, blue sky still needs to be hit with a stick."

When you are enlightened, you should completely forget about enlightenment. This is great practice. This is called letting go. But this is a very hard practice. All the distinguished teachers abide in glory and enjoy bringing up the past. Compared to this, Ikkyu was great. He said, "I don't remember making a mistake called enlightenment." This is good. He doesn't look outstanding or distinguished, and he doesn't have the stink of enlightenment. Needless to say, he doesn't act violently, like swinging a fist, or hitting with a stick, or giving a shout. Here is the true dropping-off.

Then what is "this no-trace continues endlessly"? Because enlightenment must not remain, you grind it off completely, until there is not even a speck of enlightenment. When you reach this point of "no stink of enlightenment," where there is no trace, you vow with great determination to let the absence of enlightenment continue long, long, long, like a single rail of iron for myriad miles. This is, again, great practice that encompasses the entire future. When you say, "Plunge in and work secretly like a fool, like an idiot," or when you say "no more enlightenment," you must not stop there.

As the host within the host, birth after birth, world after world you never cease, even when you get to the time of Maitreya Buddha descending. You go all the way, together with sentient beings, transmigrating through the six realms. This is indeed great practice. Look at this closely. Practice has to be like this. It's stupid to be puffed up over a handful of enlightenment, like a long-nosed goblin who is proud of getting hold of a demon's head.

Instead, you let the absence of a trace of enlightenment emerge long, long, long. You must travel through the three realms magnificently with this absence of a trace of enlightenment throughout the three asamkyaya *kalpas*, and a hundred more. This is it. The forty-two ranks is the long, long, long emerging of this absence of the trace of enlightenment. Bodhisattvas of great power, appearing in various forms responding to circumstances, are the bare magnificence of this absence of any trace of enlightenment. Body and mind dropping off is the beginning of practice. Adding practice-enlightenment to this body-mind dropping off is indeed the *Genjo koan* of the Buddha-ancestors' practice-enlightenment.

SECTION 9

When you first seek dharma, you imagine you are far away from its environs. At the moment when dharma is correctly transmitted, you are immediately your original self.

The first sentence of *Genjo koan* expresses body-mind study of the Way, following the passage "to study the Buddha Way is . . ." In other words, the direction of practice-enlightenment is demonstrated with the principle of "no dharma outside of the mind." This is not limited to the beginner's mind. It is the moment of going toward *Buddha dharma* with the awareness that there is practice-enlightenment. This has to happen.

But it is very strange. We usually say, "The first thought of enlightenment arises simultaneously with complete perfect enlightenment," but this is not what is meant here. What it means is: When you first go toward the *Buddha dharma*, you are already standing back to back with the dharma. It's strange, isn't it? Why do we face away from dharma? Why are we so far away from its environs? Here, no dharma comes from outside the mind.

When the self is in the midst of the original path, without confusion, and without topsy-turvy views, without increase or decrease, and without mistakes, there is not one thing that is lacking. To seek for enlightenment outside of this is already being far away from the environs of dharma.

Not only that, there is originally not one speck of dharma to seek for in the *dharmadhatu*. There is no self, no person, no sentient beings, and no beings with eternal life. Because of this, in the *Prajnaparamita Sutra* it is said, "The five *skandhas* are all empty," "not born, not attainable." As the Fourth Ancestor said, "All dharmas are ultimately liberated." What on earth do you seek for in the midst of dharma? As soon as you arouse the idea of seeking for something, you have gone astray thousands of myriads of miles from the Way.

This is what Dogen Zenji says, based on the original thusness of dharma. From the viewpoint of the original thusness of dharma, there are no myriad dharmas outside of the self. And there is no self outside of the myriad dharmas. The path is originally complete and pervades everywhere. However, you try to attain something by practicing something new. This is like seeking dharma outside the mind.

But we should be aware of the tendency of beginners to say, "It's not good to seek for dharma, so I will not pursue it." Don't make this mistake. Dogen Zenji says this from the viewpoint of the original thusness of dharma. It is not possible to perfectly fit with dharma at the beginning of our practice. So not seeking for dharma is out of the question. You must endeavor with urgency, even sacrificing filial piety for your own mother. By doing so, you come to understand that non-attainment is the true face of dharma.

In this way, the difference between the original thusness of dharma and the guidelines for beginners is like the distance between heaven and earth. In the scriptural school, there is something called the abiding mind of desire, where desire for good dharma is encouraged. If your doubt is big, then your enlightenment is strong and big. Only when you get to the extreme of seeking mind do you arrive at no-seeking. Therefore, you must start out with a great determination to practice thoroughly, study with a teacher, study the scriptures, and study the 3,000 rules for monks and 80,000 detailed activities.

Here, it is explained from the viewpoint of the original thusness of dharma. However, you can't see this, if you have even a little seeking mind or a bit of attainment. So it is said that the seeking mind immediately ceases. Even when someone calls, you don't look back. And you go away covering your ears. Only thus is the activity of the one thusness of the *dharmadhatu* actualized. Only then does face-to-face transmission between buddhas and ancestors happen.

The second sentence of the opening paragraph shows the dynamics of attaining dharma and realizing the intimate merging. But this is funny. It is said that when dharma is already recognized and correctly transmitted, you are immediately your original person.

But, in fact, there is no before or after. It is pecking inside and outside of the shell at the same time. When the dharma is transmitted to the self and you say, "Ah ha!" you are your original person right then, and you don't have even a particle of seeking mind. It is strange that when you don't have a conception of the self, dharma is correctly transmitted. However much you hope for *Buddha dharma*, you cannot get it as long as you have hope.

Only when you forget yourself and forget *Buddha dharma* is dharma transmitted to you. When Dogen Zenji said [to Rujing], "Master, please do not give your seal of approval so easily," it was indeed body and mind dropped off. The time of body and mind dropped off is the place of no seeking. It is as plain as a blank wall.

You have been busily running around like a thirsty person looking for water. But now, when you become your original person, what will you think? You understand that even before taking one step there was already the original face and eye and the complete *Buddha dharma*, abiding where bodhi-mind first arose. This cannot be understood without twenty or thirty years of endeavor in the face of extreme hardship.

If you look from here, even a speck of seeking mind creates a gap between heaven and earth. So Deshan says, "Before you get back into the boat, I will give you thirty blows." Dogen Zenji explained this from the viewpoint of original thusness of dharma.

SECTION 10

When you ride in a boat and watch the shore, you might assume that the shore is moving. But when you keep your eyes closely on the boat, you can see that the boat moves. Similarly, if you examine myriad things with a confused body and mind you might suppose that your mind and nature are permanent. When you practice intimately and return to where you are, it will be clear that nothing at all has unchanging self.

The first line represents the principle of "all dharmas are without self," criticizing the view of a permanent, single, presiding self, ordinarily held by people outside the Way. The metaphor of the boat moving or the shore moving is presented. But this is only a partial metaphor. Now, you should have a good understanding what a metaphor is. In general, metaphors look like they are hitting the mark, but mostly they don't. Most of the metaphors presented by buddhas and ancestors are only partial metaphors. Some of the partial metaphors express most of the points, but others express only a small part. So it is foolish to create interpretations saying that the boat means "this" and the shore means "that." Here, the comments of *Gosho* are suitable and appropriate: "It is a crooked view to say that the body is impermanent and the self-nature is permanent. It is as wrong as saying that it is the shore that moves. This is just a metaphor. Look, the confused view, regarding what actually is impermanent as permanent, is illustrated by seeing the shore as moving while actually it is the boat that is moving."

The second line talks about confused body and mind, which is deluded thinking. That is thinking without looking at the dharma body. This is intended to criticize and exclude the theory of an established *atman*, saying that the self-existent body is permanent and universal, which is presented by the theory of the twenty-five categories of truth in the *sastras* of the Sarvastivadins, or the six definitions in the *Paramartha-satya-sastra,* and the view of Srenika that the soul is permanent but the forms perish fits into this category.

Broadly speaking, most students nowadays are stuck with this view, separating body and mind and being content with deluded thinking. To caution against such ideas, Dogen Zenji set up a section for discourse. There are many people who know that "mind is permanent but form perishes" is a view outside of the Way. And even though they say so, they nevertheless fall into this view. Theorists of cause and effect talk about the karmic reaction in the three worlds, and teachers of scripture talk about Buddha's practice throughout the *asamkyaya kalpa.* Also nowadays, there are those who talk about an eternal soul. They are all stuck with a poisoned view. This is a mistaken ordinary view that separates body and mind.

In general, to see body and mind as separate is the mistaken view of people outside of the Way. *Buddha dharma* is one thusness of body and mind, the non-duality of nature and form. In this way, if the mind is permanent, the body is permanent. And if the mind is impermanent, the body is impermanent. Although everyone agrees that the body is born and dies in each instant, many people regard mind alone as impermanent.

How is this so? *Buddha dharma* is never like that. When you say permanent, the entire heaven and earth are permanent. But this permanence is not apart from impermanence, and this impermanence is not separate from permanence. Because of this, the Buddha says, "All dharmas have the true mark. The self permanently abides in nirvana." An ancestor says, "The green mountain is always walking. A stone woman gives birth to a child in the night."

However, people outside the Way say that there is one permanent thing within the mountain of the five *skandhas,* and it presides over myriad things. This is a greatly mistaken view. When we look at the four limbs and the five divisions of the body, there is nothing to be recognized as atman or a divine self, or anything like the form of a self. If you say that the self is universal, permanent, and one, the body that comes from it must also be permanent and one.

However, the form of the body is born and dies every moment and keeps moving without ceasing even for an instant. The form of mind is said to be born and die fifty times within the cycle of a day and a night. People ordinarily think that their body and mind are permanent because they use them continuously all their life. But if you reflect on yourself intimately, what we call self-mind and self-nature perishes in each moment. The self-mind and self-nature are annihilated when this body is destroyed. There is no place where this so-called divine self abides. The notion of the divine self is criticized in many sutras and commentaries. Compared to them the text here is short, but what is said is profound.

The last sentence mentions "where you are," which is the backside of *this*. It means turning around the light and illuminating inside. If we turn around and see "What is self-mind, what is self-nature," there is not even a particle of anything like divine self or anything like permanence. There is only mind-consciousness that corresponds to the power of action, which does not stop even for a moment.

"Myriad dharmas are without self" means that myriad dharmas have no self. Now it is clear that we don't have self. As myriad dharmas are without self, we are without self. In this way, myriad dharmas are taken up to show the principle that the self has no self. Now, even if you understand the principle, you need to have a great capacity to be free from the dualistic views of annihilation and permanence, and freely utilize annihilation and permanence. The view that holds that heaven and earth perish is the view of annihilation. The view that holds that heaven and earth continue to exist forever is the view of permanence.

The views of annihilation and permanence are not necessarily invalid. Heaven and earth function in these two ways and would not be maintained apart from this. However, those who fall into either of these views go against the true body of dharma. For that reason, to maintain the self beyond these two views, using them freely and not getting stuck with either one, indicates a great capacity. Annihilation and permanence are the left and right of dharma just where you are.

SECTION 10B

*Firewood becomes ash, and it does not become firewood again.
Yet, do not suppose that the ash is after and the firewood before.
You should understand that firewood abides in the phenomenal
expression of firewood, which fully includes before and after and
is independent of before and after. Ash abides in the phenomenal
expression of ash, which fully includes before and after. Just as
firewood does not become firewood again after it is ash, you do not
return to birth after death.*

*This being so, it is an established way in Buddha dharma to deny
that birth turns into death. Accordingly, birth is understood as
no-birth. It is an unshakable teaching in Buddha's discourse that
death does not turn into birth. Accordingly, death is understood
as no-death.*

*Birth is an expression complete this moment. Death is an expression
complete this moment. They are like winter and spring. You
do not call winter the beginning of spring, nor summer the end
of spring.*

This is an essential point, so all the teachers made a great effort to comment on it. In the end, this is the teaching of the undivided activity of birth and death. It is meant to replace the dualistic views of worldly people by demonstrating the clear understanding of birth and death in the Buddha Way. We often say to fully experience one dharma. You should understand this here. It sounds like pushing forcefully, things that are scattered in many places, into one dharma. But that is not so. Essentially, all dharmas are fully experiencing one dharma.

There are many kinds in one, and there is no duality in two. There is not a single piece in all dharmas that falls into a second head. Fully experiencing one dharma is an actual form of the *dharmadhatu*. And this is *Genjo koan*. The *Buddha dharma* of Dogen Zenji speaks about the going beyond of going beyond. This is fully experiencing one dharma.

But if you want to take care of everything by fully experiencing one dharma, disregarding its context, that is ignorance of one dharma.

Fully experiencing one dharma is not like that. All dharmas as they are are fully experiencing one dharma.

"Firewood becomes ash and it does not become firewood again." Most people misunderstand this metaphor. When the record of my lecture on this subject was published, one priest who didn't understand matters and principles criticized harshly that Nishiari has the view of annihilation. This text appears to be so if you take it hastily. But study it carefully.

In heaven and earth, and in the *dharmadhatu,* that which perishes is bound to perish. And that which is permanent is bound to be permanent. With poisonous views you fall into either the view of annihilation or the view of permanence. This is a disease. But annihilation and permanence are both the true marks of heaven and earth, the *dharmadhatu.*

That priest does not yet seem to understand the annihilation and permanence of *Buddha dharma,* misunderstanding the true marks of heaven and earth and calling it the view of annihilation. This is where we need thorough study. Look at the first metaphor: Firewood becomes ash. What is this compared to?

It's compared to the undivided activity of birth and death. Birth is undivided activity and death is undivided activity. Birth and death are not like what people ordinarily think. It is not that someone who is alive dies. Rather, birth is birth all the way, and death is death all the way. When you say birth, there is no death. And at the time of death, there is no birth.

Firewood becomes ash. And when it becomes ash it never returns to firewood. Firewood is at the singular state of firewood all the Way. Ash is at the singular state of ash all the Way. Birth and death are just like this. There is only birth at the time of birth. Similarly death does not return to birth. There is only death at the time of death. It is not that birth becomes death. This is explained using the metaphor of firewood and ash. This metaphor has a stronger tone than the previous one of the shore and the boat. In this metaphor firewood represents birth and ash represents death.

Now, following this metaphor, you can clarify the original cause of birth and death and investigate thoroughly the settling point of birth and death according to the understanding of the Soto School. The true great settled mind cannot be attained through the power of Amitabha Buddha or through the merit of chanting Buddha's name. The final guidance at the end of your life must be brought forth by you yourself while you are alive. This is indeed necessary, but hard to attain.

First, "Firewood becomes ash," and then there is a pause. "It does not become firewood again." Then there is another pause. Now look. How about this? This is the point of Dogen Zenji's great settled mind. Can each of you affirm this and attain the settled view? You may not be able to do it so quickly.

The reason for this is, having learned about cause and effect in the three worlds and transmigration throughout the six realms; having maintained the precepts and having practiced for good causes and good effects, you may have the conventional view of counting on what you cannot count on, with the wish to become a buddha someday. But upon hearing that firewood becomes ash and does not become firewood again, it may come up against your conventional view. And you may be astonished and disappointed. But it doesn't help to see in that way. You should make an effort to realize this.

After firewood becomes ash it will never return to firewood. After the present you dies, you will never return to the former you. Returning is inevitably cut off. Even if you enshrine the Buddha's relics, the Buddha won't come along with them. Tathagatas in the ten directions are like firewood that perishes in the fire. All you can do is to build a stupa and conduct a condolence ceremony. Dogen Zenji will not return and Bodhidharma will not be resurrected. In the same manner, the Nishiari of today will not be the Nishiari of tomorrow. When the continuation of one lifetime stops, the former Nishiari will not appear again.

Today is only today. Yesterday is only yesterday. This is the landscape of discontinuation in the *dharmadhatu* without self. You may think that Nishiari of the present will continue without being cut off because cause and effect or action and result extend throughout the three worlds. But this is an ordinary view. The Nishiari of today will never appear again, even in one million years. Birth does not become death. Death does not become birth. Birth is only birth. Death is only death. And they never overlap each other.

Therefore we should experience all the way to the bottom today. We should open to one phrase and practice just one practice and get all the way to the bottom of the independence of the self, thoroughly experiencing this birth. Even if you become a buddha in the future, you of the present will never be seen. It is just one time, one direction. If we think about it, what seems to be just an ordinary person's petty realm today is indeed very precious.

"Yet, do not suppose that the ash is after and the firewood is before." But it is hard to understand only through hearing these words. Dogen Zenji sometimes switches the orders of things. To say that ash is before and firewood is after may seem like confusion of before and after.

Since it is said, "Firewood becomes ash," you might hold to the view that firewood is before and ash is after. Likewise, you might think that birth is before and death is after, and birth turns into death. This is a delusion where two views are in opposition to each other. Because of holding such a dualistic view, ordinary people can never achieve settled mind. If we are without this dualistic view, we can experience the great settled mind and great emancipation right on the spot.

Now this is most important. Let me tell you why Dogen Zenji excluded before and after so much. Because of this thought of before and after, we are pulled by birth and death. We cannot die thoroughly. Because of this view, we cannot stop breathing. Even if it is said, "Firewood becomes ash," it is not that firewood turns into ash. Firewood is firewood. Ash is ash. One direction that is all-inclusive, one time that is all-inclusive. It is being independent of before and after. Birth and death are like this. It is not that birth turns into death or that death turns into birth. Birth and death are independent dharmas. Now at the place of one time, one direction, lies the bull's-eye of great settled mind.

Go where there is ash and ask, "Right now you have a very fluffy body. But you used to be called firewood, which was very solid and flammable when put into a fire. You got burned little by little and got yourself to where you are now." Do you think the ash will agree to this? It will certainly reply, "Nonsense! I have never met anyone called firewood." In this way, the view that firewood is before and ash after is from the perspective of being outside. The ash itself is not concerned with it.

Understand in this way. It may appear that the thought before arose in the past and the thought after will arise in the future. All of you may think that the thought after continues from the thought before. Is it that the thought before stops at the point when the thought after occurs? Or is it that the thought after arises when the thought before is exhausted?

This will be like a single-span bridge with no interruption. The thought before simply stops. The thought after simply arises. Before and after are cut off and dropped off. The moment before and the moment after are cut off and dropped off. When the thought after arises, if you say to it, "You are a recurrence of the thought before," it will be astonished. In this way, the thought before does not know the thought after, and the thought after does not know the thought before. The thought that arose in the past will never arise again, even in the distant future, when Maitreya appears in this world. All dharmas are like this.

Now, you should ponder closely. People abiding within birth ordinarily look upon death with fear. What is the use of being fearful? Can you maintain the mind within birth at the moment of death? Speaking of death, can you bring death here while you are alive and meet with it? It is nonsense. So you should give up your dualistic view.

To give up your dualistic view is to realize the undivided activity of birth and death. Truly experience the all-inclusive activity of birth while you are within birth, and practice fully without neglecting even for a moment the everyday activity of raising up and putting down the foot. There is no need to think about death beyond this. Thinking won't help at all.

This is the decisive point of the settled mind. Instead of worrying, you just die. Boom! Without any delusion. To die—Boom!—mean to not be rigid. Death is a moment of death that does not require anything extra from us. It cuts off our breath from its own side. We should die in the way that death takes us. Then why can't we do this? The reason is that we normally have a dualistic view of birth and death as separate.

This is because you cannot fully experience the all-inclusive moment of birth and the all-inclusive moment of death. If you experience birth through the undivided activity of birth, then death is experienced as it is. You should fully investigate this point.

The principle of thoroughly experiencing one dharma can be understood through the example of beans and tofu. Beans become tofu.

From the tofu maker's point of view, beans are boiled and are turned into tofu. It appears that beans are before and tofu after. But this is a perspective from outside. If you say to tofu, "Your former body was a hard material called beans, which I boiled, ground, and strained and hardened with nigiri, and now you have a soft body with a rectangular face, so different from your former body," then tofu would say, "This is nonsense." Tofu can never meet beans again. Beans are beans, tofu is tofu. It is not that "this" turns into "that," but there is only one direction at one time, there is only one undivided activity at one time.

In the same manner, it is not that the eighth son in the former life is born now as the ninth son. The eighth son in the former life was just the eighth son, and the ninth son in this life is just the ninth son. All dharmas are like that. This is the actualization of undivided activity. Birth is just birth. Death is just death. Birth and death are never opposed to each other.

Apply this principle to the realm of our daily activity. You may be calculating how to do "this" this year and "that" next year and become the Head of the School at sixty. But what is the use of it? However hard you scheme, this may not come true. We should rather endeavor moment to moment, acknowledging that today is the only day.

You endeavor and endeavor and when you are exhausted you can go ahead and die. As long as you endeavor completely, within your endeavor you will shine without trying to shine. A painting by Okyo will remain valuable even if it is left alone on the shelf. A painting by a mediocre artist will be worthless even if it is treasured in a double box of kiri wood. In this way, each person should just endeavor. Evaluation will be done by others. You will not need to strive for achievement in order to receive recognition.

A sweet cake does not fall down from heaven no matter how much you wish for it. But as it is commonly said:

> God of fortune
> collecting with empty hands
> New Year's Eve

In this way, normal everyday behavior is essential. As long as your daily behavior is correct you will receive a good result without effort at the appropriate time. In this way you should guide yourself toward death within the course of your ordinary daily activity.

What is guidance for yourself? It is to endeavor on each moment, without ignoring or obscuring each moment. This is the dharma gate of the mind of great ease. If you look for the mind of ease outside of this, it is not the Buddha Way. To talk about before and after is the view of someone outside of the Way. Neither firewood nor ash has before and after. We just say "as it is."

Some people interpret this teaching as the true mark of all dharmas for "mind only." But this falls into theory, which it is not. When you say firewood, the *dharmadhatu* is firewood. When you say ash, the entire heaven and earth is ash. The before and after are cut off. In this way, at the moment of birth the entire heaven and earth is birth. At the moment of death, the entire *dharmadhatu* is death. It is the root of delusion to see birth against death, to regard death as opposed to birth, and to see before and after in birth and death.

The mind of ease is to be free from these views. At the time of birth you exhaust the entire portion of birth and don't see death. At the moment of death you exhaust your entire portion of death and don't see birth. This is the immediate mind, the immediate buddha. It is called emancipation from birth and death. It is the dharma gate of great ease and bliss.

"You should understand that firewood abides in the phenomenal expression of firewood, which fully includes before and after." In the previous section it was cautioned against arousing the view of "before and after." Now at this point, independence of before and after is taught.

"Abid[ing] in a dharma position" does not mean any particular position or direction. That firewood is firewood and ash is ash is called abiding in the dharma position. "Firewood abides in the dharma position of firewood and there is before and after." This is true. Firewood has a time when it was standing in the mountains as a tree, and it has a time when it is cut down and made into firewood. It also has a time when it is stuffed into a kiln and burned. Therefore it has before and after. Although it has before and after, before and after are cut off. To put the moment when it was in the mountains in opposition to the time when it was burned, saying, "This is before and this is after," is an outsider's view. The firewood itself does not have before and after at all. Each moment is the entire time.

"Ash abides in the phenomenal expression of ash." It has its after and it has its before. It is commonly viewed that firewood gradually collapses as it turns to ash. Yet one moment is an entire moment for ash too. Firewood and ash should not be in opposition to each other as "before" and "after." Firewood is the entire portion of firewood, exhausting heaven and earth. Ash is the entire portion of ash, exhausting the entire *dharmadhatu*. In the same manner, birth has hundreds of varieties of before and after, and so does death. Although there is before and there is after, before and after are cut off and "one moment" is the "entire time." In this way, to see before and after in birth and death is a deluded view ordinarily held by people. The Buddha Way is "dropping off" moment by moment. This is described as, "Birth is an expression complete this moment. Death is an expression complete this moment."

Just as firewood does not become firewood again after it is ash, you do not return to birth after death." Here everyone is astonished. The reason is that your understanding of birth and death is based on the common view. You get disappointed because you have a view of permanence.

Dogen Zenji is not talking about such a view. He is actually pointing out the position of one moment that is the entirety of time, and the view that birth is the actualization of undivided activity and death is the actualization of undivided activity. Even if there is rebirth, that does not mean that death becomes birth. There is just birth. Even when we say someone has died, it does not mean that birth turned into death. At the time of death there is just dying.

In this way, birth is birth as a single rod of iron for 10,000 miles. Death is also a single rod of iron for 10,000 miles. Even if innumerable *kalpas* have passed, death does not turn into birth. You should fully understand this "one moment is entire time." Indeed, there is no way other than to say that today is one moment. You might talk about the twelve hours, the twenty-four hours, one year, one hundred years, or ten million years. What is this? It is only the customary thinking of folks.

Such symbols are used in a relative way. It has to do with before and after. Time itself does not have one hundred, or one thousand. Furthermore, it is never stuck with the twelve hours. In this way, when we say time we should say, "just one moment." Past and future are cut off.

This very person makes a face. It manifests at just this moment. You can see this from the fact that the human world has the twelve hours, but dogs and cats don't care about it. In the world of roosters, there is only the fact that the eastern sky becomes red but they don't call it dawn. In the *Lotus Sutra* there is a phrase, "sixty small *kalpas* are like a mealtime." Basically, time is not long or short. Long and short lie only in human thought. To view one moment and to view incalculable *kalpas* are just illusions of human beings.

People ordinarily are worried about birth, death, and reincarnation. But in the end there is no birth or death. Birth and death are just time. There is no suffering and no pleasure, there is just time. If you are enlivened in each moment of time, you are indeed a great iron person.

The celestial realm is time; *naraka* (hell) is time. Arousing the Way-seeking mind, practice, bodhi and nirvana are nothing but actualization on each moment. To be aware of just this moment and practice thoroughly is the practice of just this day.

People ordinarily go back and forth between before and after, time never becomes this very time. When Dogen Zenji says "each moment," he shows the concept of the thorough practice of "this moment" as "the time."

If we see that sixty small *kalpas* are not long and one moment is not short, but that they are both the actualization of time, then raising and lowering the foot of today is never ignored. In this way, if we understand that the so-called coming and going of birth and death is nothing but the flow of time, we realize that intrinsically there is no birth and death to trouble us.

This is the turning point for the mind of great ease. You should all be enlivened here. While you are dilly-dallying around, where is your power? I don't get it. It may look foolish to some people that an eighty-year-old person like me is just taking care of monks. But I don't understand people who dilly-dally, having no idea of being alive or dead.

You should all make a determined effort. You don't have to do anything for the nation or for our school. You only need to establish your own realm and endeavor. As long as you endeavor, you will naturally become a person, although we can't promise beforehand.

We have this body that does not become young after being old and does not revive being once dead. If you cannot possess the great capacity on this day of this lifetime, when can you get it? A teacher of old said, "As I have a great power I fall down when the wind blows." You may think that having great power means not to fall down. But it is not so. A great power is to fall down all the way at the time of falling.

You are all cowards and paralyzed, so you are already dead before you die. But that is not how it should be. So look at this great power. Death never becomes birth. Bokusan here will never revive even after a million years. Then however coarse I am, I will practice as Bokusan throughout my lifetime. This is undivided activity. The great power of undivided activity of birth and death lies here. If, without realizing this, you count on that which cannot be counted on, then today is always absent. Instead, understand this undivided activity.

"This being so, it is an established way in *Buddha dharma* to deny that birth turns into death. Accordingly birth is understood as no-birth." At this point, the principle of no-birth and no-cessation is explained.

This is where Tenkei's *Benchu* and my thought mysteriously come together after a space of 300 years. The text of *Genjo koan* mentions no-birth. But wouldn't no-death make more sense than no-birth here? If birth does not turn into death it means no cessation.

The next line says, "It is an unshakable teaching in Buddha's discourse that death does not turn into birth. Accordingly, death is understood as no death." Wouldn't it make more sense to say "no birth, no death" here? When I was young, I did not understand, and I had great doubt about it. I sometimes thought that perhaps the word order had been misplaced. But as a result of reading further and investigating more and more, I came to understand that this was correct. Why then did Dogen Zenji turn around the way of expressing it? I kept a record of my understanding in my notes: "As it is birth of no birth, it does not become death. As it is cessation of no cessation it does not become birth." This happens to coincide with the explanation of Tenkei. I'm very happy about it. This is the deeply profound and subtle point that Dogen Zenji is expressing.

"To deny that birth turns into death." You should see this through the dialogue of Jianyuan and Daowu. Whenever he was asked, Daowu said, "I won't say, I won't say." Look at this. When you are asked what it is, whether birth or death, what would you say? Do you say death because you think the person inside is dead? Then who is dead?

Or do you say at birth, "Who is being born?" You should investigate this thoroughly.

We say "no birth, no death." But the four great elements and our five *skandhas* might now have just shown up, being attracted by karma. There should not be anything called birth at all. The reason for this is that one's karma does not have lumps. Conditions are not goods. Therefore, for everything there is no birth. Furthermore, when we die, we do not leave even one speck of dust. It is completely no death. The commentary of Tenkei, who saw through this, is indeed excellent.

The *Lotus Sutra* describes the Buddha who achieves eternal buddhahood, and explains that eternal buddhahood is no birth/no cessation. It is explained as the permanent true mark. So you may misunderstand, thinking that the buddha nature is permanent. If your dharma eye is not open, you fall into the view of permanence. In the "Eternal Life" chapter of the *Lotus Sutra*, it says, "multiply these numbers." This is quoted by Tenkei, which is excellent. We say, "Death does not turn into birth, birth does not turn into death." After all, there is no birth or death. When we say no birth and no cessation, there is nothing that is born. Therefore, there is nothing that ceases.

What on earth is this body? Being pulled by one's karma and various conditions, just this much is showing. Originally it is unborn. The body has manifested in this way while unborn. When a wind blows, the cloud moves. The cloud arises just because of the wind. There originally is nothing called cloud. A human being is only the causes and conditions of karma that consists of ignorance and attachment.

If we open up the buddha eye and the dharma eye and look, there is nothing that passes away, and there is nothing that is born. This being so, there is nothing that dies. See through the ancient past as well as the present. There is indeed no birth and no cessation. In order to illustrate the root of no birth and death, Dogen Zenji turned around the words *birth* and *death* here. In Tenkei's *Benchu* he shows that he has a clear understanding.

"Birth is an expression complete this moment. Death is an expression complete this moment." What is prominent—unborn and unceasing—appears in the form of birth and death as an expression of this moment. "Birth and death" is just an expression, just time. It is not that death becomes birth or that birth becomes death. When a birth of no birth becomes a birth, it is the total actualization of birth. It is the complete exertion of one dharma within birth. When the cessation of no cessation is actualized as death, it is the thorough manifestation of death, a complete exertion of our dharma as death.

"They are like winter and spring." It is a simile for each direction. Winter is only winter. Spring is only spring. At each moment there is one direction. In this way, when we say "spring," it does not mean spring that is opposed to winter. In the same way, we don't say that spring becomes summer. This sounds understandable, but it does not reach our gut. The reason is that we lack true practice. Although we talk about "each moment," we actually obscure time. However, this is truly the point of arriving at a settled mind in our school. You should hang this from your neck day and night and investigate thoroughly.

SECTION 11

Enlightenment is like the moon reflected on the water. The moon does not get wet, nor is the water broken. Although its light is wide and great, the moon is reflected even in a puddle an inch wide. The whole moon and the entire sky are reflected in dewdrops on the grass, or even in one drop of water.

Enlightenment does not divide you, just as the moon does not break the water. You cannot hinder enlightenment, just as a drop of water does not hinder the moon in the sky.

The depth of the drop is the height of the moon. Each reflection, however long or short its duration, manifests the vastness of the dewdrop, and realizes the limitlessness of the moonlight in the sky.

"Enlightenment is like the moon reflected on the water" shows the principle of non-hindrance between a person and the dharma. The dharma enters the person and the person enters the dharma. In this way, the person and the dharma do not have separate bodies. In the *Heart Sutra* it says, "Avalokitesvara Bodhisattva, when practicing deeply the *Prajnaparamita* . . ." It means the entire body of Avalokitesvara Bodhisattva is deep prajna, and the totality of deep prajna is Avalokitesvara Bodhisattva.

The person and the dharma or the buddha and the dharma are one body and not two. Because of that, when we experience the person, there is only person. As soon as we say that a person attains the dharma or enlightenment, there is a gap. We are not talking about such a sluggish thing. The entire body of Avalokitesvara is itself dharma. Such an intimate point is "the moon reflected on the water."

However, as *Gosho* points out, there are seemingly contradictory similes: "Unlike the moon and its reflection in the water, when one side is illuminated the other side is dark," and, "Enlightenment is like the moon reflected in the water." The former crushes the dualistic viewpoint of the moon in the water. The latter points out that the water and the moon are truly intimate and not obstructing each other.

Then what is this intimacy? "The moon does not get wet, nor is the water broken." The moon is reflected in the water without moving a speck of dust or without changing a single form. Since the water is the moon and the moon is the water, there is no way that either is broken. It is just as Avalokitesvara makes deep prajna her entire body, while prajna is not broken or crushed.

"Although its light is wide and great, the moon is reflected even in a puddle an inch wide." It is said in Buddhism that the size of the moon is fifty *yojanas* (wide). Indeed, its light is wide and great. And yet, the moon is reflected in a puddle an inch wide or in a dewdrop on the grass.

Don't think that a puddle an inch wide is incapable of containing the moon that is fifty yojanas wide. The dharma of the entire *dharmadhatu* gets into this body that is five feet fall and this five-foot-tall body actualizes the enlightenment of the entire *dharmadhatu*. This body becomes the body of the entire world. The body and the dharma neither turn away nor touch each other.

"The whole moon and the entire sky are reflected in a dewdrop on the grass or even in one drop of water." The sky is said to be 400 *yojanas* wide. Such a huge sky abiding in a dewdrop on the grass or even in a drop of water. What an amazing thing! This transcends large and small, wide and narrow, where large is not large and small is not small. In this way, the dharma of the entire world abides in us. This body itself contains the dharma of all buddhas. This body is the dwelling place of all buddhas, all dharmas, and all precepts. This is how a person does not hinder enlightenment or dharma.

"Enlightenment does not divide you, just as the moon does not break the water." Just as the moon reflected on the water does not drill holes in the water, enlightenment does not crush the person. As the entire water is the moon and the entire moon is water, neither of them breaks or wets the other. They are intimate indeed. It is not the intimacy of two separate things. But they are extremely intimate, because they are exactly one.

"You cannot hinder enlightenment, just as a drop of water does not hinder the moon in the sky." This line forms a pair with "Enlightenment is like the moon reflected on the water." Even if a person is opened up for enlightenment, the *dharmadhatu* does not turn triangular or square. Nothing can be done to our eyes, which are horizontal, or our noses, which are vertical. How so? Because the person sees the *dharmadhatu* fully engaging body and mind, the person and the *dharmadhatu* are not two. Because they are not two, there is no way that they hinder each other. Because of the moving body, Avalokitesvara Bodhisattva is deep prajna, Avalokitesvara does not hinder deep prajna, but instead appears in thirty-three kinds of bodies.

Nothing is hindered when the entire moon and the entire sky abide in the thirty-three kinds of bodies, or in dewdrops on the grass. The whole body abides completely in large bodies of water, or it abides completely in a small puddle of water. Now you need to reflect on your own steps. On the conduct of each one of us, whether the matter is large or small, the entire personality, as well as the entire practice, is reflected. Therefore, if you look at tiny things, you can see the totality of the person. This is a scary thing. You should reflect deeply on this and be mindful. One phrase is the result of a lifetime, one action is the accumulation of the power of practice throughout your life.

"The depth of the drop is the height of the moon." If the moon palace is fifty *yojanas* high, then its reflection in the water is fifty *yojanas* deep. This is a small body with the height of about five feet, but when the deep prajna of the entire world practices, then this body is the body of the entire *dharmakaya*. When even for a moment you express the

Buddha's seal in the three activities of body, speech, and mind by sitting upright in *samadhi,* the entire world becomes enlightenment. The body that is sitting upright is itself the body of the entire *dharmadhatu,* the body of the entire empty sky. In this way, the size of a person and the size of dharma are the same. Therefore, in our daily actions the measure of the power of our practice is expressed. The measure of enlightenment is the measure of our power of practice.

"Each reflection, however long or short its duration, manifests the vastness of the dewdrop, and realizes the limitlessness of the moonlight in the sky." An *asamskyaya kalpa* plus a hundred more *kalpas* is not necessarily a long time—the duration of a finger snap is not necessarily short. In one instant there are sixty *kalpas* and in the span of a finger snap there are immeasurable *kalpas.* "Wherever for a moment you express the buddha's seal in the three actions of body, speech, and mind by sitting upright in *samadhi,* the whole phenomenal world becomes the Buddha seal and the entire sky turns into enlightenment." In this way, this very moment is the time that penetrates the entire past and the entire future. Whether the duration of the reflection of the moon on the water is long or short, it is entire time.

In a large amount of water a huge moon is reflected. In a small amount of water a small moon is reflected. The moon is reflected as large where it is supposed to be reflected as large. The moon is reflected as small where it is supposed to be reflected as small. But the moon itself does not change its size. The duration of time, long or short, is just like that. When it needs an *asamskyaya kalpa,* it takes an *asamskyaya kalpa.* When it takes a finger snap, it is complete in a finger snap. After all, long or short, large or small, all are *Genjo koan.*

SECTION 12

When dharma does not fill your whole body and mind, you may assume it is already sufficient. When dharma fills your body and mind, you understand that something is missing.

For example, when you sail out in a boat to the middle of an ocean where no land is in sight, and view the four directions, the ocean looks circular, and does not look any other way. But the ocean is neither round nor square; its features are infinite in variety. It is like a palace. It is like a jewel. It only looks circular as far as you can see at that time. All things are like this.

Though there are many features in the dusty world and the world beyond conditions, you see and understand only what your eye of practice can reach. In order to learn the nature of the myriad things, you must know that although they may look round or square, the other features of oceans and mountains are infinite in variety; whole worlds are there. It is so not only around you, but also directly beneath your feet, or in a drop of water.

The first line corresponds to the previous line, "When you first seek dharma you may assume that you are far away from its environs." It is like reinterpreting this previous line. When our investigation of *Buddha dharma* with our body and mind is shallow and when we are standing at the threshold, we tend to feel that we have achieved enough dharma. The great ocean of *Buddha dharma* becomes deeper and deeper as we enter. To become a long-nosed goblin is proof that *Buddha dharma* has not yet become one's own. As it is said, "When the dharma fills your body and mind, you understand that something is missing." The more deeply you study, the more things you find that you don't understand. A scholar said, "It's a real problem to be an expert." Usually it's easy to get away with not claiming expertise in a certain field, but an expert cannot do this.

When a person acquires a small amount of money, he may feel that he could rule the entire world. On the other hand, a ruler of a nation seems to have plenty, but has to be concerned with the governing of the nation from morning till night and cannot enjoy the wealth. Likewise, when we first see and hear about *Buddha dharma* and pass a few *koans,* we feel extremely encouraged and are awakened to the great matter, or feel that we understand tremendous things. But when we arrive at the ultimate realm, things become unattainable; enlightenment disappears. It's not only that "something is missing," but the entire body becomes lacking; this is interesting.

The Second Ancestor's "unattainable," the Fourth Ancestor's "emancipation," the Sixth Ancestor's "not one thing," and Dogen Zenji's "body and mind dropped off" are all lacking. The extreme end is ultimately "not doing and not attaining." So there is nothing that is sufficient. "When one side is illuminated, the other side is dark." To think that something is missing is reality or is true, and to think that what is there is sufficient is false. Therefore, to grab one phrase or half a phrase and think that you have obtained something is a grave mistake.

It's just like four views of the same water [a palace, a jewel, pus and blood, and water]. You only see things through analytical views, which are not different from those of ordinary people. But the actuality of dharma can only be seen when such karmic views are exhausted. Now, you should understand the correct marks of *Buddha dharma*.

"For example, when you sail out in a boat to the middle of an ocean where no land is in sight, and view the four directions, the ocean looks circular . . ."

When Dogen Zenji went to Great Song, he had an actual experience of crossing the ocean. He now comments on it from the viewpoint of practice. This is a teaching based on his memory. Now when you go out in the ocean, there is no mountain, land, or anything that obstructs your eyes. Then does it only look circular?

"But the ocean is neither round nor square." This is the meaning of "the ocean looks circular." The ocean looks circular as far as our eye can see. But the ocean is neither round nor square—it has an infinite variety of features.

"It is like a palace. It is like a jewel." This refers to the four views of a single body of water. Fish see water as a palace; celestial beings see it as a jewel ornament. Hungry ghosts see it as pus and blood; humans see it as water. These are the views corresponding to each being's karmic limitation. None of these views is complete. In the same manner, to see the ocean as only circular is a limited, tentative view. It is not, of course, exhausting all the features of the ocean, which is neither circular nor square. Not being able to see the ocean in the correct way, people ordinarily cannot see all things as they are because they have views corresponding to their own capacity, limited by karma.

"Though there are many features in the dusty world and the world beyond conditions, you see and understand only what your eye of practice can reach." The world beyond conditions is outside of the ordinary world. Both in the dharma of the ordinary world and the world outside there are infinite features and unlimited characteristics. But we can only see and understand what our eye of practice can reach among these dharmas. Therefore, those who have not had their body and mind filled with dharma think that what they have is sufficient. And those whose whole body and mind are filled with dharma know that there are many other characteristics. And yet there is nothing that is not dharma.

People understand only according to their capacity. A tall person has a tall dharma body; a short person has a short dharma body. Yet, dharma is not limited to this. So it is said, "In order to learn the nature of the myriad things, you must know that although they may look round or square, the other features of oceans and mountains are infinite in variety."

In the practice of the Buddha Way, to understand the nature of the myriad things, we must know that for infinite *kalpas,* with our eyes wide open, there are innumerable dharma gates and paths of investigation besides what we can see. When I say this you might think that we study with a vast view and we are looking somewhere afar somewhat vaguely. But don't be mistaken. Vastness without limitation is immediately underfoot. You may think a great ocean is vast and distant, but it is no other than the cup of tea you are drinking right now. Where there is walking forward there is walking backward. Where there is something aside there is something right here. Understand this point clearly and do not arouse the thought that you have understood enough.

SECTION 13

A fish swims in the ocean, and no matter how far it swims there is no end to the water. A bird flies in the sky, and no matter how far it flies there is no end to the sky. However, the fish and the bird have never left their elements. When their activity is large their field is large. When their need is small their field is small. Thus, each of them totally covers its full range, and each of them totally experiences its realm. If the bird leaves the air it will die at once. If the fish leaves the water it will die at once.

Know that water is life and air is life. The bird is life and the fish is life. Life must be the bird and life must be the fish.

Besides this, further steps can be taken. Thus there are practice and enlightenment, which encompass both eternal life and limited life.

Now if a bird or a fish tries to reach the end of its element before moving in it, this bird or this fish will not find its way or its place. When you find your place where you are, practice occurs, actualizing the fundamental point; for the place, the Way, is neither large nor small, neither yours nor others'. The place, the Way, has not carried over from the past, and it is not merely arising now.

Accordingly, in the practice-enlightenment of the Buddha Way, to attain one dharma is to penetrate one dharma, to meet one practice is to sustain one practice.

Here is the place; here the Way unfolds. The boundary of realization is not distinct, for the realization comes forth simultaneously with the mastery of Buddha dharma.

A fish is free in the water, and a bird finds its freedom in the air. Even though a bird flies every day, it does not fly beyond the limit of the sky. There is no fish that has exhausted the boundary of the water although it swims around all day long. A fish lives in the water and forgets the water. A bird stays in the sky and does not notice the sky. They are free only in water and sky.

"When their activity is large their field is large. When their need is small their field is small. Thus, . . ." In this way, little sparrows in the yard are busy picking up fallen seeds on the ground, while a great roc flaps its wings in the vast sky and flies 90,000 miles in one movement. According to the scale of its activities, there is a corresponding result. In the same manner, the myriad things in heaven and earth for us and the myriad things in heaven and earth for all sages are just dharmas as they are. There is no difference, but they can be wide or limited according to the activities of each.

"Thus, each of them thoroughly covers its full range and each of them totally experiences its realm." A roc is a roc, and a sparrow is a sparrow. The scale of their activity is different. Yet they do not depend on the power of others. Each of them flies off on its own. Each of them comes and goes without hindrance. In the emptiness of primary significance, fish are also like this.

And yet, "If the bird leaves the air it will die at once. If the fish leaves the water it will die at once." We too are like that. The three worlds are the pure land of ease and bliss. So we don't need to get out of the three worlds. To get out of the three worlds is something extra. The fact that we are bound by the three worlds is our fault and it is not the fault of the three worlds.

If we "abide in the world as emptiness, just as the lotus blossom is not attached to the water," we will not be bound by the three worlds. There is nothing lacking in the three worlds, as they are the settled abode of the buddha. The buddha dies when he is outside of the three worlds. We die when we get outside of the water of true empty nature.

"Know that water is life and air is life." The life of all buddhas is the three realms. Life for us is zazen. Fish and birds make the water and sky their life.

But that is not all. "The bird is life and the fish is life. Life must be the bird and life must be the fish." In this way it is not that all buddhas make the three worlds their life, but all buddhas *are* the three worlds. The water *is* fish and the sky *is* birds.

Furthermore, when we speak, the entire bodies of all buddhas are life. The entire bodies of fish and birds are life. Life and all buddhas are not two. Life and fish are not two. Life and birds are not two.

Our daily activity of the present moment is done freely without hindrance in this water, the water of dharma nature. In the emptiness of primary significance we fly around freely without contriving. As soon as we depend upon any scheming or manipulation we immediately lose the wisdom and life of buddhas and ancestors.

"Besides this, further steps can be taken. Thus there are practice and enlightenment, which encompass both eternal life and limited life."

This means that we should not be stuck in our place. Just as it is said in the fascicle of *Bendowa:* "Although this inconceivable dharma is abundant in each person, it is not actualized without practice, and it is not experienced without realization."

Then how do we take further steps? What kind of practice and enlightenment will be there by taking one more step? When we hear "life is the bird and life is the fish" it is a very concise statement where subject and object are no longer standing against each other. But if we say that we regard life as the bird or the fish it sounds like we are separating life from the bird or the fish. This being so, it ought to be that water is water and bird is bird.

If we inherit the Buddha Way we experience the unlimited life as well as the limited life of the Buddha Way. If we inherit the three kinds of poison we experience the unlimited life as well as the limited life of three kinds of poison. Therefore it is essential to inherit Buddha's unlimited life by taking further steps and attaining enlightenment.

For a bird air is life, and for a fish water is life. For us zazen, the emptiness of primary significance and Buddha's dignified bearing, are life. If we leave these elements we will die right away.

"If a bird or a fish tries to reach the end of its element before moving in it, this bird or this fish will not find its way or its place." This is a point that requires particular attention. If you try to find the end of the limitless sky and water before you travel in it, you can't do so. The reason is that there will be no moment when we have exhausted the limitless sky or water.

This being so, if we do one thing today we thoroughly practice this one thing. If we encounter one practice we do it thoroughly. This is the practice of those who study the Buddha Way.

As there is no beginning for the origin, there can be a practice for *asamskyaya kalpas*. It's not something you can exhaust in a moment. Dogen Zenji said, "Although there are thousands of myriads of things that we don't know, just try not to go against *Buddha dharma*." You need to keep in mind in your everyday life the one road of "not going against."

"When you find your place right where you are, practice occurs, actualizing the fundamental point. When you find your way at this moment, practice occurs, actualizing the fundamental point."

Great fish live in the great ocean. Small fish live in a narrow stream. Water is not limited to large or small. The realm of freedom lies within the capacity of the fish. It is not that the great sky was formed for a great bird, it is not that a great ocean was created for a large fish.

It is just that a person and the environs correspond to each other. In the realm where you go about, a world that corresponds emerges. You can only make use of the world according to your own capacity.

Enlightenment does not appear beyond what you have practiced.

"Practice occurs, actualizing the fundamental point." In actualizing the fundamental point, the "fundamental point" is a synonym of "actualizing." Dogen Zenji often uses words in such a way.

"The place, the Way, is neither large nor small." When we have the dharma in hand, this practice of *Buddha dharma* emerges without limitation. Then what is "the Way"? It is *annuttaru-samyak-sambodhi*. It is the primary emptiness. It is dharma nature water. It is neither large nor small, neither self nor other. Because it does not appear without practicing, it is not like dharma suchness, which is originally existent. Yet, it is not anything you acquire just now. As it is said [in *Bendowa*], "This inconceivable dharma is abundant in each person, yet it is not actualized without practice, and it is not experienced without realization."

Because the Way and the place—the treasure place—are such, practice follows and the fundamental point is actualized. If you get this point, you are done with the eight volumes of the *Lotus Sutra*.

"Accordingly, in the practice-enlightenment of the Buddha Way, to attain one dharma is to penetrate one dharma, to meet one practice is to sustain one practice." This being so, if you engage one dharma you should penetrate that dharma. There is no need to hurry, no need to get another dharma or another practice. When you eat rice you should become rice. Then it is not likely that you would bite down on a small stone.

When you do zazen, you should become zazen thoroughly. There is no need to bring in the *koan*s. If you work on *koan*s during zazen, the *koan* becomes the master and zazen becomes the attendant. Thus zazen is no longer zazen. To abide at ease in steadfast non-thinking is the bull's-eye of zazen. Other schools aside, the dharma descendants of Dogen Zenji should study Dogen Zenji's *Buddha dharma*.

When we practice our dharma thoroughly in this way, "Here is the place; here the Way unfolds. The boundary of realization is not distinct, for the realization comes forth simultaneously with the mastery of *Buddha dharma*."

There are various ways of reading: "The boundary of realization is not distinct." The commentary *Shiki* reads it as "not clear." It's all right, but if we read the text as "The boundary of realization is not known," it can make sense.

Although there are myriad dharmas to be known "out there," it is not known that the single practice that is being practiced now encompasses myriad practices. Although it is not known, there is no problem about not knowing. Knowing means that studying one dharma is studying myriad dharmas, and practicing one dharma is mastering myriad practices.

When we talk about zazen in the realm of thoroughly experiencing one dharma, invariably myriad dharmas arise altogether, study together, and practice simultaneously. Although this is not recognized, in fact neccesarily there is simultaneous arising and simultaneous studying together; all dharmas and all practices are merged in darkness and practice in darkness.

This is to practice together with the entire *dharmadhatu* and to practice together with all sentient beings. If we look at the text in this way, "not distinct" means not to be known. The dharma that is not to be known "comes forth simultaneously with the mastery of *Buddha dharma*." If we understand in this way, it is completely all right that what is to be known is not known.

Why is it so? The reason is that where the *Buddha dharma* to be known is thoroughly experienced, the myriad dharmas and myriad practices that are not yet known arise together and study together, coexisting simultaneously. That is why there is no problem. This is the meaning of the phrase [in *Bendowa*], "When even for a moment you sit upright in *samadhi,* the whole phenomenal world becomes the Buddha's seal and the entire sky turns into enlightenment."

In the common world it is said, "Filial piety is the source of a hundred practices." This means that filial piety extends to a hundred practices. If you have filial piety toward your parents, you will be loyal to your lord, you are faithful to your friends, and do not lose track of the order of relationships. Everything goes that way. It is that way right now. It is not that filial piety brings forth a hundred practices, but filial piety is itself a hundred practices.

All dharmas are unobtainable and are without self-nature. Ordinary people set up their abiding place and approach the dharma with their own views. But they should abide at ease in their place of no-abiding. When we say "abiding at ease immovably," it does not mean to be immovable by being bound up. A wheel turns around regardless of day or night. Turning is the "abiding at ease immovably" of the wheel. Not turning is a disruption for the wheel.

There is a verse, "Encountering spring for many years, the heart does not change." Does "the heart does not change" mean that sprouts do not come forth from a decayed tree or flowers do not bloom? No, it doesn't. To sprout in spring is the heart that does not change. To bloom in spring is to abide at ease immovably. "I have a great power. I fall down when a storm blows." This is "abiding at ease immovably." Because you abide at the place of no abiding, your mind is at ease. When you thoroughly exhaust one practice after another at this place of ease, each practice is the path of *anuttara-sammyak-sambodhi*, which arises and is practiced simultaneously with thorough actualization of *Buddha dharma*.

Section 14

Do not suppose that what you attain becomes your knowledge and is grasped by your consciousness. Although actualized immediately, the inconceivable may not be apparent. Its appearance is beyond your knowledge.

Zen Master Baoche of Mount Mayu was fanning himself. A monk approached and said, "Master, the nature of wind is permanent and there is no place it does not reach. Why, then, do you fan yourself?"

"Although you understand that the nature of the wind is permanent," Baoche replied, "you do not understand the meaning of its reaching everywhere."

"What is the meaning of its reaching everywhere?" asked the monk again. The master just kept fanning himself. The monk bowed deeply.

The actualization of the Buddha dharma, *the vital path of its correct transmission, is like this. If you say that you do not need to fan yourself because the nature of wind is permanent and you can have wind without fanning, you will understand neither permanence nor the nature of wind. The nature of wind is permanent;*

because of that, the wind of Buddha's house brings forth the gold of the earth and makes fragrant the cream of the long river.

Written in mid-autumn, the first year of Tempuku [1233], and given to my lay student Koshu Yo of Kyushu Island. Revised in the fourth year of Kencho [1252].

The first line points to the dynamics of thorough realization. This corresponds to the previous line: "In the practice-enlightenment of the Buddha Way . . ." What you "attain" is the power of sustaining one practice when you meet one practice. When you practice you may get some feeling that "Aha, this is it!" But don't assume that this is reflected in your perception, and that you can recognize this as enlightenment. If there is someone who knows and something that is known, this is duality and not enlightenment. Here in this sentence, discriminating mind is rejected and the point of thorough realization is demonstrated.

"Although actualized immediately, the inconceivable might not be apparent." When you practice *Buddha dharma* genuinely, you will certainly experience thorough realization as "Oh, this is it." This is what is called a great opening of enlightenment—thorough realization. But here it is said "actualized immediately." Practice and realization are actualized simultaneously; it is quick. Sitting buddha, killing buddha, the actualization of thorough realization, is intimately with you. So when you grasp it, there is not even a small particle of realization.

Therefore it is intimate. Discrimination, whether it is hidden or revealed, is useless. Where there is practice, there is also realization. But when we want to pin down what is revealed that is "beyond your knowledge," and there is nothing in particular, subject and object both disappear. The *dharmadatu* is one thusness, and ultimate existence is beyond your knowledge. At this time you clearly fit the dharma and the dharma reveals itself unmistakably. Thorough realization is like this. Seemingly impenetrable, it is nothing special. Here Dogen Zenji explains the matter of realization in an intimate way.

"Zen Master Baoche of Mount Mayu was fanning himself. A monk approached and said, 'Master, the nature of wind is permanent and there is no place it does not reach. Why, then, do you fan yourself?'"

Mayu is a dharma heir of Mazu and was a distinguished master.

Although the nature of wind is omnipresent and all pervading, it doesn't manifest when it is not called forth. Only when it is called forth does it manifest. However, this monk fell into the view of spontaneous arising [of enlightenment] and did not understand the meaning of omnipresent and all pervading. So he said that basically the nature of wind is permanent and there is no need to use the fan.

This is the same as saying, "If we are originally the body of dharma nature we do not need to rouse the mind of enlightenment and practice." This is not correct. Precisely because we are the body of dharma nature, dharma becomes ours when we rouse the mind of enlightenment and practice. What is originally ours becomes truly ours. It is just like that in this case. Since the nature of wind is permanent, the wind appears when the fan is used. If there were a place where the nature of wind did not reach, the wind would not appear even if we use the fan.

Although Mayu said this, the monk did not understand and said, "What's the meaning of its reaching everywhere?" And the master just kept fanning himself. Without questioning whether it comes from the east, south, west, or north, he was demonstrating the principle, that the wind manifests when being called forth. "The monk bowed deeply." This is a place where you cannot do anything but bow.

"The actualization of the *Buddha dharma*, the vital path of its correct transmission, is like this." To use a fan though the nature of wind is omnipresent means to arouse the aspiration, practice, bodhi, and nirvana, even though we all have Buddha nature by origin. This is the wind [teaching] of the Buddha's house and the vital path of its correct transmission.

". . . [T]he wind of Buddha's house brings forth the gold of the earth and makes fragrant the cream of the long river." Although the entire earth is the earth of gold, it does not become gold unless you go through the process of making it gold. Although what flows through the river is pure milk, it does not yet have the taste of cream. The radiance of our original nature manifests only when we practice and actualize the buddha nature. We should not fall into the view of spontaneous enlightenment. This is the vital matter.

II.
Commentary by Shunryu Suzuki

Edited by Dairyu Michael Wenger and Sojun Mel Weitsman
Assisted by Jeffrey Schneider

INTRODUCTION:
Suzuki Roshi and the *Genjo koan*

SHUNRYU SUZUKI was born in 1904. Like his father before him,
he became a Zen priest. As a young man he met Nona Ransom, an
English woman who was a tutor to the last emperor of China. From
her he learned English. He did chores for her, and she, through him,
became interested in Buddhism.

Shunryu soon became interested in bringing Buddhism to the West—
specifically, Dogen's teachings and the practice of zazen. It wasn't until
1959 that conditions were right for him to leave his temple and come to
America. At that time, he applied for and was appointed to a three-year
term as priest of Sokoji Temple in San Francisco, an old synagogue in
Japantown that served the Japanese congregation.

Shunryu sat zazen in the pews. Artists, painters, poets, and seek-
ers of all shapes and sizes heard there was a Zen master in town and
made their way to see Shunryu Suzuki. He invited them to sit meditation with him early in the morning. He gave lectures on the Blue Cliff
Record and Dogen's teaching. Shunryu had studied Dogen's teachings with Kishizawa Ian, who had studied with Nishiari Bokusan. He
taught a *Genjo koan* lecture series in 1965, '66, '67, '69, '70, and '71. We
do not have a complete record of any of the series, so we present here
talks from all of them, to give a commentary of the whole work. He
taught that the *Genjo koan* and the practice of zazen are inextricably
bound.

The *Genjo koan,* distilled through his years of practicing zazen, was
at the core of Shunryu's teaching. Shunryu did not travel around the
country. He planted himself in San Francisco, and with zazen practice
as his focus the center grew. In 1966 Tassajara Zen Mountain Center
was added to the mandala. It grew into becoming a monastic temple

in the Los Padres National Forest. In time, his students matured and started centers in Mill Valley, Los Altos, and Berkeley. At his death in December of 1971, he had founded a vibrant meditation community through which Dogen's teachings could be expressed in America.

Shunryu Suzuki Commentary
on *Genjo koan*

THE SECRET of all the teachings of Buddhism is how to live in each moment, how to obtain absolute freedom moment after moment. This is the theme of the *Genjo koan*. Moment after moment, we exist in interdependency with past and future and all existence. In short, if you practice zazen, concentrating on your breathing moment after moment, you will be keeping the precepts, helping yourself and helping others, and attaining liberation.

We do not aim for or emphasize some particular state of mind or some particular teaching. Even though it is a perfect and profound teaching, we do not emphasize the teaching only. Rather, we emphasize how we understand and how we bring the truth into practice. This practice does not mean some particular practice only. When we say "Zen," Zen includes all the activity of our life.

Dogen Zenji said meditators practice like water and milk. When each one of us is concentrated on Zen practice, we are not just separate beings. The oneness of all the students or monks is manifest. When you live in each moment, each one of you is both an independent being and a dependent being. Each one of you has absolute independence. You attain the same buddhahood that Buddha attained. Living in each one's absolute freedom we attain the same attainment. Each one of us is independent in the same realization. When this reality is understood, there are students, there are teachers, there is someone who serves tea, there is someone who drinks the tea, and they are independent beings. By practicing the practice that was started by Buddha, Buddhism is carried forth.

Though Buddha was born 2,500 years ago, Buddha is right here when we practice his practice. Buddha lives in our age with us. Buddha is Buddha, and we are students. You may say there is student and teacher, but we are all the same—we are practicing the same practice in the same way as our buddha ancestors did in their time. Actually, we are all practicing the same practice *with* them. Whatever we do, that is Buddha's practice. This is how we keep the precepts.

In Buddha's day, the practitioner's way of life was Indian—in China there was the Chinese way of life, in Japan today there is the Japanese way of life. Although the way of living is different, actually what we do is not different from what Buddha did. We all express absolute freedom. There are not two absolute freedoms.

In China when they were too interested in Buddhist philosophy, they ignored how to live in Buddha's way. In other words, they ignored how to keep the precepts. To keep the precepts is not to keep the Indian way of life. When you eat here, you should eat here. You cannot eat in India all the time. Strictly speaking, if you want to keep the precepts literally, you have to go to India. Then you can keep the precepts completely. There is an interesting story about a monk from India. When he came to China, he could not observe Indian precepts because the customs were different. So he returned to India because he was so afraid of breaking Indian precepts.

If you do not know how to observe the precepts, or if you emphasize just written precepts without knowing how to keep them, then Buddhism will die immediately. If you know how to keep the precepts, Buddhism will continue, and it will develop as Zen developed in China. Various Mahayana schools observed them as Indian Buddhists did. They thought that this is Buddha's Way. So Buddha's Way eventually separated from their everyday life. Zen students understood the precepts as their way of life. They were sure that their way of practice was to actualize Buddha's teaching—to live in this moment, to attain enlightenment. To be Buddha is to attain perfect freedom. How to attain perfect freedom is how to live in this moment.

In China, Zen Buddhists established new precepts, which are called pure rules. For other Buddhists, precepts were some rules Buddha observed; but for Zen Buddhists precepts were their own way of life— how to live in this moment in this place. When we are not so sincere about our practice or about our way of life—about ourselves—we may say, "I am a priest, but they are laymen." "I am a priest, and Buddhist teaching is written in some particular book." If you understand Buddhism in that way, you ignore the precepts. But if you realize that religion is for everyone, that is our way of life. Precepts that are written in some particular book cannot be actualized—cannot be brought into everyday practice. When we become sincere about our everyday life and the meaning of religion, we cannot live with old precepts that were set up for someone else. We should have our own precepts.

Thus, Hyakujo Zenji established Mahayana precepts in the eighth century. Mahayana Buddhism was introduced to China in the fourth century. For many years, Indian precepts were observed. It is impossible for Chinese people to observe Indian precepts. It is ridiculous. They were observed by the priest only, ignoring the life of ordinary people.

Zen Buddhists were very serious about their way of life and the people's way of life—they revised the Indian precepts. In India they could practice zazen all day long, because the monks were supported entirely by the people. After they finished their household life, they became monks, and their children supported them. But Chinese monks supported themselves and could not sit all day long. Whatever they did should be Zen. So they adapted the practice more to everyday life. Chinese Zen was more practical. They knew how to apply Zen in everyday life.

How to apply Zen in everyday life is not difficult. If we live in each moment, that is Zen, whether you are sitting or working. Living in each moment is Zen. Zen is in our everyday life. You may say the Indian way was rather lazy, not active enough. Indian Zen emphasized some mysterious state of mind, but in China they emphasized direct experience.

In this way, Buddhist philosophy was actualized in Zen practice. The oneness of zazen practice as everyday activity was brought to society. So Zen is the source of the philosophy, and the source of art, and the source of religious life. Now let's turn to the *Genjo koan.*

GENJO K'OAN

As all things are Buddha dharma, *there is delusion and realization, practice, birth and death, and there are buddhas and sentient beings. As the myriad things are without an abiding self, there is no delusion, no realization, no buddha, no sentient*

*being, no birth and death. The Buddha Way is, basically, leaping
clear of the many and the one; thus there are birth and death,
delusion and realization, sentient beings and buddhas. Yet, in
attachment blossoms fall, and in aversion weeds spread. To carry
yourself forward and experience myriad things is delusion. That
myriad things come forth and experience themselves is awakening. Those who have great realization of delusions are buddhas;
those who are greatly deluded about realization are sentient
beings. Further, there are those who continue realizing beyond
realization, who are in delusion throughout delusion. When buddhas are truly buddhas they do not necessarily notice that they
are buddhas. However, they are actualized buddhas, who go on
actualizing buddhas.*

In the first paragraph of *Genjo koan,* Dogen Zenji gives us the whole
pattern of the Buddhist way:

When all things are Buddhist phenomena . . .

—when all things are Buddhist teaching—

We have enlightenment and ignorance . . .

—something to study or to observe—precepts, or sutras, or a problem for philosophical discussion of life and death, enlightened ones, or
ignorant ones.

*When all things are without self, we have no ignorance, no
enlightenment, no buddhas, no people. No life and no death.*

When all things are without self what we do is done in the realms of self-
lessness, like milk and water. When the whole fabric is woven completely
in various colors, what you see are not pieces of thread, what you see is
one whole cloth. Do you understand? There is no need to say, "This is
water" when you drink water and milk, and there is no water and milk.

Dogen continues:

When all things are without self, we have no ignorance, no enlightenment, no buddhas, no people. No life and no death.

The Buddhist way is beyond being and non-being. We know each colorful thread and we know the whole woven cloth. We observe things in two ways without any contradiction. But when we are not sincere enough, we may say, "This is Buddhism [*laughs*], and this is another religion. We are monks, and they are laymen, that's all." You don't understand the whole beautiful cloth.

The Buddhist way is beyond a thread or a textile. Therefore we have birth and death, ignorance and enlightenment. Still we see the various colors in the woven cloth, and we appreciate the pattern of the cloth.

We have life and death, ignorance and enlightenment, people and buddhas.

—so many interesting colors in the one whole piece of cloth.

However, flowers fall with our attachment, and weeds grow with our detachment.

As Buddhists, we live with people observing the flower fading away day by day. We bring forth the weeds day after day with our detachment.

So in the second paragraph he says:

That we move ourselves and understand all things is ignorance.

Here in the second paragraph, there are various ideas and various practices, not only Zen but also the Pure Land School. But for Dogen, they are one beautiful cloth. A piece of thread alone is not useful. When you make a beautiful cloth with it, it becomes useful—it becomes perfect religion.

Buddhism and various religions find their own meaning in big, human, religious life. It makes sense to weave a beautiful cloth with thread. Each religion is just a piece of thread. Maybe it is colorful, maybe it is beautiful, but if you weave something with it, you can make a beautiful robe.

In this sense our way has two facets. One is the true meaning of religion. On the other hand, each school is one of the many ways of religious practice.

I have two facets. I belong to the Soto School. I am just a piece of thread [*laughs*]. I know how to make myself a piece of useful material. This is the Soto way. Without knowing how to make ourselves useful, to observe some lofty activity does not make much sense.

We are not just Soto priests. We are Buddhists. But we cannot practice all the ways of practice. Although we practice just the Soto way, we are, nevertheless, Buddhist. That's all.

> *That things advance and understand themselves—that is enlightenment. It is buddhas who understand ignorance.*

Who is Buddha? Buddha is someone who understands ignorance. Who are people? People are ignorant of enlightenment.

> *It is people who are ignorant of enlightenment. Further, there are those who are enlightened about enlightenment, and those who are ignorant of ignorance. When buddhas are truly buddhas, they are not necessarily aware of themselves as buddhas. But they are enlightened ones and advance in enlightenment.*

To live in each moment makes everything possible—the precepts, attaining enlightenment, and attaining absolute freedom from sectarianism. This practice makes it possible to attain perfect, complete satisfaction in our life.

Sometimes we say, comparatively, "This is good, this is bad." These two ways of understanding life are necessary. Sometimes we compare one thing to another. This is very important, but this comparative good or bad has created a lot of difficulties. Comparison is the basic attitude of science and philosophy. It intellectualizes our life. When you intellectualize life, it will eventually come to a dead end. That is why we have difficulties. Originally, it is just relatively good. We are comparatively better than some people. That's all. But nowadays we say, "Absolutely good." Here is the big mistake. Nothing is absolutely good.

When you say "absolutely good," it does not mean good anymore.

It is the same thing as bad. You are forcing the Way. You are depriving the freedom of others. Dogen Zenji says in *Genjo koan*:

> *That we move ourselves and understand all things is igno-rance. That things advance and understand themselves—is enlightenment.*

He is talking of the complete understanding of life. What is igno-rance and what is enlightenment? What is good and what is bad?

We say "ignorance" or "enlightenment" without knowing what is ignorance and what is enlightenment. But when we say "ignorance" or "enlightenment," we should know what is ignorance in its true sense and what is enlightenment in its true sense. "That things advance and understand themselves is enlightenment." When we have no particular concrete idea of good and bad, we expose ourselves and accept criti-cism; that is enlightenment.

We may do many things intellectually and intentionally, in the realm of consciousness, but most of these activities are more unconscious than conscious. What is the true expression of yourself—the conscious one or the unconscious one? Of course, 99 percent of your activity is unconscious, and this is the true expression of yourself. If you say, "I am right," that is just a small part of your expression. As you understand yourself, we don't know what we are exactly. "Don't know" is right.

Those two statements about ignorance and enlightenment are based on one big understanding of life. Enlightenment is something that will happen to us sometime, and ignorance is something that will come over us sometime. We are a big box including enlightenment and ignorance.

In our everyday life, there is enlightenment and ignorance. You can-not escape from ignorance to attain enlightenment, because enlighten-ment is not somewhere else. Dogen says, to know what is ignorance is enlightenment. And to be ignorant about enlightenment is ignorance. Something good is something bad. If I say something is good, then that something should be bad. Because it is the same thing if I say, "Good morning. You came on time this morning. That is good." That means you do not come on time usually. So it's the same thing. We should not be disturbed by the words "ignorance" or "enlightenment."

If we understand ourselves completely, there is no special thing as enlightenment or ignorance. Ignorance is enlightenment, enlightenment is ignorance.

> *It is buddhas who understand ignorance.*

Dogen says, "It is buddhas who understand ignorance"—their own ignorance. Buddha was enlightened about his ignorance, and it is people who are ignorant of enlightenment. So there is no difference between Buddha and people—same thing, same human being. But buddhas understand their ignorance, and we are ignorant of enlightenment. But, if I say this, then there will be no need to practice zazen. If we are the same as Buddha, why should we practice zazen? When you understand this philosophy or statement just intellectually, you will have this problem.

Dogen continues:

> *It is people who are ignorant of enlightenment. Further, there are those who are enlightened beyond enlightenment, and those who are ignorant of ignorance.*

"Enlightenment beyond enlightenment." If you retain consciousness of enlightenment, that is not good enough. So you should go beyond enlightenment. If you attain enlightenment, that enlightenment means enlightenment above enlightenment above enlightenment and above ignorance. So eventually you will go toward ignorance. When you say, "I have attained enlightenment consciously," that consciousness is delusion. About what have you attained enlightenment? You attained enlightenment about ignorance. What you grasp is ignorance, not enlightenment. There is nothing to understand but ignorance for the enlightened person. There is nowhere to go.

"Enlightenment beyond enlightenment" means conscious enlightenment is not good enough. You have to give up enlightenment at the moment you attain enlightenment. When you actually attain enlightenment, what you grasp is ignorance. When you understand how ignorant you have been—that is enlightenment.

So it is impossible for an enlightened person to forget about enlightenment. It is impossible because you have found something that you already have. So how can you forget about enlightenment? You should abide in enlightenment forever with people who all have the same nature as you.

If you think, "I attained enlightenment" (although most haven't attained enlightenment yet), that is a *big* mistake. That is just delusion. You didn't grasp anything. It will soon vanish from memory, from experience.

Even though it looks like we are doing the same thing, there is some difference between those who have attained enlightenment and those who haven't. But for an enlightened one, constant effort continues with people wherever one is.

> *. . . and those who are ignorant of ignorance.*

"Ignorant of ignorance" means people will eventually attain enlightenment. Those people who are ignorant of ignorance are just ignorant of their own ignorance. You don't feel that you have the same quality or same nature as an enlightened person. Once you become enlightened of your ignorance you will be saved.

> *When buddhas are truly buddhas, they are not necessarily aware of themselves as buddhas.*

If there is someone who has attained enlightenment they will go back to ignorance, and although someone is ignorant of ignorance, eventually that person will become enlightened about ignorance. It is not necessary to become aware of your buddha-nature. We have it. The difference is, there are those who are awakened to their true nature, and there are those who are ignorant of ignorance. That is the difference. So strictly speaking, it is not necessary to be aware of ourselves as Buddha to be Buddha.

That is why I say you will come back. Even though you are a thousand miles away from this *zendo,* you are included in this *zendo.* With this understanding, whether you are here or not is not the point. Do you understand?

You may ask, what is the purpose of practice? Actually, there is nothing special for you to do. Why then did Dogen Zenji strive for many years, until he attained enlightenment and dropped off his ideas of body and mind? He says, "Flowers fall with our attachment, and weeds grow with our detachment." In spite of detachment, the flower will fall. This is life. And if you do not try to understand this point fully, those profound teachings are nothing. Actually, it is necessary to continue our practice in the realm of duality as unenlightened people. We should all be unenlightened people and we should strive for enlightenment. While you are striving for it, you will really understand what Dogen meant. Intellectually you have understood it already. But do you remain doing nothing in a sunny place, eating what you want? Can you always lie down in your bed reading some interesting stories? Can you do that? No, you cannot. For a while you can do it. When you are tired of reading, you will go out, or you will work. And if you earn some money and are lazy, you will stop working. If you continue your life in this way, you will not find any meaning in your life. Someday you will deeply regret what you have done: you will be disgusted with yourself. You will feel unable to help people, or unable to love anyone. You will be completely isolated from this world.

You may care for something good—something that is absolutely true—and try to escape from this world, or if that doesn't work, commit suicide. This is what we do with our life. But there is a way to resume a deeper understanding of life and work with people, without any prejudice or discrimination, and help each other with mutual understanding. The only way is to share our joy of a deeper understanding of life with people, and to participate in worldly life with more sincere effort. Then you will be a perfect human being, as well as a perfect Buddha's disciple.

A new student who was studying Indian philosophy asked, "I read many books about Zen, and they use the term 'oneness of duality.' But actually, what is 'oneness of duality'?" I had no time to discuss with him the oneness of duality. He understood intellectually pretty well what is the oneness of duality. I wanted to help him, but I knew that it was impossible to help him. Until he suffers, until he tries to find out what *is* the oneness of duality, it will take a pretty long time. By long effort, his understanding will be better and better, until, "Oh, this is oneness of duality." You will reach this kind of understanding by suffering in your actual life, by thinking more about your life, or by practicing zazen.

So to practice Zen in a noisy place is itself a very dualistic way. [*Traffic noises can be heard.*] Try to be calm. This is an extremely dualistic way, but in this effort there is a big hint.

So after all those sharp, profound teachings, Dogen writes:

> *However, flowers fall with our attachment, and weeds grow with our detachment.*

> *When we see things and hear things with our whole body and mind, our understanding is not like a mirror with reflections, nor like water under the moon. If we understand one side, the other side is dark.*

These three lines are impossible. You cannot do anything with them. It takes a long time to understand this. "When we see things and hear things with our whole body and mind"—without any idea of enlightenment or ignorance—when we *do* something and go beyond ourselves, this is to be enlightened.

"Our understanding is not like a mirror with reflections." You say the moon is in the water, but it is not like that. When you watch the beautiful moon, or waves of water, or calm silent still water, that is the moon. So when you see the moon in the water, that is the moon. When you see the moon in the sky, that is the moon. It is impossible to see the moon in the water and the moon in the sky at the same time.

The only way is to appreciate the beauty of the moon in the water or the moon in the sky. But intellectually we say "enlightenment" or "ignorance." It means you are very busy watching. What shall I do? If you sit here, you have a disturbance in your mind. If you are at home, you want to sit. When you sit, your mind is there. When you are there your mind is here, and you are going back and forth. Beautiful moon. Very busy moon.

Dogen says it is not like a mirror with reflection, nor like the water under the moon. If we understand one side—the sky or the water—or some images in the mirror, we cannot see both sides at once. If we understand one side, the other side is dark. This is two. But usually you want to see the one side only, having some idea or some desire for the other side. So you cannot accept what you are doing. You always have something else in your mind. The perfect way is just to watch one side. That is enough. This is pretty strict. Before you understand it will take time because you always have the opposite in your mind.

Actually, Zen is something more than just sitting in the cross-legged position. But if you understand what that something is, you will practice it in the cross-legged position. There is no other way. One side is enough.

You may say, just to sit on your black cushion will not do anything for you. You cannot solve the problems of our life by just sitting. You may say so, but it means you are trying to watch both sides—up and down. Pretty busy. In that way, your practice will not work. If you say, "I have to sit. That's all. Period," there is no need for you to think of the meaning of zazen, even if you just sit. That will work out beautifully. This is zazen.

One practice is enough. This is not just an intellectual understanding. Intellectual understanding is the moon in the water or things in the mirror. But true understanding or direct experience is not like water under the moon or mirrors with reflections.

This understanding brings our practice into everyday life. "When we understand one side, the other side is dark." So for us the most important thing is to carry out our activity with sincerity. That is the Way to attain enlightenment, whether or not we realize it.

> *To study Buddhism is to study ourselves. To study ourselves is to go beyond ourselves. To go beyond ourselves is to be enlightened by all things. To be enlightened by all things is to free our body and mind, [and] to free the bodies and minds of others. No trace of enlightenment remains, and this no-trace continues endlessly.*

Here he says that in the direct experience there is no subjectivity or objectivity. So to study ourselves is to study everything. This is study of Buddhism.

> *To study ourselves is to go beyond ourselves. To go beyond ourselves is to be enlightened by all things.*

So enlightenment comes from all things to us. And when we attain enlightenment, everything comes. You may say, "They made me enlightened," or "I attained enlightenment." It is the same thing in direct experience, but in intellectual experience it is not the same. I understand something. But in direct experience, "I understand something" means a truth came to me, although I didn't expect it. I didn't try to understand the truth, but understanding came.

To go beyond ourselves is to be enlightened by all things. To be enlightened by all things is to free our body and mind, and to free the bodies and minds of others.

So no trace of enlightenment remains, because there is no subjectivity or objectivity in our enlightenment.

When first we seek the truth, we are far away from its environs.

When you say, "I have attained enlightenment," you are far away from the direct experience of enlightenment.

When we discover the truth that is already being correctly [inherently] *transmitted to us, we are ourselves at the moment of enlightenment.*

It is not a matter of effort or practice anymore. Our practice is not just effort. You come here and study or practice zazen so that you can understand what is Buddhism. I'm making an effort to give you some understanding of Zen. That is true. That is actually what we are doing here. I shall be very much disappointed if you come to zazen thinking, "Now I know what Buddhism is." If you think there will be no need to practice zazen, to study Zen, I shall be very disappointed. I want you to come here even though you understand what Buddhism is. I am not selling you something, but I want you to be my customer. And I want to live with your support and I shall be very glad if you have some joy in practicing here. This is actually Buddhism. It is not a matter of enlightenment or understanding.

To perfect our character, we continue this kind of practice. We cannot force anything on others. But it is necessary to do things over and over again until you acquire a perfect acquisition, which will not vanish from you. It is like pressing your dress or trousers. You want an iron. Just to fold your trousers is not good enough. You should press. If possible, you should put something on it even after you iron it. This kind of effort is necessary; but, it does not work when it is forced on you. That kind of effort should be continued without effort, with mutual encouragement. This way our practice will continue.

When we think we know what truth is, it is not enough. We are "far away from its environs. When we discover that the truth has been transmitted inherently to us, we are ourselves at that moment." When we find our true nature or our way of life, that is enlightenment.

At first it looks like you are trying to get something; but when you understand that the purpose of practice is to understand your nature, you realize you don't know it. We may feel someone is always mean to us and someone is forcing the practice on us. "I have practiced for a long time. It may be enough for me. And it doesn't look like I made any progress." If you go to Eihei-ji you may say, "I have been at Eihei-ji for one year. I cannot speak any Japanese, and intellectually I cannot study anything here. What we are doing, just to eat and work and recite sutras and practice zazen in the same way. What does it mean? I know everything already," you may say.

So as long as you try to find your true nature by practice, you cannot find it. But if you find your true nature in practice, or if you think the practice itself is your true nature, that is enlightenment. Past sages found their true nature in practice. We should find our true nature in the same practice. That is true realization.

The practice is not some means to attain enlightenment. Before you attain enlightenment, you are just an ordinary person. After you attain enlightenment, you are a sage. "That we move ourselves and understand all things is ignorance." When we try to attain enlightenment by practice, we are ignorant. Truth will come by itself, and we will find ourselves in the truth, in the practice. That is enlightenment.

So practice is first; enlightenment is second. You should be absorbed in practice until you become one with practice, until you build up your character by practice, until you become Zen practice itself. Like a rock. That is enlightenment. A rock doesn't know what it is.

"When we discover that the truth has been transmitted inherently," even before we are born, that is true enlightenment. And we find ourselves in transmitted, inherent Buddha-nature in our practice. That *is* enlightenment. So, when we discover that the truth has already been *inherently* transmitted is better. Correctly is not strong enough. Inherently is better. "Inherently transmitted to us"—even before we are born, it was transmitted to us, and when we realize that true nature in our practice, that is enlightenment. The moment we practice with our utmost effort, that is enlightenment.

> *If we watch the shore from a boat, it seems that the shore is moving. But when we watch the boat [directly]—we know that it is the boat that moves. If we examine all things with a confused body and mind, we will suppose that our self is permanent. But if we practice closely and return to our present place, it will be clear that nothing at all is permanent.*

We are caught by some ideas—some permanent, some impermanent. As long as we practice our practice in this way, we cannot realize what is true. Just when we do it, we will understand what is our true nature.

> *Firewood becomes ash and it does not become firewood again. Yet, do not suppose that the ash is future and the firewood past. You should understand that firewood abides in the phenomenal expression of firewood, which fully includes future and past. Just as firewood does not become firewood again after it is ash, you do not return to birth after death. This being so, it is an established way in Buddha dharma to deny that birth turns into death. Accordingly, birth is understood as no-birth. It is an unshakable teaching in Buddha's discourse that death does not turn into birth. Accordingly, death is understood as no-death. Birth is an expression complete this moment. Death is an expression complete this moment. They are like winter and spring. You do not call winter the beginning of spring, nor summer the end of spring.*

In this paragraph, Dogen Zenji says that the absolute independence of our existence covers everything. Because it includes everything, it is independent being. So here we find absolute liberation. When we practice zazen, concentrating on each breath, we are absolute, independent beings.

We should not say "firewood becomes ash." Ash is ash, firewood is firewood. Firewood is independent being. But ash includes firewood. And firewood includes the ash. Ash not only includes firewood, but it includes everything. So firewood is independent being; and ash is also independent being; so one breath after another, you obtain absolute freedom when you practice.

> *Now it is specifically taught in Buddhism that life does not become death. For this reason, life is called "no-life." It is specifically taught in Buddhism that death does not become life. Therefore, death is called "no-death."*

> *Life is a period of itself; death is a period of itself. They are like winter and spring. We do not call winter the future spring, nor spring the future summer.*

It is not a matter of life or death. When death is accepted as death through-and-through, it is not death anymore. Because you compare death with life, it is something. But when death is understood, completely, as death, death is not death anymore. Life is not life anymore when life is life through-and-through.

But this life and death does not just mean the problem of life and death. By "life and death" Dogen means understanding of existence and non-existence, or unconditionality and conditionality. When you practice Zen, the purpose of religion or goal of religion is not to attain some state of mind called non-existence. We want to attain enlightenment in both the realms of non-existence and existence. This is the Buddhist way of practice.

"Now it is specifically taught in Buddhism that life does not become death." Life is one conditioned period. Life is a conditional expression of unconditionality that is unconditionality itself. So we do not say "life becomes death." Life and death are the same.

"For this reason, life is called 'no-life.'" Life is the conditionality of unconditionality. So death is the conditionality of unconditionality. So there is no difference. So in Buddhism we do not say "life becomes death."

It is specifically taught in Buddhism that death does not become life. Therefore death is called "no-death." This "no" means emancipation or liberation. The statement points to the thing itself. It is not negative. Death is death. Life is life. When we point out something directly, we say "no." Because when you say "death," you are comparing death to life. When we reach this understanding, death is death, life is life. And death and life are the same. Both are conditionality of unconditionality. They are like winter and spring. Winter is the conditionality of the unconditional climate. And summer is also some special season based on one universal weather.

So: "We do not call winter the future spring, nor spring the future summer." When we say spring we want to know whether it is warm or cold. When we say spring—"Oh, that's wonderful!" If I say, "This is future summer," you will feel funny. Future summer or future winter. You feel as if you are going back. So when spring comes you should feel very warm and you should feel very happy. That is why we say it is spring now. So it is ridiculous to say that this is a future winter. It is ridiculous to say life is future death. You may say death is future life. This statement gives you some hope. Still, you will have some anxiety until you see it.

When we say we ordinary people attain enlightenment just as firewood becomes ash, this is a mistake. We should not think of it in that way. You say, "I will attain enlightenment tomorrow." And ordinary people become sages, firewood becomes ash. Dogen says ordinary people are ordinary people. A sage is a sage, and ash is ash, and firewood is firewood. Firewood has its own past and future, and ash has its own past and future. Future will be a sage, and a sage has its own past and future. In the past, he is an ordinary person. What is the difference? It's the same thing. So we should not say ordinary people become sages, as we shouldn't say firewood becomes ash.

You are Buddha anyway. You cannot escape from it. But you make some excuse why you are not Buddha, that's all. Maybe it is convenient for you. But because you are actually Buddha, you do not feel so good when you make some excuse. That is what Dogen says.

Therefore, the sage is called "no-sage." Ordinary people, no difference. When we practice in this hall, there is no teacher and no student.
We are all sages. Even though your practice is not good enough, we
cannot say your practice is not good enough. It is good anyway. You
have your own past and future. You have a bright future—to be a sage.
Don't worry.

"Life is a period of itself; death is a period of itself. They are like
winter and spring. We do not call winter the future spring, nor spring
the future summer."

An enlightened sage is a period of time itself, and ordinary people are
like winter and spring. We do not call winter the future of spring, so we
shouldn't call ourselves future sages. You are a sage, not a future sage.
If you practice it by yourself without any aid, you are a sage. Even though
you are a sage, you do not lose your nature or form or character.

> *Enlightenment is like the moon reflected in the water. The moon
> does not get wet, nor is the water broken. Although its light is wide
> and great, the moon is reflected even in a puddle an inch wide.
> The whole moon and the entire sky are reflected in dewdrops on the
> grass, or even in one drop of water. Enlightenment does not divide
> you, just as the moon does not break the water. You cannot hinder
> enlightenment, just as a drop of water does not hinder the moon
> in the sky. The depth of the drop is the height of the moon. Each
> reflection, however long or short its duration, manifests the vast-
> ness of the dewdrop and realizes the limitlessness of the moonlight
> in the sky. We gain enlightenment like the moon reflecting in the
> water. The moon does not get wet, nor is the water broken.*

"We gain enlightenment like the moon reflecting in the water." Even
though your practice is not good enough, you may say—"The moon
does not get wet"—the moon itself is your practice—"nor is the
water broken."

You will not be broken. You are just as you are. And when you are
just as you are, through and through, there is enlightenment.

"Although its light is wide and great—although enlightenment or
truth, is wide and great—the moon is reflected even in a puddle one
inch wide." The whole moon and the whole sky are reflected in a drop

of dew in the grass. So in your practice there is enlightenment.

Enlightenment does not destroy the person, just as the moon does not break the water. The person does not hinder enlightenment, just as a drop of dew does not hinder the moon in the sky. The depth of the drop is the height of the moon. The period of the reflection, long or short, will prove the vastness of the dewdrop and the vastness of the moonlit sky.

The kind of wonderful composure, the absolute meaning of our life, will be realized when we reach this understanding. There is no more problem of big or small. Each moment of our life is an expression of conditionality of one unconditional being. It is not a matter of long or short.

According to some psychologist, one moment for us is three to six seconds. When we say, "I see something," that means the image will stay embedded in your mind for three to six seconds. After three to six seconds it will turn into some idea. So direct experience stays from three to six seconds only. But strictly speaking, the moment you see, there is no length of time. It is not even one second. In that moment the object you see will be clear and genuine. But in the next moment it will change into something else.

What is this world? It is silly to try and find out something just in our conscious world. Dogen says there is no more problem of good or bad, long or short. "The moon is reflected even in a puddle an inch wide. The whole moon and the whole sky are reflected in a drop of dew in the grass."

We cannot say the moon is bigger than the drop of dew. It is the same. It is one period of our life, long or short. Three to six seconds is one period of our life. And seventy or eighty years of your life is also one period of life. Which is long and which is short? You cannot compare. This way of understanding life is different. But the life is originally the same. There is no particular life for us. We are just expressing our unconditioned being, which is universal to everyone.

"The moon does not get wet." Even though the moon is in the water, it does not get wet. ". . . nor does the water get broken." There is no trace of the moon. You may seek for an enlightenment which is some special experience, where you will have no problems, where you will get rid of all your vicious habits. Once you have attained enlightenment, you will not drink any more sake. That may be the kind of enlightenment you are seeking. But actually, if you liked sake, even though you gain enlightenment, you will have a hard time getting past the store where sake is sold. Things will still happen to you even though you attain enlightenment. So the water is not broken, nor does the moon get wet. The same water and the same moon will be there.

"Although its light is wide and great . . ." You may say the moon's light is bright and great, while the moon in the dew is so small. The moon in the sky is also in the drop of dew. Even though it is in the drop of dew, it is the moon. Even though you may say your attainment is too small, enlightenment is enlightenment. There is no difference.

"The moon is reflected even in a puddle an inch wide. The whole moon and the whole sky are reflected in a drop of dew in the grass." Enlightenment does not destroy the mind or help the mind. The mind does not hinder enlightenment, just as a drop of dew does not hinder the moon in the sky. The depth of the drop is the height of the moon. Because you compare something to something else, you have this kind of misunderstanding or confusion. But firewood is firewood, ash is ash. Ash and firewood are perfect, because they are whole, independent beings, or independent realities. This kind of understanding is beyond our thinking. You can explain it with logic, but the explanation will not be perfect.

When dharma does not fill your whole body and mind, you think it is already sufficient. When dharma fills your body and mind, you understand that something is missing. For example, when you sail out in a boat to the midst of an ocean where no land is in sight, and view the four directions, the ocean looks circular, and does not look any other way. But the ocean is neither round nor square; its features are infinite in variety. It is like a palace. It is like a jewel. It only looks circular as far as you can see at that time. All things are like this. Though there are many features in the dusty world and the world beyond conditions, you see and understand only what your eye of practice can reach. In order to learn the nature of the myriad things, you must know that although they may look round or square, the other features of oceans and mountains are infinite in variety; whole worlds are there. It is not only around you, but also directly beneath your feet or in a drop of water.

"When the truth does not fill our body and mind, we think that we have enough." Because you do not know the truth, you may say there is no need to practice. When you obtain truth, everything obtains truth. Everything is Buddha's teaching. There will be no need even to listen to it, because we already know it. That is a common mistake when you do not know what truth is.

"When the truth fills our body and mind, we know that something is missing." When truth actually fills your body, you think that something is missing. Do you understand what he means? "Something is missing" means that if you understand the actual truth, it reveals itself in the eternal present. Not only this moment, but also eternally it will continuously reveal itself through our activity. What we do just now is not enough. We have to do another activity in the next moment.

That is the true meaning of "to drop off our body and mind," or "nothing to grasp," or Bodhidharma's "I don't know." "I don't know" means there are many things to know. Because I don't know, I have to know many things. That is the true meaning of truth. Truth is not some particular thing. If I say "truth," you think it is some special mathematical theory or scientific theory. But we don't mean such concrete, static logic by "truth." Truth is unconditionality or eternal reality. Reality does not take any particular form. That is why we call it reality. There is no other word for that. So sometimes we say unconditionality. Because it is unconditionality it takes various conditions. If so, there should be innumerable variety in its form and color.

"When truth fills our body and mind, we know that something is missing." When we become one with truth, we take up various activities according to the circumstances. We feel something is missing. So we will start continuous study, continuous practice, because we feel we should study more. When you think truth is some particular theory or teaching, you may think it is enough. So you don't want to study more. But when you realize what is truth, you feel you should do it, then you will start continuous true practice.

You may think the truth is some particular thing—some concrete theory. That is exactly the same as saying the ocean is round or square. It is not square or round. There are infinite features. "It is like a palace. It is like a jewel." For a dragon it may be like a palace. For a fish it may be like a jewel.

"It seems circular as far as our eyes can see at the time." Dogen had a pretty hard voyage when he went across the ocean to China. He is referring to the voyage here. "As far as our eyes reach, the ocean is circular." That is only at that time. When storms come with black, dark clouds, there is no circular ocean. We don't know what kind of ocean we will have tomorrow. Everything is like this. Though there are many features in the so-called "defiled life" or "pure life," we only understand what our study can reach. We say, "This is awful," or, "This is wonderful." That is our particular understanding—one of many understandings of life at that time. In our study of all things, we must appreciate that although they may look round or square, the features of oceans or mountains are infinite in variety.

If we actually understand what the truth is, we will feel that what we do is not enough. This feeling should follow when you realize the truth. "I am not so good," you may say. Why you say so is because the truth is within yourself. The truth says, "I am not so good." But if you think, "I feel I am not so good," that is a self-centered idea.

"It is so not only around ourselves, but also directly here—even in a drop of water." If someone asks you what is truth, you may say, "I don't know," or you can say, "What is it?" "What is it!" means you stop and think, you can appreciate life in that moment. We live in the eternal present, but we know that we are not even aware of the present time.

When you are actually one with the truth, the things which happen in your life are your true life. The more you discuss what the truth is, the more you will be separated from the truth. But it's all right—if you ask me a question while I'm eating, I may say, "Don't be silly, I am just eating."

You may say you attained some stage in your practice, but that is just a trivial event in your long life. To say the ocean is round or the ocean is like a jewel, or the ocean is like a palace for a fish or dragon, the ocean is a big house. For a human being, the ocean is water. So there are various understandings of this.

When the ocean is a palace, you cannot say it is not a palace. For a dragon it is actually a palace. If you laugh at a fish who says that it is a palace, Buddha will laugh at you when you say it is two o'clock or three o'clock. It is the same thing. So if we know this fact, we cannot laugh at a fish. When we do not know the truth, we think we found out something. But when we think in that way, we are far from enlightenment.

If we know the truth, we think something is missing. In Japan, the famous writer Fumiko Hayashi always said, "This work is not all my ability." This is a very interesting statement. She wrote and wrote. And at last she became a very famous writer. People say she is a good writer, but she says, "This is not all my ability." People say she is good, but she says, "I am not a good writer. I cannot express my feelings yet. There is more I want to express." "Something is missing" in this sense. When you are ignorant through-and-through, when you are unable to explain yourself through-and-through, it is good. When she says, "This is exactly what I wanted to say," she may not be such a good writer.

A fish swims in the ocean, and no matter how far it swims there is no end to the water. A bird flies in the sky, and no matter how far it flies, there is no end to the sky. However, the fish and the bird have never left their elements. When their activity is large their field is large. When their need is small their field is small. Thus, each of them totally covers its full range, and each of them totally experiences its realm. If the bird leaves the air it will die at once. If the fish leaves the water it will die at once. Know that water is life and air is life. The bird is life and the fish is life. Life must be the bird and life must be the fish. It is possible to illustrate this with more analogies. Practice, enlightenment, and people are like this.

Now if a bird or a fish tries to reach the end of its element before moving in it, this bird or this fish will not find its way or its place. When you find your place where you are, practice occurs, actualizing the fundamental point. When you find your way at this moment, practice occurs, actualizing the fundamental point; for the place, the Way, has not carried over from the past and it is not merely arising now. Accordingly, in the practice enlightenment of the Buddha Way, meeting one thing is mastering it; doing one practice is practicing completely.

Mortality, practice, eternity, enlightenment, and ignorance should be understood in this way. But before you understand the true meaning of mortality or eternity or enlightenment or ignorance just by intellect, without having a deep understanding, mortality is something which is different from eternity. Enlightenment is something which is different from ignorance. You may say practice is some means to attain enlightenment, and practice and enlightenment are two completely different things. After you attain enlightenment, there is no ignorance, but if you understand what enlightenment is in its true sense, enlightenment is ignorance too. When one is not aware of one's own ignorance, that is not enlightenment.

Asahina Sogen was the abbot of Engakuji, a Rinzai temple. Long after he attained enlightenment, he got married. And his followers, I think, must have been disappointed. But what he said is very meaningful and interesting. He knew that people might be disappointed with him. But he felt "something is missing." So he wanted to be an ignorant, ordinary fellow after he attained enlightenment. He acknowledged his humanity. I think that is *true* enlightenment. He does not say so, actually. He is laughing at himself. This is very meaningful.

Once he resided in a remote mountain with his good friend, a Soto priest. They practiced in the mountains because they were not satisfied with their practice. The house they built was very far away from the village. They raised their own food and supported themselves. His practice was so hard; and after hard practice like that, he got married to his girlfriend. People who understand mortality and eternity, ignorance and enlightenment in a different way will be disappointed with him.

But eternity is immortality. When we are a mortal being, through-and-through, we will acquire the immortal life. When we are absorbed in the fear of pure ignorant practice, we will have enlightenment. After all, how to be a true Buddhist is to find the meaning of life in your limited activity. There is no need for you to be a great person. In your limited activity, you should find out the true meaning of yourself . . . if you pick up even a small stone, you have the whole universe.

"When a fish swims in the ocean, there is no end to the water." This is a very important point. There is no end to our practice. Because there is no end to our practice, your practice is good. Don't you think so? But usually you expect your practice could be effective enough to put an end to hard practice. If I say, "Practice hard for just *two* years," you will lose interest in our practice. If I say, "You have to practice your *whole life*," then you will be disappointed. "Oh, Zen is not good. Zen is not for me." But if you understand what practice is, and if you are interested in practice, the reason that you are interested in practice is that practice never ends. That is why I am interested in Buddhism. There is no end. Even if human beings vanish from this earth, Buddhism exists. That is why I am interested in Buddhism. Buddhism is not always perfect. It is not perfect at all. Because it is not perfect, I like it. If it is perfect, many people will be interested in it, so there is no need for me to work on it. Because people are very much discouraged with Buddhism, I feel someone must practice it.

The other day in morning service, I thought it might be better to bow nine times. But they said if you bow this way, people may be discouraged. It is true, very true. I *know* people will be discouraged. I bow nine times, and I know exactly how they feel. Buddhism wants our effort always. Eternally it wants our constant effort. That is why I like Buddhism.

Until you are interested in this point, you cannot understand Buddhism. In this way—mortality makes eternity. Eternity makes mortality. Enlightenment makes practice. Practice makes enlightenment. In this way "further analogies are possible to illustrate our practice." Bird makes sky, sky makes bird. Fish makes bird, bird makes fish. In this way, there must be further analogies possible, further illustrations of our practice. So, in short, it is enough if you do one thing with sincerity. That is enough. There is no need to try to know the vastness of the sky or the depth of the sea.

A bird just flies. A fish just swims. There is no end of the water or the sky for the fish or the bird. A fish does not realize it is swimming. A bird does not realize it is flying. But where the fish swims, where the bird flies, there is water or sky.

"When the use is large, it is used in a large way. When the use is small, it is used in a small way. Though it flies everywhere, if the bird leaves the air, it will die at once." So, when you practice Zen, you practice enlightenment. Enlightenment and practice are not different.

Dogen says, "When the use is large, it is used in a large way. When the use is small, it is used in a small way." But you cannot compare which is large, which is small, which is good and which is bad. So each practice is absolute—each practice is enlightenment itself, as when birds fly, there is sky. There are not two kinds of water for big and small fish. The water is the same.

Now, here is the problem: "If a bird or a fish tries to reach the end of its element before moving in it, this bird or this fish will not find its way or its place."

True practice will be established in defilement. Before we are aware of enlightenment, we attain enlightenment. It is impossible for a bird or a fish to know what air or water is before they move in it. So enlightenment should be attained before we are aware of it. Do you understand? True practice should be established before we attain enlightenment, before we know what enlightenment is. If you move in the practice, you cannot know the end of air or water. You cannot know what enlightenment is or what defilement is before you practice it. When you practice it, enlightenment is there. If you doubt it, you are trying to know what enlightenment is. You are a fish or a bird who wants to practice, who wants to move realizing the end of the water or the sky.

"If a bird or a fish tries to reach the end of its element before moving in it, this bird or this fish will not find its way or its place. When we find our place at this moment, when we find our way at this moment, the practice follows and this is the realization of truth." This is pretty difficult to accept. Pretty difficult to be a fish or a bird who just moves in water or sky. Because we are not a fish or bird, we try to know the end of the sky or water before we move in it. It may be quite natural for you to want to know what is enlightenment, what is water or sky before you practice or before you move in it. That is why I'm trying to explain what enlightenment is, why Dogen worked so hard to explain what enlightenment is. But before he wrote so many works to let you know what water is, what sky is, he said you should not wait to understand Buddhism intellectually before practicing. That is like a bird who tries to move in the sky after he knows the end of the sky.

Of course, we do not ignore the intellectual understanding of Buddhism, or someone who has the time to explain it intellectually. It is their duty to explain it intellectually. But for us, it is necessary to start practice, so you will understand completely what Buddhism is. You will have no time to realize what Buddhism is.

There is no subject who practices and no object which is practiced. When you practice, reality appears. Reality did not exist before you practiced it. "They have not existed in the beginning, and they are not in the process of realization." Each moment is realization and is not in the process of realization. Do you understand? It is not a process. At the same time, it is in the process of changing into some other practice. But although your practice is a continuous one, it is discontinuous at the same time. Today you have done something, and what you have done will be continued tomorrow. But even though we do not know anything about tomorrow, tomorrow is included in the present. Your work has its own tomorrow and past. Tomorrow what you have done will have its own past and future. What you have done today will belong to the past tomorrow. So it is not the same. Not the same at all. Tomorrow is independent, and today is independent.

There must be some relationship, but although there is a relationship, you cannot compare what you have done today to the things you will do tomorrow. So you must be satisfied with what you did today. Tomorrow you should be satisfied with what you will do tomorrow. So when you compare what you have done today with what you will do tomorrow, it is like trying to mix oil with water. You cannot compare them. Oil is oil and water is water. You should not compare.

"They have not existed from the beginning, and they are not in the process of realization." Your practice is not in the process of realization. So will you give up? This kind of practice is not our practice. Even though you practice our way for a whole lifetime, some of you attain enlightenment and some may not. You see? If so, do you give up your practice?

When you are busy working on something, it is not possible to see what you have done. If you want to see, you have to stop doing it. "When the truth does not fill our body and mind we think that we have enough. When the truth fills our body and mind, we know that something is missing." This "something is missing" has a different meaning. We know that that is not enough; at least, we know that we should continue. It is not the end of it all. Moment after moment we should work on it. We feel this way. There is no time for us to lie down and sleep. We must go on and on and on. And we have our ideal ahead of us. Usually without knowing this, you are caught by your ideal, which is not possible to attain. You will just suffer until you commit suicide.

Enlightenment might be just an ideal for you, but even enlightenment is not always the same. It will make some progress. I cannot explain it just now because you will be mixed up. There may be big enlightenments and small enlightenments, as the biographies of the great masters say—countless small enlightenments and several big enlightenments. This kind of description means that enlightenment is not always the same. Enlightenment after enlightenment, we should practice our way. You feel that something is not enough. Even though you feel good, even though you feel that you had enlightenment, that is not enough. When you feel this way, that is true enlightenment. But when you think you have had enough, that is not true enlightenment.

A monastery is not some particular place. Whether you can make Tassajara a monastery or not is up to you. It may be even worse than city life. But when you have the wisdom of the *Prajnaparamita Sutra*, even though you are in San Francisco, that is the perfect monastery. This point should be fully understood.

Here is the place; here the Way unfolds. The boundary of realization is not distinct, for the realization comes forth simultaneously with the mastery of Buddha dharma. Do not suppose that what you realize becomes your knowledge and is grasped by your consciousness. Although actualized immediately, the inconceivable may not be distinctly apparent. Its appearance is beyond your knowledge.

Even though you have it, you don't realize it. You don't feel you have it. But you have it. How can you have this kind of matured practice instead of lazy practice—always sitting on your black cushion, with mosquitoes and false pride? That is not actually real practice. Why we practice so rigidly is to acquire that kind of practice, little by little. While you are doing rigid practice, sometimes it is fighting with the dragon and sometimes you are bothered by many ideas that come.

Anyway, you try to sit. While you are sitting in that way, little by little, without knowing when you acquired the power, you will own zazen, zazen will become your own. And you will not feel you are practicing zazen. Even though you are sitting, you will not feel you are practicing zazen. Even though you are doing something else, you will not feel: "Oh, it is good to do something after zazen." You will not feel so much difference between zazen practice and everyday activity, because you are familiar with your practice. Old students say, "I have been sitting for eight years with you but nothing has happened." Nothing happening is *very* good.

> *Zen master Baoche of Mount Mayu was fanning himself. A monk approached and said, "Master, the nature of the wind is permanent, and there is no place it does not reach. Why then do you fan yourself?" "Although you understand that the nature of wind is permanent," Baoche replied, "you do not understand the meaning of it reaching everywhere." "What is the meaning of it reaching everywhere?" asked the monk again. The master just kept fanning himself. The monk bowed deeply.*

> *The actualization of the Buddha dharma, the vital path of its correct transmission is like this. If you say that you do not need to fan yourself because the nature of wind is permanent and you can have wind without fanning, you will understand neither permanence nor the nature of wind. The nature of wind is permanent; because of that, the wind of the Buddha's house brings forth the gold of the earth and makes fragrant the cream of the long river.*

Dogen Zenji refers to the *koan* of Zen Master Hotetsu of Mount Myoho fanning himself. He was a disciple of the famous Hyakujo Zenji, and he was a very good Zen master.

"Hotetsu Zenji of Mount Myoho was fanning himself. A monk approached and said, 'Sir, the nature of wind is permanent, and there is no place it does not reach. Why then must you fan yourself?'" Do you understand? Even though you understand that everyone has Buddha nature and form is emptiness, you do not understand that emptiness is form.

"'What is the meaning?' asked the monk. The master just fanned himself." He did not answer, just fanned himself. There is a very great difference between a man who fans himself and one who does not fan himself. One will be very hot, and one will be very cool, even though wind is everywhere. "The master just fanned himself. The monk bowed with great respect."

This is an experience of the correct transmission of Buddhism. Dogen Zenji said, "Those who say we don't need to use a fan because there is wind everywhere know neither permanency nor the nature of wind. The nature of wind is permanent. The wind of Buddhism actualizes the gold of the earth and ripens the cheese of the Long River."

"Ripens the cheese of the Long River"—this is a quotation from the *Gandavyuha Sutra*. The water of the Long River is supposed to be pure milk. But even though the water of the Long River is pure milk, if it doesn't go through the right process, it cannot become cheese. Milk is milk and cheese is cheese. So if you want to ripen cheese, you should work on it. Even though there is wind, if you do not use your fan, it will not make you cool. Even though there is a lot of gold on the earth, if you do not pick it up, you cannot get gold. This is a very important point.

People may think Zen is a wonderful teaching. If you study Zen, you will acquire complete freedom. Whatever you do, if you are in a Zen Buddhist robe, it is all right. We have that much freedom in our teaching. This kind of understanding looks like observing the teaching that form is emptiness, but what I mean by "form is emptiness" is quite different. Back and forth we practice; we train our mind and our emotions and our body. And after that process, you will acquire the perfect freedom.

And perfect freedom will only be acquired under some limitation. When you are in one position, realization of the truth will be there. But if you don't work from where you are, wandering about from one place to another without knowing where you are, without knowing the place on which you work, there will be no chance to realize your true nature. Even though you use something to make yourself cool—a Japanese round fan, a Chinese fan, and a big electric fan—if you are always changing from one to the other, you will spend your time just changing your equipment. And you will have no time to appreciate the cool wind. That is what most people are doing. Reality will be experienced only when you are in some particular condition. That is why we say emptiness is form. Emptiness will be very good, but it can only be appreciated in some form or color or under some limitation.

But you cannot be attached to your understanding. You should appreciate, moment after moment, what you are doing right now. First, you must know under which condition you actually are. If you are a teacher, you should behave like a teacher. When you are a student, you should behave like a student. You should know what your position is, or realization of the truth will not happen to you. This is how we should understand our way. To realize our position and find ourselves is the Way.

"Reaching everywhere" means that the activity of the cool wind, which is blowing in a certain direction, in some spirit, covers everything. At that moment, the movement of the wind is the whole world, and the independent activity of the wind. Nothing can be compared with the wind under this condition. Ash is ash, having its own past and future; and firewood is firewood, having its own past and future. Firewood and ash are thoroughly independent. So is the wind. This is how wind reaches everywhere, and this activity is beyond the idea of time.

When we attain enlightenment, all the ancestors attain enlightenment at the same time. You cannot say Buddha is before and we are after. When you understand enlightenment, you are independent from everything; you have your own past and future, as Buddha has his own past and future. And his position is independent, as your position is independent. If so, this realization is beyond time and space. In this way, the wind reaches everywhere. Do you understand? You cannot say Buddha is before and we are after, like ashes are after and firewood is before. In this way, you should realize the nature of wind is permanent. The monk did not have any understanding of this kind. For Hotetsu Zenji, it was impossible to explain this direct experience of reality, so he just fanned himself, appreciating the cool wind.

This is a very famous statement: "The wind of Buddhism actualizes the gold of the earth and ripens the cheese of the Long River." Only by your practice, when you practice zazen in this way, aiming at this kind of goal, will you have a chance to attain true enlightenment.

III.
COMMENTARY BY KOSHO UCHIYAMA

Translated by Shohaku Okumura

Introduction: Uchiyama Roshi's
Teisho on Genjo koan

Journey for the Truth

KOSHO UCHIYAMA ROSHI was born in Tokyo, Japan, in 1912, the
final year of the Meiji era (1867–1912) and also the first year of
Taisho era (1912–1926). When he was a teenager, he thought that his
life was like a fresh blank canvas, and he wished to paint a painting
with the title "Truth." And yet he did not know what the truth is. That
was his starting point of his journey to find the truth. He thought the
time and place he was living in was an intersection of Eastern tradition
and Western culture, introduced since the Meiji era. Because of this,
he could study both Eastern spiritual tradition of searching for peace
of mind and Western rational way of thinking, which pursues progress
of material civilization. He was inspired to create something new and
meaningful by studying both of them.

In search for the truth of life, he first studied Western (mainly Ger-
man) philosophy at both the undergraduate and graduate school
at Waeda University in Tokyo. After finishing in 1937, he became a
teacher at a Catholic seminary in Oita Prefecture, Kyushu, and taught
philosophy and mathematics. He also studied Catholic theology,
because he thought that, in order to really understand Western philosophy, he needed to understand Christianity. After six months, he
gave up the idea to become a Catholic, because he could not fit into its
institutionalism.

In his twenties, he married twice. His first marriage was while he
was a university student. His wife died from tuberculosis, and he also
contracted the illness. After coming back from the Catholic seminary
to Tokyo, he married again. While his second wife was pregnant, she
became sick, and after a few days she died. This tragic experience made

him take the decisive step to become a Buddhist monk and practice zazen under the guidance of Kodo Sawaki Roshi. Sawaki Roshi gave him priest ordination on December 8, 1941, when Uchiyama Roshi was 29 years old. That was the Buddha's Enlightenment Day, and also Pearl Harbor Day in Japan, when World War II began.

PRACTICE UNDER SAWAKI ROSHI

At that time Sawaki Roshi was the *godo* of Sojiji Monastery, one of the two main monasteries in Soto Zen Buddhism. Sawaki Roshi borrowed a temple named Daichuji in Tochigi Prefecture and let his disciples and students practice together; he named the place Tengyo Zen'en (Heavenly Dawn Zen Garden). They had two *sesshins* a month. In one, Sawaki Roshi came to Tengyo Zen'en to lead, and they had Sawaki Roshi's *teisho*, services, work period, etc. In the other *sesshin,* they practiced by themselves, without the Roshi. They sat all day. They repeated fifty-minute zazen and ten-minute *kinhin* (walking meditation) from two a.m. until midnight. They took turns carrying *kyosaku* (hitting stick to wake up) each period. Only from midnight until two a.m., they did not carry *kyosaku,* so they would sleep sitting on the cushion. Uchiyama Roshi said after each *sesshin* his shoulder swelled up badly. This *sesshin* was called *sannai sesshin* (*sesshin* only for residents of the temple), and this was the origin of the modified five-day *sesshin,* also called *sannai sesshin,* which Uchiyama Roshi started when he became the abbot of Antaiji.

His life completely changed when he became a monk. Before that he was an intellectual person, immersed in philosophical thinking and reading books. Since he was from quite a rich family, he had never washed even his handkerchief by himself. He started to practice using his body and mind with strong determination. He felt very refreshed and delighted to do so, even though it was extremely hard practice particularly for a person like him who was highly intellectual and physically weak. He wrote the following poem about his practice.

POEM FOR LEAVING HOME

Like the sunbeam
In a beautiful

Autumn
Morning,
I, both body and mind, would like to
Completely become one
With the transparent,
Wholehearted
Practice.

Sawaki Roshi's disciples had to leave Daichuji after three years, because schoolchildren evacuated from Tokyo came to live at the temple buildings. In 1944, Uchiyama Roshi went to a place in a deep mountain in Shimane Prefecture to do charcoal making during the winter, and then to a beach in Shizuoka Prefecture to work making salt. During this time, he suffered from malnutrition. Almost all Japanese people were starving because of the war.

In 1945, after Japan lost the war, he moved to a temple in Hyogo Prefecture. In 1948, he moved to a temple in Nagano Prefecture. And in 1949, he moved to Antaiji in Kyoto. Since Sawaki Roshi did not have his own temple and was always traveling, his nickname was *Yadonashi* (Homeless) Kodo. Sawaki Roshi's disciples also had to be "homeless" and moved from one place to another. But after moving to Kyoto, he settled down at Antaiji and lived there for 26 years, until 1975.

In 1963, when Sawaki Roshi was 83 years old, he stopped traveling to teach because of his physical condition; until then, Sawaki Roshi had always traveled by himself all over Japan. Sawaki Roshi spent his final days at Antaiji for two years, until 1965. Uchiyama Roshi and his dharma sister Reverend Joshin Kasai, together with a few younger monks, attended and took care of Sawaki Roshi until his death. In the '70s Joshin-san visited the San Francisco Zen Center several times, to teach sewing, *okesa,* and *rakusu.*

When Sawaki Roshi passed away, according to Sawaki Roshi's will, Uchiyama Roshi did not have a funeral ceremony. Instead, he had a 49-day funeral and memorial *sesshin* for his late teacher. They sat eight periods a day for 49 days. Whoever came to Antaiji to make a call of condolence, he asked to sit zazen in the Buddha hall/zendo in front of Sawaki Roshi's relics.

BRIEF HISTORY OF ANTAIJI

Antaiji was founded in 1921, based on a layperson's vow to help produce eminent scholars/practitioners who could expound Soto Zen teachings in the modern society. Sotan Oka Roshi was invited as the founding abbot. He was the president of Sotoshu University (presently Komazawa University) and the abbot of Shuzenji and Daijiji. Ian Kishizawa, Eko Hashimoto, Kodo Sawaki, and many other prominent teachers practiced under the guidance of Oka Roshi. Unfortunately, right after the opening ceremony of Antaiji, Oka Roshi became sick and passed away several months later. Reverend Zuirin Odagaki, the brother of the founding patron, served as the second abbot with the guidance of Reverend Kyugaku Oka, a dharma heir of Sotan Oka.

Antaiji was a study monastery. A small number of selected students (about ten) graduated from Komazawa University and were allowed to stay at Antaiji to do further study of Dogen Zenji's teachings. Ian Kishizawa Roshi was the third abbot, and Reverend Sokuo Eto, the eminent Soto scholar and the president of Komazawa University, was the fourth abbot of Antaiji. Many eminent students who later became well-known Soto scholars and masters — such as Professor Kodo Krebayashi (president of Komazawa University) and Renpo Niwa (abbot of Eiheiji) — studied at Antaiji before the war.

After World War II, Antaiji lost the financial foundation and no priest lived there. In 1949, Sawaki Roshi asked Reverend Sokuo Eto, who was the president of Komazawa University and did not live at Antaiji, to borrow the temple and allowed his disciples to stay and practice. Sawaki Roshi took over Antaiji from Reverend Eto and became the fifth abbot of Antaiji only by name. He continued to be a professor of Komazawa University and traveled all over Japan to teach. He visited Antaiji once a month to lead a *sesshin*.

UCHIYAMA ROSHI BECOMES THE ABBOT OF ANTAIJI

Uchiyama Roshi and his elder dharma brother Sodo Yokoyama Roshi lived together at Antaiji from 1949 for about ten years. Sodo-san left Antaiji and lived in Nagano Prefecture. He sat alone at a park named

Kaikoen every day for the rest of his life. He became famous for his music with a grass flute, poems, and calligraphy.

Since Antaiji had no family members and no income at all, they had to support their practice by begging (*takuhatsu*). When Sawaki Roshi died in 1965, Uchiyama Roshi planned to leave and move somewhere else. But the temple priests near Antaiji asked him to be the abbot and take care of the temple. Otherwise, Antaiji would be abandoned without a caretaker again. Uchiyama Roshi accepted the request, but he declared that he would be the abbot of Antaiji only for ten years, from 1965 to 1975. When Sawaki Roshi died, people said that he was the last true Zen monk in the traditional sense, but Uchiyama Roshi said he would be the first Zen monk for the ages to come.

ANTAIJI PRACTICE UNDER UCHIYAMA ROSHI'S GUIDANCE

When Uchiyama Roshi became the abbot, he was a relatively unknown teacher. But after a few of his books were published, more people came to practice with him. When I first went to Antaiji, in January 1969, although many people participated in the monthly five-day *sesshin,* the residents were only five Japanese monks. In the next year, 1970, when I was ordained, Antaiji had about ten resident monks. Since then the number of resident practitioners and *sesshin* participants continued to increase. In 1975, when Uchiyama Roshi retired, we had about thirty residents, both monks and lay practitioners, including some foreign practitioners.

During the monthly five-day *sesshin,* we usually had about fifty to sixty people. One third were the resident practitioners; one third were Japanese people from outside; and another third were foreigners from America, Germany, England, France, Australia, etc. Many of them lived in various parts of Kyoto and came to sit *sesshin* regularly. Some of them lived in a neighborhood of Antaiji and came to sit every morning and evening. One apartment house near Antaiji was almost completely occupied by foreigners. Uchiyama Roshi sponsored some of those people.

Although there were many Westerners who regularly came to sit at Antaiji, Uchiyama Roshi himself did not speak any foreign languages. He always had a vast perspective of the history of human spirituality, and he thought the twenty-first century must be the age of spirituality. And he often said that the world needed people who had thorough experience of zazen practice to express the significance of zazen in foreign languages. I was very much influenced by his long-range view and wide-scale vision. He encouraged his students to be pioneers, instead of simply following the fixed tradition. However, he always said that if it was too difficult for me to study English, I could quit anytime. He never forced people to do anything, but always encouraged us and let us do with our own spontaneous determination.

After I started to study English, I became one of the "English-speaking" monks. Many Westerners became my friends. To practice zazen with Westerners became a very natural thing to me. My current activity in the USA is a tiny fruit of Uchiyama Roshi's boundless vision of the significance of zazen practice in human spirituality. If I did not meet him, my life would be completely different.

Antaiji still had no family members or particular patrons. Monks there had to support their practice by *takuhatsu*. Uchiyama Roshi's practice of *takuhatsu* was continued by his disciples. We monks went out to do *takuhatsu* two or three times a month, to support our practice and purchase foods for the *sesshin*. He never requested *sesshin* participants to pay anything. He only asked them to bring one cup of rice or a meal they wanted to have during *sesshin*.

When he became the abbot of Antaiji, he started the five-day *sesshin* as he described in his book *Opening the Hand of Thought*. That was the modified version of the *sesshin* Sawaki Roshi's disciples had at Daichuji without the Roshi. From his own experiences of the *sesshin* with extremely long sitting, Uchiyama Roshi thought that to sit twenty-four hours a day without lying down was not meaningful. Human beings need a certain amount of sleep. Otherwise, no matter what kind of posture they might take, they fall into sleep. He decided that to sleep seven hours should be sufficient. Then people had no excuse for sleeping during zazen. He gave no lectures during the *sesshin*; it was completely silent.

Uchiyama Roshi gave two ninety-minute lectures on the occasion of Sunday Zazen-kai he had twice a month. He talked about various chapters of Dogen Zenji's *Shobogenzo*, *Chiji-Shingi* (pure standard for temple administrators), *Shodoka* (song of enlightenment), etc.

Sawaki Roshi never had his own temple or monastery, so his disciples did not have many occasions to live with him. But Uchiyama Roshi tried to stay at Antaiji, except a few times a year when he was invited to teach at some temples. We could live together with him on a daily basis. After each meal he came to have tea and talk with practitioners. We could ask him any questions, and he often asked how each of us was doing. If we had particular questions we wanted to talk with him personally about, we could visit his room when he was available.

Antaiji was different from most Soto Zen monasteries in Japan. We had a five-day *sesshin* a month, zazen-kai twice a month. The rest of the month, we sat three periods in the morning, from five to eight and two periods in the evening, from six to eight. After breakfast, if we had some community work, all people worked together. Otherwise, each person did personal work according to one's own responsibility.

Since we cooked and made a bath with firewood, preparing firewood all year round was one of the big projects. Especially at a temple like Antaiji, which is in a city, to find wood was sometimes difficult. We had a small vegetable garden. Temple cleaning and weeding of the temple grounds was also important work.

The most characteristic aspect of Antaiji was that we had almost no ceremonies. We had no morning, noon, or evening service, except during the summer special period for two weeks in August, mainly for college students. The rest of the year, the only time we chanted was when we went to *takuhatsu* and when we came back from *takuhatsu*. We chanted the *Heart Sutra* and *Shosaimyo-kichijo-darani*. We had meals at the dining room using *oryoki*, but we did not chant the meal verses. Antaiji monks had a bad reputation when we went to other monasteries to practice, because we could not even chant the *Heart Sutra* without seeing a sutra-book.

All monks took turns cooking every three days. Our meals were very simple. In the morning, usually we had rice gruel made from the leftover rice from the day before, and pickled *daikon* or another vegetable. For lunch, we had brown rice, miso soup, and some pickled vegetables.

Since Antaiji was a small temple, although we had a strict zazen practice, we could not get any qualification as teachers of Soto School. We needed to go to other official monasteries to get qualification to become a temple priest. Uchiyama Roshi said that the practice at Antaiji had no bait. We needed to just practice for the sake of practice, without any expectation of desirable results. And in Uchiyama Roshi's teachings, this practice without any expectation was very important.

FINAL DAYS OF UCHIYAMA ROSHI

In February 1975, Uchiyama Roshi retired from Antaiji at 63 years old and started to live with his wife, Keiko-san, in Ogaki, Gifu Prefecture. A few years later, he moved to Noke-in Temple in Kohata, Uji, near Kyoto City. It is said that Kohata was where Dogen Zenji was born. After retirement, he said that his practice was to see his own life and death and to make reports for the younger people.

While he stayed at Noke-in, for about the first ten years, he gave *teisho* at Sosenji Temple in Kyoto on various chapters of Dogen Zenji's *Shobogenzo,* once a month when his health allowed him to do so. Those lectures were transcribed and edited by his students and published in many volumes. More than twenty books either written by him or recording his lectures were published. In the summer from May to September every year, because it was too hot and humid in Uji, he stayed at a house offered by a lay student in Nagano Prefecture.

In his early seventies, he made a collection of poems about life and death. Following are some of the poems Daitsu Tom Wright and I translated.

MY PRAYER

A higher even more comfortable life
Everyone seeking only to inhale
Exposing themselves to the crisis of suffocation
This twentieth-century age of the masses
I pray for the day
When the ultimate wisdom may work in human beings
And that we may become aware
That inhalation and exhalation are one breath
Life-and-death together from one life
That a completely new prototype of human being

Vividly living out the true life force as it is
Inclusive of life and death
Glowing from the depth of life
May be held up brightly for the people of the twenty-first century.
We can see that even when he was seeing closely at his own
    life and death, he was always together with all beings.

LIFE-AND-DEATH

Water isn't formed by being ladled into a bucket
Simply the water of the whole Universe has been ladled
    into a bucket
The water does not disappear because it has been scattered
    over the ground
It is only that the water of the whole Universe has been
    emptied into the whole Universe
Life is not born because a person is born
The life of the whole Universe has been ladled into the
    hardened "idea" called "I"
Life does not disappear because a person dies
Simply, the life of the whole Universe has been poured out
    of this hardened "idea" of "I" back into the universe

SAMADHI OF THE TREASURY
OF THE RADIANT LIGHT

Though poor, never poor
Though sick, never sick,
Though aging, never aging
Though dying, never dying
Reality prior to division—
Herein lies unlimited depth

Kosho Uchiyama Roshi passed away on March 13, 1998, at Noke-in, Uji. He was 85 years old. In the lunar calendar, the day was the fifteenth of the second month. That was Shakyamuni Buddha's Parinirvana Day.

Uchiyama Roshi's *okusan* (wife), Keiko Uchiyama, wrote about his final day in the afterword of the book *Inochi Tanoshimu* (*Enjoying Life*, a collection of Roshi's unpublished essays and poems compiled by Reverend Shusoku Kushiya and published by Daihorinkaku):

"On the day, after he ate late breakfast at almost noon, he smoked a cigarette and in good mood, he talked about *Buddha dharma* to me for about forty minutes and asked me, 'Do you understand?' When he was about to finish the talk, he said with smile, 'This is why I am delightful. I am joyful.'

"In the evening, he fell down in the bathroom, but when I gave my hands, he stood up and sat down on the chair and started to brush his teeth. He looked back to me and said with very gentle smile, 'I am OK.' I felt relieved with his smile and said, 'I am going to have a drop of tea. Please wait here.'

"When I went back to the living room and had a few drops of tea, I heard a sound of a cup fell down. Because he sometimes dropped a cup or toothbrush, I thought he did it again. Without worrying, I rushed to the bathroom. To my surprise, leaning toward the sink, he fell on his face.

"I laid him on the rag there and made a phone call to the doctor's home, because it was already in the night, and asked him to come immediately. I also asked one of our neighbors to come to help and we waited for the doctor. During that time, he could say a few words in a very soft voice. However, when the doctor came, he could not say anything. He could understand that the doctor came for him; he looked at the doctor's face with gratitude. Soon after, one of his disciples Shusoku Kushiya and Mr. Takayuki Maeda came. Four of us moved him to the bedroom. For about one hour, he breathed quietly and passed away so peacefully as it was difficult for us to tell when he died."

According to Keiko-okusan, although he usually wrote in his diary before going to bed, on that day, he wrote in it sometime before evening. He wrote, "Last night, my legs moved convulsively without cease. When legs moved furiously, I woke up. The legs did not stop moving. I slept only a few hours. I visited the Ojizo-sama and took a walk as far as the *hendensho* (transformer). But, today finally, I have completed the poem, *Ogamu* (*Bowing*) in the most refined form."

His final poem is as follows.

BOWING

Put right hand and left hand together as one and just bow
Just bow to become one with God/Buddha
Just bow to become one with everything I encounter
Just bow to become one with all myriad things
Just bow in the Way Life becomes Life

Reverend Doyu Takamine hurried to Noke-in when he received the notice of Roshi's death. He wrote that when he arrived there the temple was illuminated by pure and bright full moon light and was covered with deep silence. Uchiyama Roshi was sleeping peacefully, with a very quiet smile.

I would like to express my deepest gratitude for his teaching and his own way of life, always focused on the reality of life that includes all beings in the whole universe. Without his teachings and example, I really did not know how to live my own life.

Shohaku Okamura

A TRANSLATION OF
SHOBO GENZO GENJO-KOAN

THE FIRST CHAPTER OF *SHOBO GENZO* (*TRUE DHARMA EYE TREASURY*): *GENJO KOAN* (*ACTUALIZATION OF REALITY*)

1
When all dharmas are the *Buddha dharma,* there are delusion and realization, practice, life and death, buddhas and living beings.

2
When the ten thousand dharmas are not [fixed] self, there are no delusion and no realization, no buddhas and no living beings, no birth and no death.

3
Since the Buddha Way by nature goes beyond [the dichotomy of] abundance and deficiency, there are arising and perishing, delusion and realization, living beings and buddhas.

4
Therefore, flowers fall even though we love them; weeds grow even though we dislike them. Conveying oneself toward all things to carry out practice-enlightenment is delusion. All things coming and carrying out practice-enlightenment through the self is realization. Those who greatly realize delusion are buddhas. Those who are greatly deluded in realization are living beings. Furthermore, there are those who attain realization beyond realization and those who are deluded within delusion.

5

When buddhas are truly buddhas, they don't need to perceive they are buddhas; however, they are enlightened buddhas and they continue actualizing Buddha. In seeing color and hearing sound with body and mind, although we perceive them intimately, they are not like reflections in a mirror or the moon in water. When one side is illuminated, the other is dark.

6

To study the Buddha Way is to study the self. To study the self is to forget the self. To forget the self is to be verified by all things. To be verified by all things is to let the body and mind of the self and the body and mind of others drop off. There is a trace of realization that cannot be grasped. We endlessly express this ungraspable trace of realization.

7

When a person first seeks the dharma, the person strays far from the boundary of the dharma. When the dharma is correctly transmitted to the self, the person is immediately an original person. If a person is riding in a boat watches the coast, the person mistakenly perceives the coast as moving. If one watches the boat, then one notices that the boat is moving. Similarly, when we perceive the body and mind in a confused way and grasp all things with a discriminating mind, we mistakenly think that the self-nature of the mind is permanent. When we intimately practice and return right here, it is clear that all things have no [fixed] self.

8

Firewood becomes ash. Ash cannot return to firewood again. However, we should not view ash as after and firewood as before. We should know that firewood dwells in the dharma position of firewood and has its own before and after. Although before and after exist, past and future are cut off. Ash stays in the position of ash, with its own before and after. As firewood never becomes firewood again after it has burned to ash, there is no return to living after a person dies. However, in *Buddha dharma*, it is an unchanged tradition not to say that life becomes death. Therefore we call it no-arising. It is the established way of Buddha's turning the dharma wheel not to say that death becomes life. Therefore, we call it no-perishing. Life is a position in time; death is also a position in time. This is like winter and spring. We don't think that winter becomes spring, and we don't say that spring becomes summer.

9

When a person attains realization, it is like the moon's reflection in water. The moon never becomes wet; the water is never disturbed. Although the moon is a vast and great light, it is reflected in a drop of water. The whole moon and even the whole sky are reflected in a drop of dew on a blade of grass. Realization does not destroy the person, as the moon does not make a hole in the water. The person does not obstruct realization, as a drop of dew does not obstruct the moon in the sky. The depth is the same as the height. [To investigate the significance of] the length and brevity of time, we should consider whether the water is great or small, and understand the size of the moon in the sky.

10

When the dharma has not yet fully penetrated body and mind, one thinks one is already filled with it. When the dharma fills body and mind, one thinks something is [still] lacking. For example, when we sail a boat into the ocean beyond sight of land and our eyes scan [the horizon in] the four directions, it simply looks like a circle. No other shape appears. This great ocean, however, is neither round nor square. It has inexhaustible characteristics. [To a fish,] it looks like a palace; [to a heavenly being,] a jeweled necklace. [To us] as far as our eyes can see, it looks like a circle. All the myriad things are like this. Within the dusty world and beyond, there are innumerable aspects and characteristics; we only see or grasp as far as the power of our eye of study and practice can see. When we listen to the reality of myriad things, we must know that there are inexhaustible characteristics in both ocean and mountains, and there are many other worlds in the four directions. This is true not only in the external world, but also right under our feet or within a single drop of water.

11

When a fish swims, no matter how far it swims, it doesn't reach the end of the water. When a bird flies, no matter how high it flies, it cannot reach the end of the sky. When the bird's need or the fish's need is great, the range is large. When the need is small, the range is small. In this way, each fish and each bird uses the whole of space and vigorously acts in every place. However, if a bird departs from the sky, or a fish leaves the water, it immediately dies. We should know that [for a fish] water is life, [for a bird] sky is life. A bird is life; a fish is life. Life is a bird; life is a fish. And we should go beyond this. There is practice-enlightenment[2]—this is the Way of living beings.

12

Therefore, if there are fish that would swim or birds that would fly only after investigating the entire ocean or sky, they would find neither path nor place. When we make this very place our own, our practice becomes the manifestation of reality (*Genjo koan*). When we make this path our own, our activity naturally becomes actualized reality (*Genjo koan*). This path, this place, is neither big nor small, neither self nor others. It has not existed before this moment nor has it come into existence now. Therefore, [the reality of all things] is thus. In the same way, when a person engages in practice-enlightenment in the Buddha Way, as the person realizes one dharma, the person permeates that dharma; as the person encounters one practice, the person [fully] practices that practice. [For this] there is a place and a path. The boundary of the known is not clear; this is because the known [which appears limited]

2 This phrase is a reference to the traditional koan story of a dialogue between the Sixth Ancestor of Zen, Dajian Huineng (Jap. Daikan Eno), and his student, Nanyue Huairang. An account of their first encounter reads as follows:

Huineng said to Nanyue, "Where do you come from?"
Nanyue said, "I come from Mount Song."
Huineng said, "What is it that thus comes?"
Nanyue could not answer.
Eight years later, Nanyue attained enlightenment. He told the Sixth Ancestor, "I now understand."
The Sixth Ancestor said, "What is it?"
Nanyue said, "To say it exists misses the mark."
The Sixth Ancestor said, "Then does it exist or not?"
Nanyue said, "I don't say that it does not exist, but it cannot be defiled."
The Sixth Ancestor said, "This 'cannot be defiled' is what has been confirmed and maintained by all buddhas. You are thus and I am thus."
Dogen's phrase "there is practice-enlightenment" refers to the Sixth Ancestor's question, "Then does it exist or not?"

is born and practiced simultaneously with the complete penetration of the *Buddha dharma*. We should not think that what we have attained is conceived by ourselves and known by our discriminating mind. Although complete enlightenment is immediately actualized, its intimacy is such that it does not necessarily form as a view. [In fact] viewing is not something fixed.

13

Zen Master Hotetsu of Mount Mayoku was waving a fan. A monk approached him and asked, "The nature of wind is ever present and permeates everywhere. Why are you waving a fan?"

The master said, "You know only that wind's nature is ever present—you don't know that it permeates everywhere."

The monk said, "How does wind permeate everywhere?"

The master just continued waving the fan.

The monk bowed deeply.

The genuine experience of *Buddha dharma* and the vital path that has been correctly transmitted are like this. To say we should not wave a fan because the nature of wind is ever present, and that we should feel the wind even when we don't wave a fan, is to know neither ever-presence nor the wind's nature. Since the wind's nature is ever present, the wind of the Buddha's family enables us to realize the gold of the great Earth and to transform the [water of] the long river into cream.

Translated by Shohaku Okumura

Dogen Zenji's
Shobo genzo Genjo koan

With Commentary by Kosho Uchiyama Roshi
Translated by Shohaku Okumura

UCHIYAMA ROSHI'S *TEISHO*
ON *GENJO KOAN*

I N THE *Shobo genzo,* all words should be understood as meaning beyond dichotomy.

Since ancient times, many commentaries have been written on the *Shobo genzo.* Among them, *Gosho,* written by Senne Zenji, is especially valuable for us as practitioners of the Buddha Way. Since Senne Zenji personally studied with Dogen Zenji, his commentary gives us helpful guidance about the fundamental attitude we should keep in mind when we read the *Shobo genzo.* That is to say that each word used in the *Shobo genzo* should be understood as a word of the *Buddha dharma.*

To read the words of the *Shobo genzo* as the words of the *Buddha dharma* is, in short, to understand them beyond any dichotomy. We have to accept them free from any comparison or relativity. Usually all words we use have meaning only in opposition to one another. For example, poverty has meaning in relationship to wealth. Unhappiness has meaning in relation to happiness. Delusion has meaning in comparison to enlightenment. Thus, living beings are the opposite of buddhas, and life is paired with death.

A simple example is the dichotomy of big and small. Big is relative to small and small is relative to big. This is simply a matter of comparison. Actually, there are comparatively bigger and bigger things endlessly, and smaller and smaller things also endlessly. Without comparison, we cannot say that a thing is big or small.

However, usually people think that there are big things and small things and never question this. But big or small in conventional usage has meaning only in comparison. This is truly an incomplete way. When the word *big* is used in the *Buddha dharma,* it goes beyond such comparison and relativity. To understand words in this way is to read words as the *Buddha dharma.*

In Senne's *Gosho*, first he discusses the title *Genjo koan* and teaches us how to understand each word, *gen, jo, ko,* and *an* as the *Buddha dharma*.

I am sorry that, at the very beginning of my lecture, I have to talk about the following quotation from *Gosho,* which is difficult to read and understand. However, since this is important, I will quote the original sentences from *Gosho* and discuss the meaning of *Genjo koan.*

First, *Gosho* says about *genjo:*

"*Genjo* (appear, become) does not mean that something which was concealed appears at this moment. We should not understand *genjo* as opposed to 'hidden.' *Gen* (appearing) has nothing to do with the dichotomy of hidden and apparent. *Jo* (becoming) has nothing to do with effort and study."

Based on this comment, Nishiari Zenji said in his commentary on *Genjo koan* in *Shobogenzo-Keiteki:* "*Gen* is something which is beyond hidden and apparent and *jo* is something beyond becoming and decaying."

The common meaning of *gen* is to appear. How can we say that something appears at a certain moment? It is a matter of degree. When we compare past and present, or when something becomes clearer than before, we say it appears. *Jo* is the same. However, a discussion based on such comparison is incomplete. We should go beyond comparison or dichotomy and say that true *gen* is beyond appearing and disappearing, existence and non-existence, and *jo* is beyond creation and destruction.

Next, *Gosho* says about *koan:*

"This word *koan* came from lay society. We can understand this word in both mundane and supramundane senses. The definition of *ko* (public) in its mundane usage is to equalize inequality. To equalize a world which is unequal and unfair is the essence of being public and beyond self-concern. To govern with virtue is equalizing inequality. *An* means to keep to one's sphere in life. In whatever situation, to know one's place is the meaning of *an.*"

Originally the expression *koan* was not a Buddhist term. The original meaning of *ko* (public) in the secular world is to equalize the world when it is disordered and unequal, and *an* is keeping one's position without disturbing others. *Gosho* also says:

"To understand the expression *koan* as equalizing inequality and keeping one's position is not a correct Buddhist understanding. It is difficult to define inequality and unfair situations. With what criteria can we determine equality and inequality? Once we understand that equality and inequality are not separate, it is not possible to say that I can equalize an unequal and unfair situation. Keeping one's position is also not the *Buddha dharma* when there is a boundary between one person and another. The *Buddha dharma* is inequality and keeping one's position as total dynamic function (*zenki*)."

In the worldly sense *Gosho* defines *koan* as "equalize inequality" and "keep one's position." When we speak of the *Buddha dharma* beyond comparison and dichotomy, where is the boundary between equality and inequality? Actually there is no such distinction. Therefore, the true meaning of "public" is the "not-two-ness" of equality and inequality. What is the "position" when we say to keep one's position? Originally, there is no such fixed position. *An* is beyond such boundaries.

For example, if we slightly injure our little finger, it becomes a great existence. In doing anything, we have to protect it. However, when we have no problem, eyes are eyes, ears are ears, hands are hands, feet are feet—they are different from each other and they work in different ways ("unequal"). Thus, they function by keeping their position. And yet they are nothing special, just ordinary and equal. This is the oneness of equality and inequality and the meaning of being public (*koan*).

I have explained the Buddhist understanding of *Genjo koan* according to Senne Zenji. In this traditional interpretation, each word means just "this is it," being beyond any comparison and dichotomy. Each word in this expression *gen-jo ko-an*, here and now, must have its unique meaning. By tasting the meaning of each word, I have made a liberal translation of *gen-jo ko-an* into modern Japanese: "the ordinary profundity of the present moment becoming[3] the present moment."

---

3 Because the present moment is always the present moment, there is no way the present moment can become something else. And yet, because our mind often wanders here and there, in the past or in the future, we lose sight of the present moment, and therefore we need to practice letting go of thought and returning to here/now. This returning to here/now is nothing special, it is a really ordinary thing, because through this practice, the present moment simply becomes the present moment. However, within this ordinary practice through which we become simply ordinary, there is infinite profundity.

Why did I render *Genjo koan* in this way? As I have discussed, *gen* has nothing to do with appearing and disappearing. What is *gen*? As long as we think of anything as outside of ourselves, there is nothing that either appears or disappears. We should find *gen*, something that neither appears nor disappears, within ourselves. When we look for *gen* in our actual life experience, it is only this present moment. For us, this present moment is the only thing, which cannot be hidden at all. Even if we say, "my present moment is hidden and does not exist," we have the present moment which is hidden and does not exist. Since this present moment cannot be hidden, it cannot appear or reveal itself; therefore, this is *gen,* which has nothing to do with appearing and disappearing. Furthermore, this *gen* is more intimate when we understand it as the *gen* of *gen-zai,* meaning the present moment.

However, we can lose sight of this *gen* which is neither hidden nor revealed and has nothing to do with appearing and disappearing. Although even when we "lose sight of" the present moment, that is the quality of our present moment. The present moment is not really lost. The present moment is never hidden or revealed. But, we "lose sight of" it. Therefore, we have the present moment that is actually the present moment, as well as the present moment in which we lose sight of the present moment.

How can we determine if we are in the present moment? There is no fixed criterion to measure this because it is never hidden or revealed. At any moment, the present moment is the present moment without fail. Therefore, in our lives, the present moment is the present moment anytime and anywhere. However, if we say that the present moment has become the present moment, it is too much because it is already in the past. At that point, it is not the present moment anymore. If we say the present moment will become the present moment, it is not sufficient because it is still in the future. At that point, the present moment has not yet become the present moment. In whatever situation, the present moment is the present moment. And yet, it is possible to lose sight of the present moment. At that time the present moment is no longer the present moment for us.

It goes without saying that air is more important for the physical life of human beings than money or diamonds. However, actually there are many people who put more value on money or diamonds than air.

Although we cannot be alive for a moment without air, we often lose sight of this truth. Even if we lose sight of it, we will not die from suffocation right away. But, if we continue to pollute the air for the sake of maintaining our luxurious lives as we do today, the time may come when we will suffocate. Therefore it is a problem for us to lose sight of the importance of air.

Thus we are always living in the present that has nothing to do with appearing and disappearing. The present moment is always the present moment. But if we do not value the present moment as the present moment and instead use it to fulfill our illusory thoughts, we will certainly suffocate. It is truly important to live without losing sight of the present moment as the present moment. This is why we have to endlessly deepen this *genjo*.

The present moment becoming simply the present moment is more essential than air, and at the same time it is an ordinary thing. Therein lies the infinite profundity. We should work with our whole energy to embody such profundity. As Senne said, "This is inequality and keeping one's position as the total dynamic function." Therefore, I translate *Genjo koan* as "the ordinary profundity of the present moment becoming the present moment." I render *genjo* as "the present moment becoming the present moment," *ko* as ordinary, and *an* as profundity.

As I said, it is really so ordinary that we always live in this present moment. However, within this ordinariness in which the present moment becomes the present moment, there is *infinite profundity in ordinariness becoming ordinary*. This ordinariness is not merely a fact, it is an inquiry. To express the nature of *Genjo koan* as a question, I render *an* as profundity [in which we have to deepen ourselves].

Even though I say infinite profundity, it is not something mysterious that is enveloped in a dense mist and cannot be seen. It is completely off the mark to think that this infinite profundity is some kind of rare or special state of mind, which is beyond our reach. Rather it is a question of how we do things in this present moment, using our hands and feet in our ordinary day-to-day lives.

For example, in the story which Dogen Zenji quotes at the end of *Genjo koan,* we have to use a fan to actualize the universal wind-nature as wind, right now and right here. Even though the nature of wind is ever present in the whole heaven and earth, we can have wind only when we use a fan. When we don't wave a fan, we have no wind. Then how much shall we fan? When can we graduate from fanning the wind? There is no graduation from fanning the universal wind-nature. Anyway, in the same way as we have to continue breathing in each moment, we have to continue fanning to make wind in this moment. The reality of life is thus. In *Genjo koan,* Dogen Zenji talks about such profundity as the reality of life.

In many commentaries, *Genjo koan* is interpreted as "the true form of all beings" or "in the whole world, nothing is hidden." And both are correct. But if we simply grasp *Genjo koan* in this way, Dogen Zenji's teachings become too plain and simple. I believe that this chapter is entitled *Genjo koan* instead of "the true form of all beings" or "in the whole world, nothing is hidden" because Dogen Zenji wanted to express the profundity of our practice. Therefore, I have translated *Genjo koan* into modern Japanese as "the ordinary profundity that the present moment becomes the present moment." Please read the whole chapter and taste it for yourself, then decide whether my rendering is appropriate or not. Dogen Zenji also expresses the idea of *Genjo koan* as "practice based on enlightenment" or "practice and enlightenment are one."

"What is *Buddha dharma?*" is the essential question.

(1) *When all dharmas are the* Buddha dharma, *there are delusion and realization, practice, life and death, buddhas and living beings.*

(2) *When the ten thousand dharmas are not [fixed] self, there are no delusion and no realization, no buddhas and no living beings, no birth and no death.*

(3) *Since the Buddha Way by nature goes beyond [the dichotomy of] abundance and deficiency, there are arising and perishing, delusion and realization, living beings and buddhas.*

Now we can begin to investigate the text of *Genjo koan.* I have heard from many people that these first three sentences express the innermost secret of *Buddha dharma.* They say that if we understand these sentences, we can grasp the essence of *Buddha dharma.* Japanese people like to hear such claims as "This medicine is good for every sickness. If you take this medicine you will recover from any disease." Such phrases have been widely spread without people really understanding their meaning. Not only in the general public, but also among scholars who study *Shobogenzo,* such sayings are popularly believed.

Of course, these three sentences are important; that is true. But we cannot say that if we understand these sentences, we understand the whole of *Buddha dharma.* If we say something "expresses the whole of *Buddha dharma,*" even the colors of mountains and sounds of valley streams are also expressing the whole of *Buddha dharma.* It is not only these sentences that expound the whole of *Buddha dharma.*

Although some people think that these sentences express the whole of *Genjo koan,* it is not true. *Genjo koan* is explained throughout this entire chapter; we cannot say that if we understand only these sentences, we completely grasp Dogen Zenji's teachings on *Genjo koan.* Therefore, I would like to clearly give the final words (*indo*) and put to rest this common misunderstanding.

I think that this mistaken perception has been widely spread because these first three sentences state "ari, ari, ari (there is a, b, and c)," "nashi, nashi, nashi (there is not a, b, and c)" and again "ari, ari, ari (there is a, b, and c)" and are written with very poetic rhythms and are laden with suggestion. In other words, these three sentences are arranged in a row in the same pattern, so that we think what we cannot grasp is mysteriously expressed in these sentences. And we believe that when we understand these three sentences, will grasp the mystery. Probably this is the origin of this popular misunderstanding.

However, please read these three sentences carefully. The first sentence says, "When all dharmas (*shoho*) are the *Buddha dharma* . . ." This is clearly about *Buddha dharma.* The second sentence says, "When the ten thousand dharmas are not [fixed] self . . ." This sentence is about the ten thousand dharmas (*banpo,* all things). In *Shobogenzo Butsukojoji* (*The Matter of Going Beyond Buddha*), it is said, "*Buddha dharma* is also called the ten thousand dharmas (*banpo*)." The *Diamond Sutra* also says, "All dharmas are nothing other than *Buddha dharma.*" Thus "the ten thousand dharmas (*banpo*)" in the second sentence of *Genjo koan* also refers to *Buddha dharma.*

And yet, the third sentence says, "Since the Buddha Way by nature goes beyond [the dichotomy of] abundance and deficiency . . ." This sentence is about the Buddha Way. We must be careful that, although these three sentences are written in a beautiful way arranged in a row, the theme of the third sentence is different from the first two sentences.

However, nowadays Japanese people who study Buddhism too often say that the *Buddha dharma* or the Buddha Way cannot be explained in words. Such an excuse is accepted too easily. It seems that all questioning, thinking, or inquiring is put to an end when people encounter words such as *Buddha dharma* or Buddha Way. It is like Japanese people before World War II who received a letter with the emperor's signature and seal. Once people say they cannot explain these terms, they don't need to distinguish between them. Thus, *Buddha dharma* and Buddha Way become mixed up promiscuously. It is then very natural that when these three sentences are put in the same structure in a row, they are interpreted as if they were in the same dimension.

Of course, if Dogen Zenji used these words in such a confused way, it would be all right. But Dogen Zenji himself didn't use these expressions in such a careless way. He makes a distinction between "*Buddha dharma*" and "Buddha Way" and uses the right word in the right place. This can be clearly understood when we read the rest of *Genjo koan*.

Anyway, if we read these sentences without making distinctions, it is natural to think that what Dogen Zenji writes is something wondrous and mysterious even though we don't understand it. Also, we have a habit of thinking that precisely because it is beyond our understanding, what is written has profound meaning. Of course it is true that these three sentences have a deep meaning. However, it is not right to take for granted that there is profound, worshipful meaning simply as a result of one's chaotic feelings, without making a distinction even between *Buddha dharma* and Buddha Way. It is like believing that there must be a very deep mystery when things are veiled by a thick mist. For example, people from Tokyo, where dry winds continuously blow during winter, experience the scenery in Kyoto, where they have a lot of moisture, as very mysterious. When we visit a temple like Sanzen-in in Ohara [the northern part of Kyoto], we feel that its beautiful moss-covered garden has a very subtle and deep mystery.

In many talks on Zen, we often feel the same way. For example, [one may understand] an expression such as "oriental spirituality" merely with their chaotic feelings without clearly understanding what it means. But, once the mist clears, we may find only garbage.

True profundity is never like that. Rather, it is like the infinite depth of the blue sky that appears only after the fog of ignorance is completely blown away. What does this mean? That we should inquire into and clarify the distinction between the *Buddha dharma* and the Buddha Way.

And yet, you will see when you take a look at many of the books on Buddhism or Zen that very few of them question and inquire with fresh eyes what the *Buddha dharma* or the Buddha Way is. This is really surprising. Most books start their discussion with the assumption that the *Buddha dharma* or the Buddha Way cannot be explained in words.

We should not allow chaotic feelings based on superstition to rule our practice. The place where chaotic feelings dominate our practice is infested with rip-off artists. False priests merely act the role of venerable teachers and only promote themselves. If we worship such religious businessmen as our teachers, even though Buddhism has genuine teachings and practices which can offer true guidance for human beings today and in the future, we will consign these treasures to the grave. I am afraid of that.

We have to make a fresh start by inquiring what Dogen Zenji means by his use of the words *Buddha dharma*. When we question what *Buddha dharma* is, the most standard authority for interpreting this word "*Buddha dharma*" is a sentence in Dogen Zenji's *Bendowa*: "You should know that *Buddha dharma* is studied by truly giving up the view which discriminates [between] self and others." By giving up the view that discriminates between self and others, *Buddha dharma* becomes *Buddha dharma*.

I believe this is the essential statement for those who study *Buddha dharma*. Why has this not been discussed until now? This is strange to me. Probably because the view of self and other is difficult to give up; we struggle to understand "how" we can give it up. People think unless we give up the view of self and others, the statement "*Buddha dharma* is studied by truly giving up the view which discriminates self and others" does not make sense.

When we think that way we put the statement outside of ourselves; we want to reach a stage free from the view of self and others. We feel that until we reach such a state of mind, we cannot enter the *Buddha dharma*. In this case, the self who wants to reach the state of mind and the state of mind which is sought after become separate. Herein lies the very view or state of mind that discriminates between self and other. The important point here is that we should not put this statement "give up the view of self and others" outside of ourselves as a desirable state of mind. Rather, we should straightforwardly apply "giving up the view of the self and others" to ourselves. This is called accepting and settling right here (*jikige joto*).

When we apply this statement to our actual selves, we will see that as long as we are alive, and as long as our brains function, it is only natural to make a distinction between self and others. We always think, "I am I. Others are others." And we think the world in which we are living exists outside of ourselves. Clearly it is absolutely impossible for us to give up the view that separates the self from others. Then what on earth does Dogen Zenji mean when he says that *Buddha dharma* should be studied by giving up the view that discriminates between self and others?

This means that we should study *Buddha dharma* on the *ground* beyond the view of self and others. Even though it is not possible for us to avoid the view of self and others, it is certain that there is a ground beyond this view. For example, when we are in a deep sleep, our brains are at rest, and the view of self and others ceases. When we sleep like a rock without even dreaming, we don't think about who we are, or what this world is; all thoughts and views cease. Yet, we are actually breathing. Because we breathe so many times a minute even in sleep, when we wake up the next morning, we are not dead.

If so, it goes without question that even on the ground beyond the view of self and others, we are living. When we understand this, we will see that we live on this ground not only in our sleep during the night. For example, our stomach is always functioning without our thinking, "Now I have to put my stomach to work." Our liver is working silently as a liver.

Surgeons know what a liver looks like because they study human or animal bodies. However, a person like me only knows a liver by name since we sometimes hear the word. I have never seen a liver. And yet, still I am living. Whether I know it or think of it or not, my liver is functioning as a liver. When we are alive, we are living on the ground where actually the view of self and others has ceased. This is very clear to everyone.

Whether our brain is working or not, whether we give up the view of self and others or not, whether we think so or not, and whether we believe it or not, in fact, we are fundamentally living the reality of life prior to separation between self and other, subject and object. The ground of *Buddha dharma* is nothing other than this ground of the reality of life beyond the view of self and others and subject and object.

Further, even the function of our brains takes place on the ground of the reality of life, which is prior to any separation between self and others, and subject and object. When our brain functions, we think. The view of self and others arises and there is a separation between the subject, which is thinking, and the objects, which are thoughts. Just as when we breathe during the night, by the force of the reality of life, thoughts well up within our brains. We human beings, as the reality of life, have brains, and from our brains various thoughts are produced as secretions.

However, when I say this, there must be some people who think that this statement, "Thoughts spring from the ground of the reality of life, which is beyond thoughts," is nothing but a thought produced by our brain, and therefore, thoughts are more fundamental than the reality of life. This is true; we can say that the reality of life is grasped by a thought. And yet, simultaneously, we can ask those people, "From where are your thoughts coming? Don't they well up from the reality of life beyond thinking?"

Then as a counter-argument, they may say, "What you say is also merely a thought." I can say, "No, that is not true. Even your discussion arises from the reality of life." As a debate or theory, we can continue arguing in such an antinomic way endlessly. This is where Dogen Zenji's statement, "*Buddha dharma* should be studied by giving up the view which discriminates [between] self and others," becomes decisively and essentially meaningful.

As a conclusion, to stop viewing things on the basis of separation between self and others, and to study everything on the ground of the reality of life is *Buddha dharma*. This is the fundamental meaning of Dogen Zenji's statement, "You should know that *Buddha dharma* is studied by truly giving up the view which discriminates [between] self and others."

Therefore, precisely because breathing actually continues on the ground of the reality of life, where the view of self and others has ceased, even when we are in a deep sleep, we are alive. When we wake up the next morning, we are not dead. And when we wake up, again we have to return to the problems we had before. We have to work today in order to repay debts from the past. Even when all things are *Buddha dharma* that is the reality of life, there are myriad things. This is why Dogen Zenji says, "When all dharmas are the *Buddha dharma*, there are delusion and realization, practice, life and death, buddhas and living beings."

What Dogen Zenji says in the first sentence is a Buddhist expression, "the true reality of all things (*shoho-jisso*)." This expression, "the true reality of all things," originates in the *Lotus Sutra* and has been used from ancient times. This is not Dogen Zenji's unique idea. But when he says, "There are . . . ," he does not mean these things exist as substantial existents, as fabricated concepts, but these things "are" the reality of life, which is prior to separation into such dichotomies as self/others, subject/object, being/non-being, and life/death.

Substantial existents, as fabricated concepts, are the defining of an abstract idea. Consequently, when we say "being (*u*)," it has another side, that is, "non-being (*mu*)." But "being" as the reality of life is not a substance which can be defined by concepts. These "beings" are the reality of life before any separation between "being" and "non-being." Therefore, when we say "there are," all things are, and when we say "there aren't," all things are not. This is what Dogen Zenji says in the second section.

Buddha Dharma cannot be fully expressed using human reason, and yet it does not negate human reason.

> (2) *When the ten thousand dharmas are not [fixed] self, there are no delusion and no realization, no buddhas and no living beings, no birth and no death.*

There might be some people who wonder why Dogen Zenji says entirely opposite things when he talks about *shoho* (all dharmas) in the first sentence and *banpo* (ten thousand dharmas) in the second sentence, since they read these sentences without clearly understanding the words "*Buddha dharma*" or "ten thousand dharmas." What is the difference between *sho* (various, many) and *ban* (ten thousand)? In the past, since I didn't understand the first part of *Genjo koan*, I myself thought this way. However, what Dogen Zenji is saying here has nothing to do with such a trivial thing as the difference between adjectives. As I said before, "*Buddha dharma*" is "ten thousand dharmas" (*Beppon Butsukojoji, Another Version of the Matter of Going Beyond Buddha*). Though Dogen Zenji uses *banpo* (ten thousand dharmas), he is talking again about *Buddha dharma*.

And the "self" in "When the ten thousand dharmas are without [fixed] self" means, "The *Buddha dharma* that is the reality of life is not a substantial existence as we think in our head." This is a reasonable interpretation when we compare this sentence with the sentence in the seventh section, "When we intimately practice and return right here, it is clear that all things have no [fixed] self."

As I already said, when we talk about *Buddha dharma*, we should talk on the ground of the reality of life on which the view of self/others, subject/object is given up. It is not possible to express *Buddha dharma* with conceptual words such as "being (*u*)" or "non-being (*mu*)," which are already separated into two entities by our discriminating mind. If we still try to express *Buddha dharma*, when we say "there are . . . ," all things "are" as the reality of all things. And when we say, "there are not . . . ," all things "are not" because all dharmas are without fixed self. This is the only valid way to express the dharma.

The *Diamond Sutra* says, "The Tathagata taught that all forms are nothing other than no-form." And, "The true form is not a form. Therefore, the Tathagata calls it the true form." The true form of all dharmas (*shoho-jisso*) and "all dharmas of no-form without fixed self" are not two different things; they both express the vivid reality of life. Because Dogen Zenji is an intellectual person, when he talks about the side of true-form, he uses *shoho* (various dharmas), which is an indefinite plural noun. When he talks about the side of no-form, since a plural noun is not suitable, he uses *banpo* (ten thousand dharmas, or everything), which is a collective singular noun.

Although Dogen Zenji says here, "When all dharmas are *Buddha dharma*, there are . . ." and "When ten thousand dharmas are not [fixed] self, there are not . . . ," what he meant by "there are . . ." and "there are not . . ." are words prior to any dichotomy between "being" and "non-being."

Therefore, "when all dharmas are the *Buddha dharma*" (the true reality of all things) and "when the ten thousand dharmas are not [fixed] self" (the egolessness of all things) are not two different things. These two sentences are uttered at the same time about the same reality of life. In the chapter of *Shobo genzo* entitled *Bussho* (Buddha-nature), Dogen says that *u-bussho* (being-buddha-nature) and *mu-bussho* (non-being-Buddha-nature) are two sides of the same reality. This is the same as these first two sentences of *Genjo koan*.

Here, Dogen Zenji doesn't talk about the world in which we have to make a choice whether "to-be" or "not-to-be" on a flat two-dimensional grid. Dogen's world of reality is not something we can measure with a computer. Even though the vivid reality of life cannot be measured by a computer, it is the way things are.

Therefore, if we think about these sentences as referring to certain kinds of mental stages that are outside ourselves, our understanding is completely off the mark. I have to repeat this point again and again. Dogen Zenji is trying to show us reality itself, right now, and actually living with the life force prior to any separation between "being" and "non-being."

Whether we are conscious of it or not, whether we think so or not, whether we believe it or not—whether we discriminate or not—we live and we will die within the power of reality of life before separation into any dichotomies.

For example, now I am speaking in front of you with my full energy. On hearing my words, you may think my words are questionable. Where does the life force exist which allows me to speak in this way and allows you to question my words? We have to say this power is before the separation between "being" and "non-being." This life-force actually "is," when we talk from the viewpoint of "being." From the viewpoint of "non-being," it is without a fixed existence. For this reason, in his verse on *Genjo koan*, Giun Zenji [the fifth abbot of Eiheiji,

1253–1333] says, "What is this (*kore-nan-zo*)?" Truly, in order to express *Genjo koan* in one phrase, there is no other way but to say, "This is what (*ze-shumo*)."

Therefore, *Buddha dharma* cannot be fully expressed using human reason or language. *Buddha dharma* is nothing other than the reality of life that goes beyond human reason or language. As human beings, we have minds. Consequently, human reason functions and we use language. Therefore, the reality of life should vividly include human reason and language.

From the perspective of the human mind, which has reason and language, there are delusion and enlightenment, life and death, and buddhas and living beings. All of them "are." All beings are the true form of reality. Simultaneously, from the point of view of the reality of life, in which human reason functions, we cannot say that delusion/enlightenment, life/death or buddhas/living beings "are." All of them "are not." All dharmas are without substance. Since the reality of life includes human reason and language, we cannot one-sidedly say whether those things "are" or "are not." Life has many dimensions.

In the third section, Dogen Zenji will talk about how the self (reality of life) can vividly and flexibly function in both these ways. He points to the profundity beyond the human mind.

(3) Since the Buddha Way by nature goes beyond [the dichotomy of] abundance and deficiency, there are arising and perishing, delusion and realization, living beings and buddhas.

These first three sentences are written in a parallel form. And yet, we should pay careful attention to the fact that the subject of the first and the second sentence is *Buddha dharma* and the subject of the third sentence is Buddha Way.

What is the difference between *Buddha dharma* and Buddha Way? Previously I quoted from *Bendowa* to understand the words "*Buddha dharma*": "We should know that *Buddha dharma* should be studied by giving up the view of self and other." As the definition of "Buddha Way," I will quote the following from Dogen Zenji's *Gakudo-yojinshu* (*Points to Watch in Practicing the Way*): "Just to practice *Buddha dharma* for the sake of *Buddha dharma* is the Way."

My own rendering into modern Japanese is as follows: "Working to actualize the reality of life for the sake of the reality of life is the Buddha Way." The world of *Buddha dharma* does not deal with the two-dimensional dichotomy between this and that (being and non-being). In the case of the Buddha Way, the *Buddha dharma* works for the sake of the *Buddha dharma*. This is not a flat and simple matter. It is really complicated when we try to think about it and explain it with language. In reality, it is like driving a car.

When we drive a car, we are already in the car. This is a matter of course. In the same way, when we live out our lives, we carry out the reality of our life for the sake of the reality of life precisely because we are living out the reality of life. This is the Buddha Way for us.

When we talk about a path, we usually think of a ready-made path that is already fixed outside ourselves. Rather, the Buddha Way lies within our attitude toward our own lives.

That is why in my previous book on *Genjo koan*, *Genjo koan-ige* [*Commentary on Genjo koan* published by Hakujusha, Tokyo], I rendered "Buddha Way" into modern Japanese as follows: "[The Buddha Way] is driving the reality of life carried out by awakening to the reality of life that is beyond dichotomies of self/others or subject/object."

Recently someone visited me and we happened to begin talking about this book, *Genjo koan-ige*. The person said, "In that book you wrote that *Genjo koan* is not a simple writing. It has a multidimensional structure. It expresses a world like that of a symphony, in which various musical instruments make various sounds, and yet all play music as one. Such a world is unfathomably profound to us, isn't it?"

I actually wrote that [quotation] in the book and I want to restate it right now. And yet, if we put the Way outside ourselves by saying that it is an unfathomably profound world to us, we are completely off the mark. The Buddha Way should never be outside ourselves. It lies right in the middle of the way each one of us lives.

I think driving a car is actually the same as the world of a symphony. For hands and feet, there is a steering wheel, a brake pedal, an accelerator pedal, a clutch pedal, a gearshift, various gauges, and so on. In front of our eyes, everything is moving. The scenery is constantly changing, moment by moment. The scene is not simple. One car is in front of another. Cars are coming from the opposite direction. A car may try to pass our car. There are traffic signals and various signs we have to read and react to. A child may suddenly run into the road from an alley. We drive our cars, operating the controls, and respond to the complicated moment-by-moment changing scene in front of our eyes. This is truly like playing a symphony.

In the case of driving our life, it is much more complicated and serious. In front of us, there is money, the opposite sex, education and career goals, rivals with whom to compete, social status to reach, hard times to avoid, alcohol or gambling to tempt us, and so on. Within ourselves, there are changing physical conditions, emotions, and feelings—our own desires, thirst for fame, vanity, sense of justice, and so on. Our interior landscape is as complicated and subtle as the outside world.

In our lives, we have to drive our life, awakening to reality in the midst of the labyrinth in front of us.

In the extreme situation of directing our life, we cannot see the difference between a dream and reality.

The basic reason our lives appear to be so complicated is that we have a mind. Probably even grasses or trees have a complicated struggle about how and where to grow each leaf or small root, but since grasses and trees don't have a brain, I suppose they don't think their lives are especially complicated. In the case of human beings, because we have a thinking mind, our lives appear to be very complicated and full of contradictions. This is what I said in the first section.

Originally our mind is also a part of the universal reality of life that includes heaven and earth. And yet from the mind, self-centered thoughts well up. Not only that, we dream within this self-centered thinking and we become separate from the reality of life. This is a problem.

When we drive a car, we sometimes doze, and it may cause a big accident. What is this condition of dozing? We can understand this clearly when we sit zazen. When we sit only for twenty or thirty minutes, we will not have a problem beside the pain in our knees. But, in a *sesshin,* when we sit continuously for many hours a day, we become tired, and thoughts will come up in our mind. We are following a dream within a dream in sitting.

For example, during zazen, I may think, "The person walking behind me with the *kyosaku* (stick) is watching me; if I sit in an immovable posture without sleeping, the person will not hit me." When such thoughts come up, I am actually sleeping and dreaming that I am sitting wholeheartedly in a correct posture. Then I feel the *kyosaku* on my shoulder. It is appropriate to be cautioned, because it is clear to the stick carrier that I am actually nodding. I cannot argue since I was caught nodding and my posture was not upright. I was sleeping and following a dream of sitting immovably without sleeping. Thus I put my hands in *gassho* to prepare to be hit. In this way, zazen practitioners understand through our bodies that there is a difference between dreaming that we are awake and actually being awake.

Not only in zazen but also in daily life, this is a problem. In certain extreme situations, the difference between dreaming and reality is not perceptible by the person herself. This is really dangerous in both car-driving and life-driving (not only in dealing with day-to-day affairs but also as the direction of our whole life).

This is where "just to practice *Buddha dharma* for the sake of *Buddha dharma*" has a crucial meaning. Thus I express this as "since we are living the reality of life, we should drive the reality of life to actualize our life."

We are living out the universal reality of life, including heaven and earth. The thoughts that spring up in our minds are also a part of the interpenetrating reality of life. And yet, these thoughts are too often more self-centered than universal. Therefore, instead of throwing ourselves into these thoughts, we should open the hand of thought and drive our lives, awakening to the reality of interpenetration. The ongoing process of driving our lives in such a way is the Buddha Way.

In our lives, we desire a boy- or girlfriend, money, fame, etc., and we lose stability in our lives. Some complicated, deluded people may want to gain *satori* by any means, and thus lose sight of reality right now, right here.

However, the true Buddha Way (to practice the reality of life for the sake of the reality of life) is to breathe now at this moment. Right now, right here, always awaken and practice the reality of life at this moment. Therefore, we must be wide awake and not become spaced out and unable to make distinctions among things. "There are delusion and realization, practice, etc."

In the first sentence Dogen Zenji refers to the true form of all things and says, "there are . . ." In the second sentence, he refers to egolessness of all things and says, "there are not . . ." And in the third sentence, we have to actually and concretely practice the Buddha Way beyond the dichotomy of abundance and deficiency, that is, "there are . . ." *and* "there are not . . ." In this concrete way of life, again there are arising and extinction, delusion and enlightenment, living beings and buddhas.

As I have been explaining, even though these three sentences are written in a parallel form, Dogen Zenji is not saying the same thing. Precisely because the third sentence is different, Dogen will continue it into the next section.

> (4) *Therefore, flowers fall even though we love them; weeds grow even though we dislike them. Conveying oneself toward all things and carrying out practice-enlightenment is delusion. All things coming and carrying out practice-enlightenment through the self is realization. Those who greatly realize delusion are buddhas. Those who are greatly deluded in realization are living beings. Furthermore, there are those who attain realization beyond realization and those who are deluded within delusion.*

The first sentence in this section is usually considered a part of the last section. On the surface it seems so, but when we read it carefully, it is not. It makes more sense in this context to understand this sentence as an introduction for the sentences that follow. Here Dogen Zenji states how the distinction between delusion and realization appears, as well as the distinction between buddhas and living beings.

As I repeated, we should not objectify *Buddha dharma* as if we are looking at an exhibit in a museum. We should apply it to ourselves and see it as our own affair.

When we see *Buddha dharma* in such a way, we will see that we are living the reality of life prior to the separation between self and others, subject and object. We live within *Buddha dharma*. All things exist within the Buddha land in the ten directions. However, we cannot say that all things are the same and equal on a two-dimensional grid. There are different appearances, such as delusion and realization, life and death, and buddhas and living beings.

And yet, it is not true to say that delusion and realization or buddhas and living beings exist as fixed and substantial. We are not always deluded living beings. Such distinctions exist only in the human mind. When we see reality without fixed self, there are no such distinctions. Yet when we are driving our lives as the practice of the Buddha Way and living out the reality of life with our human mind, many different distinct forms appear.

In this fourth section, Dogen Zenji says that in driving the reality of life, these distinct forms appear in relationship with us.

> *Therefore, flowers fall even though we love them; weeds grow even though we dislike them.*

For example, suppose that you are driving a car on urgent business and need to arrive by a certain time, but are unfortunately caught in a traffic jam. Because you are in a hurry, you will become frustrated and irritated. In such a situation you feel even one minute is a long time. On the contrary, when you are driving a car with your girlfriend or boyfriend by your side and you are not in a hurry, you will not mind the traffic at all. Rather you may want the traffic jam to last forever.

When you have fun with your intimate friends and drink *sake*, you will have a good time. But even the same *sake*, if you drink it when you have to host a very important guest on the job, you may not enjoy it.

In our life-driving, we encounter a variety of scenery. [We may think:] "There are good times and hard times, pleasure and pain, happiness and sadness, and so on." Such varied scenery does not objectively exist outside us but appears relative to ourselves.

Once I read a poem by a child:
"How small it is!"
Playing at the school ground.
"How big it is!"
Weeding the school ground.
This poem also shows that the various scenery appears only in relationship with our own conditions.

> *Conveying oneself toward all things to carry out practice-enlightenment is delusion. All things coming and carrying out practice-enlightenment through the self is realization.*

This sentence is the introduction to the following sentences. All human beings live out the reality of life that interpenetrates all heaven and earth. Therefore, whether or not we think or believe it, we are one interpenetrating self (*jinissai-jiko*). And yet, even though we are one interpenetrating self, our brain constantly secretes very non-universal thoughts: "I want more money," "I want sex," "I want amusements," and so on. As a living being interconnected with the whole universe, even our brain functions as part of interpenetrating life. Yet, the contents of our thoughts, which are secretions of our brain, are not at all universal, but are very self-centered. If we hold such self-centered thoughts and try to deal with everything based on them, then such an attitude is definitely delusional.

Too many people believe that this world exists to satisfy desires, which are based on their self-centered thoughts. In reality, this world does not exist to fulfill our desires. In fact, things do not proceed in accordance with our expectations. And yet, somehow, we don't accept this. Consequently, we often complain that things do not go well, and we struggle and make a great fuss.

When we reflect on ourselves, we understand that this way of living in *samsara* is caused by our own incompleteness. So then, we want to practice to go beyond ourselves and attain enlightenment. I think many people who practice zazen originally had this thought.

And yet, there is a problem here. In the desire to go beyond ourselves and attain enlightenment, we want to make ourselves into the people we want to be. What will actually happen when we seriously practice the Buddha Way with such a desire? This is not [just] someone else's problem; I also began to practice the Buddha Way with exactly this attitude.

I wanted to throw myself into the Buddha Way and practice zazen. I was ordained by Sawaki Roshi in 1941. Following Sawaki Roshi's instruction, I started to walk the path of real zazen practice at Daichuji Temple in Tochigi Prefecture. At the time, we had two five-day *sesshins* each month. One *sesshin* was led by Sawaki Roshi, and we had services, lectures, and so on. But in the other *sesshin,* we simply repeated fifty minutes of zazen and ten minutes of *kinhin* (walking meditation) from two in the morning until midnight. We had three meals a day, and right after each meal we had thirty minutes of *kinhin.* We sat twenty-two hours a day. Even the two hours from midnight to two, we slept in sitting posture, putting our chin on a support called *zenpan*. We were in the sitting posture for almost twenty-four hours a day. Except for the two hours of sleep, someone walked around with the *kyosaku* (wake-up staff).

We had this type of *sesshin* once a month. In December we also had a seven-day *sesshin* with the same schedule. During such a *sesshin*, especially at its end, I could not keep awake. No matter how hard we were hit when we fell asleep, we could not wake up. Sometimes, my shoulder would be swollen.

Even though I practiced zazen undergoing such extremely difficult *sesshins*, during that time I settled down into the life of the Buddha Way and practiced wholeheartedly, expecting that I would improve myself and have a good result sometime in the future. Such practice lasted for exactly three years: from the fall of 1941 until the fall of 1944, which was near the end of World War II. At that time Daichuji Temple accepted many schoolchildren who had been evacuated from Tokyo for safety. As a consequence, we were forced out of the temple and moved to Shiseiryo in Shinjuku, Tokyo. Shiseiryo was a dormitory for students of Komazawa University, where Sawaki Roshi lived with his students.

If we had only practiced zazen there without working, we would have been commandeered to support the war effort sooner or later. I thought I should find some work, and I went deep into the mountains in Shimane Prefecture to make charcoal. While I was making charcoal, I had a question. When I practiced at Daichuji, I thought that if I kept practicing zazen in that way somehow I would become a better person. After several years of practice, the only clear thing I found was that no matter how many years I kept practicing zazen, I would not produce any desirable results.

Consequently, I began to wonder why I would spend my life doing such a thing. Since it was during the war, I also thought about the direction of our society, and I had become really serious about this question. Once I wrote a detailed letter to Sawaki Roshi about my question. In response, Sawaki Roshi sent a letter with Dogen Zenji's poem included in *Eiheikoroku* [Extensive Record of Eihei Dogen, Manzan-bon vol.10, #65]:

Forgetting all dichotomies
My mind is peaceful.
Within *Buddha dharma*,
All things appear at the same time in front of me.
From now on, my mind is settled,
I leave everything to causes and conditions.

Although Sawaki Roshi sent the poem, since my struggles were exactly because I wanted to attain that state of mind, it didn't help me at all.

After that, I moved to Shizuoka Prefecture and worked drawing water from the sea to make salt. Then I moved to Jippoji Temple in Tanba (Hyogo Prefecture) and again practiced zazen and frequent *sesshins,* although my life was not far from starvation. For about five years, I was in the midst of a very deep and serious distress.

While I was at Teishoji Temple in Saku, Shinshu (Nagano Prefecture) from 1948 to 1949, I was really in the dark as to my zazen practice. I could not do anything about it. I had to throw everything away: my doubts and thinking. One evening I sat alone in the zendo and I felt a release. After this experience, I wrote something like a *waka* poem:

Under the blazing sun,
Hearing a command, "Cease fire!"
I ceased fire.
Cool refreshing breeze.

Since young people today have little experience of military drills, they probably don't understand this poem. When we had mock warfare, during the daytime in mid-summer, we had to wear heavy equipment, carry guns, and run over a vast field. We were covered with sweat. In such a situation, when the drill instructor gave a command for cease fire, I felt relieved from the hard exercise, and suddenly felt a cool breeze. I experienced this during my school years. While I was sitting alone in the zendo, I again experienced this exact feeling. At the time, I didn't understand why I felt such a release. But, I thought, zazen is probably like this.

In the fall of 1949, after I moved to Antaiji in Kyoto, Sawaki Roshi said in his *teisho*, "*Buddha dharma* is immeasurable and boundless; it cannot be something which fulfills your desire for satisfaction." Upon hearing this, I felt heaven and earth turn upside down. Until then, I had been fussing and struggling with a desire to improve myself and attain enlightenment. I found that even such a small "self" was produced by the great nature of interpenetrating heaven and earth, and would not fit into my limited frame of thinking.

All of us are living out the reality of life of interpenetrating heaven and earth. And yet, we want to grasp the self and put it into a cage, or a frame of thought. We think, "This is my 'self'; I can seize it." Nevertheless, even my "self" is actually a part of interpenetrating life. We cannot seize it and put it into a framework of thought. That is all. It took me eight or nine years to understand such a simple reality.

I understood that what I could do with my thinking is really "small potatoes." If I had a desire to attain enlightenment and I attained some kind of enlightenment experience based on such a desire, this enlightenment is still within the framework of my personal desires. Dogen Zenji said, "If enlightenment depends upon the thought before enlightenment, such enlightenment is surely unreliable" *[Shobo genzo Yuibutsu-yobutsu; Only Buddha Together with Buddha]*. True enlightenment penetrating heaven and earth should be genuinely penetrating heaven and earth. It should not be seized upon and put into a framework to satisfy your personal desires.

On the contrary, several years ago, after I moved to Kohata, I wrote a poem for my New Year's greeting card titled "A Letter." I found I had settled down a bit.

A LETTER

I struggled in many ways
In my youth.
Moving here and there
Like a leaf blown in the wind.
Finally I drifted to a sunny spot
By the Jizo Bodhisattva in Kohata,
Being satisfied with dissatisfaction.
Right now, right here
I live simply.

[*Translator's note: At Nokein Temple in Kohata, Uji-shi, Kyoto, where Uchiyama Roshi lived in his final days, a statue of Jizo Bodhisattva made in the Heian period (10th–12th centuries) was enshrined.*]

I have begun to settle peacefully. Probably this has been because I am aging.

Anyway, the self is an all-penetrating self, and the reality of life is one with the whole heaven and earth. And yet, from our brain, various thoughts will come up which are not one with the whole heaven and earth. When we live out "life-driving" based on the thoughts from our brain and "convey oneself toward all things," this is certainly delusion.

To live out the self as real life, one with the whole heaven and earth, is enlightenment. Both enlightenment and delusion, buddhas and living beings, do not exist as substantial in a fixed way. Moment by moment they appear, depending on our attitude toward life.

Those who greatly realize delusion are buddhas. Those who are greatly deluded in realization are living beings.

Although both delusion and enlightenment appear simply as scenery in our thoughts, the reality of life is beyond separation between delusion and enlightenment. As the reality of life, we are living our lives before we discriminate between enlightenment and delusion. We are not fixed as deluded living beings, nor are we fixed as enlightened buddhas. Actually to awaken to the reality of life before the separation between enlightenment and delusion is buddha.

As a matter of fact, as long as we are human beings, there will be no time when delusion is completely eliminated. Because for us, to live means constantly to make a choice, what should we do? This or that? Therefore, we are always living in the midst of delusions based on discrimination between this and that. Within the midst of such delusions, the essence of the Buddha Way is to realize that discriminating thoughts are nothing other than secretions from our mind. Then we can open the hand of thoughts, and carry out "life-driving" in accordance with our scenery, which changes moment by moment. This is what Dogen Zenji meant in the *Shobogenzo Hokke-ten-hokke* (*Dharma Flower Turning*

Dharma Flower)—that when our minds are deluded we are turned by the dharma flower rather than turning the dharma flower.

Greatly realizing delusion, seeing delusion simply as delusion and awakening to the reality beyond the dichotomy of delusion and enlightenment—that is all buddhas. We are off the mark if we think Shakyamuni Buddha, Amitabha Buddha, Medicine Buddha, and so on, are other people in the past outside of ourselves. Awakening to the reality of life in each moment is buddha. Therefore, right now, in zazen, to sit and awaken to the reality of life moment by moment *is* all buddhas. In this sense, what Dogen Zenji said in *Bendowa (Talk on Wholehearted Practice of the Way)* is absolutely true: "Zazen is the true gate of *Buddha dharma.*"

Living out the reality of life, being always caught up and dragged about by thoughts secreted from our mind and losing sight of the reality of life *is* all living beings greatly deluded within realization. Delusions are also surely the reality of life. Consequently we should realize delusion as the content of reality. And yet, because we lose sight of reality, we are greatly deluded within realization.

> *Furthermore, there are those who attain realization beyond realization and those who are deluded within delusion.*

Since all of us often enter into delusions, I don't think I have to explain about those who are deluded within delusions. We should think about those who attain realization beyond realization. Briefly, this is about *butsu-kojo* (going beyond buddha), continuously and endlessly going beyond. This is not meaningful if we think this is about someone else called "Buddha." Rather, we should think about going beyond buddha as our personal business and we should illuminate our own self with this ancient teaching.

I repeatedly say that buddhas are not other people, but are an awakening to the reality of life prior to any separation into dichotomies. In a more concrete way, Dogen Zenji said in *Shobo genzo Hachidain-ingaku (Eight Awakenings of Great Beings)* that all buddhas are great beings (*dainin* in Japanese, *mahasattva* in Sanskrit). Great beings are truly matured people, not adults or grown-ups in biological terms, but rather people who are spiritually matured.

In our actual life-driving, nothing can be dealt with through making choices between this and that.

We cannot judge who is a truly mature person and who is not. We cannot say, "You are still childish. You are not yet eligible to be a mature person," or, "You are mature enough. You have passed the examination." To be buddha is to awaken to the reality of life before the separation of being eligible or not eligible, and carry out "life-driving." We should realize reality before any separation between success and failure. There is limitless profundity in realizing beyond realization. We actualize all buddhas beyond all buddhas. We become mature beyond maturity. Therein lies infinite depth.

Actually, life is a matter of profundity. It cannot be a matter of making choices between this and that, good and bad, success and failure. And yet, as this is an age of computerization, people believe that they can deal with their own lives with ideas of this and that, good or bad, success or failure. When they encounter profundity, it seems that their dualistic ways of thinking like a computer just don't work.

For example, what is more important for us in this society: to be friendly or to compete with others? What about in international relations: peace or competition and winning against other countries? These questions are matters of the basic system of values in human society. What on earth are the answers to these questions if asked from the dualistic way of thinking of computers? Computers simply make choices between this and that, right and wrong.

In modern society, people think dualistically like a computer about questions of basic values, subsequently determining the fate of human society. We have two choices: either idealistically to be friendly and peaceful, or realistically to win and be a victor. In each situation we choose one or the other without clarity as to the question. This is a kind of trick.

This kind of tricky technique is used by fake-adults who are not really matured, but it does not work in childhood education. Children show us this distorted way of modern fake-adults in a very obvious and clear way. This is why we must carefully observe what children do.

On one hand, parents and teachers say to their children or pupils that they should not fight and should be friendly, and yet on the other hand, when their children are beaten by other kids, parents or teachers may say that they should not be beaten but they should fight back and win. When the children hear both messages, it is natural that they become confused about which is more important.

In short, for parents and teachers, it is good that their children or pupils win or beat others, and simultaneously, it is good to be friendly with other children. If so, there must be other children who are beaten and are forced to be friendly. This is the natural outcome of such a contradiction. With the problem in Japanese elementary schools of bullies amongst children in classrooms, I think there is basic philosophical contradiction at the root of education. People cover up such contradictions without thinking about them deeply.

Weak and fainthearted kids who cannot beat others when they fight alone get together and discriminate against one weak kid who may be different from others and bully him. In doing this, these children feel they have carried out the teaching of their parents and teachers to be strong. Telling the victim that he should not report the cruel deeds to parents or teachers, they pretend there is no problem and that they are friendly and get along together. And thus they feel they are following the teaching to be friendly. I suppose this is the reality of the problem of bullies in Japanese elementary schools today. We didn't have such problems when I was a kid.

From the children's side, they demonstrate to their parents and teachers the result of following the contradicted teachings "to be friendly" and "to win." A child is truly a mirror that clearly shows the distortion of their parents' and teachers' way of life. By watching a child intimately we can understand our attitude toward life and we can judge ourselves.

In high school, social studies teachers may say that in this age of internationalization, peace among nations is most important. And at the same time they may say that living in a world with a struggle for existence, we must gain victory in the international arena of keen competition.

In students' day-to-day school lives, due to the competitive nature of the Japanese school system, teachers and parents drive students to think their friends are competitors and they should win against their friends. High school students who are not mature enough cannot clearly and logically understand the contradiction in what their parents and teachers say, so they cannot point it out. And yet, when the students cannot be convinced, they become irritated or frustrated and disobey and rebel against their parents and teachers.

Which is most important: to be friendly or to win a race within the community? Which is most important: peace or victory in the international arena of struggle for existence? Concerning the problem of the basic system of values for humanity, today, people deal with the dualistic ideas like a computer: this or that, good or bad. They just cover up the problems. Since people live by life-driving and society-driving forces, I think it is very natural that such social phenomena as bullying at school arise. The society is beyond judging the dichotomy of this and that, abundance and deficiency.

Regarding our present society's ideology of education, we can derive suggestions from the Buddha Way. The true way of life-driving as Dogen Zenji stated is, "there are those who attain realization beyond realization." I think that is what we have to learn from Buddhist or Dogen Zenji's teachings. Problems in our lives cannot be dealt with in such a childish manner as choosing this or that, good or bad. Rather, we have to carry out life-driving with awakened eyes. We should attain realization beyond realization; awaken moment by moment to the reality of life prior to the separation between dichotomies.

Further, in the society in which we live, it is not good simply to fight and beat each other. Nor can we be weak people of good will, victimized by avaricious people who push us around to get their own way.

How shall we live then? We should live and act with truly mature eyes, instead of judgments based on childish ideas of "this or that." We should practice life-driving freely while being continuously awake with vivid, mature eyes.

In the human life-force "car," we have an acceleration pedal of desire, a brake pedal of self-restraint, and a steering wheel to choose whether we escape, defend, or fight. It is important to have mature eyes with which to do life-driving so the life-force flows freely. We should endlessly deepen the eye of the truly mature person. In thinking about the problems in our society, what we should advocate is the creation of a society of truly mature people. Education should allow students to become truly mature people.

This is not a simple matter that can be dealt with by choosing this or that. Actually we are free and we can go in any direction. Only the profundity of our actions is important; how much we are truly mature persons. It cannot be simply two dimensions of success or failure. A person who attains realization beyond realization is a person who continuously awakens to the depth of life.

The basic profundity of a mature person in social activity is taught by Shakyamuni Buddha as follows:

"He insulted me, he hurt me, he defeated me, he robbed me. Those who think such thoughts will not be free from hate.

"He insulted me, he hurt me, he defeated me, he robbed me. Those who think not such thoughts will be free from hate."

For hate is not conquered by hate: hate is conquered by love. This is a law eternal.

[*The Dhammapada*, translation by Juan Mascaro, Penguin Books, 1973, Bungoy, Suffolk, England]

Shakyamuni Buddha said this when his clan, the Shakya, was annihilated by King Virudhaka of the neighboring country. As the capable people in the clan had left home to become Buddha's disciples, there was not a strong leader to fight against the invading army. King Virudhaka attacked the capital of the Shakya clan, killed many people, and burned the city. Before King Virudhaka attacked the Shakya clan, people from Shakyamuni Buddha's home sent messengers to Shakyamuni asking him to save them from annihilation.

On the way to the capital of the Shakya clan, the Buddha sat under a dead tree. When King Virudhaka saw the Buddha sitting under a dead tree by the road, the king asked, "Why do you sit under the dead tree?"

The Buddha replied, "The shadow of a family tree is nice and cool."

Then the king returned to his country without attacking the Buddha's clan.

The Buddha did the same thing three times to help his own clan. But the fourth time, the Buddha did not go to the dead tree. When King Virudhaka was attacking his people, the Buddha was watching the capital, Kapilavastu, burn. Form his place far away he just said, "I have a headache." And he kept sitting zazen.

After talking about this story, Sawaki Roshi commented, "At the time, if Shakyamuni Buddha had hastened back to Kapilavastu, sword in hand, to fight against King Virudhaka, saying, 'Virudhaka, you are my enemy. I will kill you!' Buddhism would not exist today. But Shakyamuni was not so impulsive. He just said, 'Hate is not conquered by hate: hate is conquered by love. This is a law eternal,' and sat silently. This is why Buddhism continues today, and is still offering us, all living beings suffering with the heat of irritation, the cool shadow of a huge tree."

"Hate is not conquered by hate: hate is conquered by love. This is a law eternal." Surely this is the final and decisive thing that everybody cannot easily do. In human relations, we say "it's a dog-eat-dog world." Human beings have internal discord and often begin to fight, even when they are working for peace. This is not an easy matter.

For instance, a mosquito alights on my body and starts to suck my blood. Do I watch it silently saying, "Hate is not conquered by hate: hate is conquered by love. This is a law eternal"? I am not such a stupid person. I will immediately squash it.

This is the reality of my self. And yet, even though I am such a person, is it certain that I will always behave in the same way? I don't think so. It is not necessarily certain. For example, when I determine to do something for the sake of all living beings, I might even throw my body away. We cannot say it is impossible. This depends on the depth of my own heart for all living beings at the time. We cannot easily tell which is more important: this or that, peace or victory. This is the way our lives actually are.

Since we are living out the reality of life that is before separation into the duality of delusion and enlightenment, there is infinite depth in both enlightenment and delusion. We should consider how deeply we are living the reality of life. People commonly think enlightenment exists outside ourselves as a fixed entity, and we realize enlightenment with a kind of mystical intuition, saying, "Wow! I've attained it." This is really simplistic and childish. Enlightenment is not like this.

After all, the self has to live the self. No one else can live for the self. How much do we progress? How much do we regress? It depends only on our selves. Realization beyond realization depends on our selves. It is not something we can observe and measure from outside. Our life has such depth. This is the depth in which the present moment becomes the present moment. Moment by moment, how much we do is how deep we are. This is why Dogen Zenji says next, "When buddhas are truly buddhas, they don't need to perceive that they are themselves buddhas."

> *(5) When buddhas are truly buddhas, they don't need to perceive that they are buddhas; however, they are enlightened buddhas, and they continue actualizing Buddha.*

People commonly think of enlightenment/delusion or buddhas/living beings as two separate and relative things. They separate them into two categories and say, "Until this point, they are deluded human beings, and after this point, they become enlightened buddhas." And yet, life does not have such a boundary. I repeat, both enlightenment and delusion, buddhas and living beings, are themselves the reality of life prior to dichotomy.

Relative ways of being, such as enlightenment/delusion, buddhas/living beings, are included in the reality of life. Precisely awakening to the reality of life is enlightenment and living in such a way is to be buddhas. Conversely, being blind to the reality of life is delusion, and people living in such a way are living beings. Therefore, this is not a dichotomy; each includes the whole reality. At the time of enlightenment, the whole reality including self and all beings becomes enlightenment. At the time of delusion, the whole reality inside and outside the self becomes deluded.

There is no place outside the self to observe the self saying, "I am a buddha." Just living out of the undivided reality of life is to be buddha. All buddhas just live out the reality of life. Conversely, to think "I have attained enlightenment, and I am a buddha," is truly ridiculous (*kokkei*) and nonsense. I always say that in zazen, we never hit the bull's-eye. Actually, while we are sitting, if we think, "Wow! My zazen is very good," we are just thinking. We are already slipping out of zazen. This is why I say it is *kokkei*, since this word means both slipping and ridiculous.

"Enlightened buddha" is doing the reality of life within the reality of life. "To continue actualizing buddha" is to live truly actualizing the reality of life.

> *In seeing color and hearing sound with body and mind, although we perceive them intimately, they are not like reflections in a mirror or the moon in water. When one side is illuminated, the other is dark.*

The reality of life, in which we see colors and hear sounds with our body and mind, is prior to the separation into an active subject and a passive object. Though I often use the word *reality*, this is not "to be real" in the ordinary meaning. Commonly, *reality* or *real thing* means something outside ourselves that is real, or not false, fake or illusory, after a separation is made between subject and object. The reality I am talking about is the reality of life before any separation into someone who sees and something that is seen.

Therefore, within such a reality of life, "although we perceive them intimately, they are not like reflections in a mirror or the moon in water." In the raw reality of life before being processed, our eyes cannot see the eyes themselves; our hand cannot grasp the hand itself. The reality of life is just doing the reality of life. We cannot be an observer or a bystander. When buddhas are truly buddhas, buddhas are just doing buddhas. To conclude this paragraph Dogen Zenji says, "When one side is illuminated, the other is dark."

Everything we encounter is our "self."

> *(6) To study the Buddha Way is to study the self. To study the self is to forget the self. To forget the self is to be verified by all things. To be verified by all things is to let the body and mind of the self and the body and mind of others drop off. There is a trace of realization that cannot be grasped. We endlessly express this ungraspable trace of realization.*

Here, Dogen Zenji discusses the Buddha Way. In *Genjo koan,* these first six sections are the outline, and after the seventh section, Dogen Zenji moves from the general to the particular. The sixth section is a summary of the previous sections. "Buddha Way" here means, as I said in my commentary on the third section, "Just practice the *Buddha dharma* for the sake of the *Buddha dharma*; this is the Way." Since we all, without exception, are living the reality of life, whether we think so or not, whether we believe it or not, we keep carrying out life-driving as the reality of life. This is the Buddha Way.

To study the Buddha Way is to study the self.

The self Dogen Zenji talks about here is not ego in terms of egoism. This is the self as *jinissai-jiko* (all-interpenetrating self) that is the reality of life prior to separation into dichotomies such as self/other or subject/object.

Previously Dogen Zenji said, "Conveying oneself toward all things to carry out practice-enlightenment is delusion." Although the self is originally living the all-interpenetrating self, my brain produces all kinds of not-interpenetrating thoughts. Thoughts well up such as: "I want money!" "I want sex," "I want a higher position!" and so on. When we are pulled by such thoughts secreted from our brain, that is certainly delusion. And yet, even though such thoughts are delusions, the fact that delusive thoughts come up is nothing other than a function of the reality of life connecting with heaven and earth. "To study the Buddha Way is to study the self" means we should study the self, which includes all heaven and earth.

Concretely speaking, we should accept everything as the contents of our "self." We should meet everything as a part of ourselves. "To study the self" means to awaken to such a self. For instance, many people visit my house or write me letters. Many of these people talk or write about their troubles and anguish and ask for my advice. I never feel troubled by such requests. As soon as I am asked about such troubles, they become my own. I meet people and problems in such a way. As long as I have such an attitude, these problems are my own. And they enrich my life. If I reject other people's problems saying, "That's not my business," my life becomes poorer and poorer. Therefore, to meet everything, without exception, as part of my life is most essential in the Buddha Way. This is what Dogen Zenji meant by saying, "To study the Buddha Way is to study the self."

To study the self is to forget the self.

An example of forgetting the self is a mother's attitude toward her child. A mother forgets herself for the sake of her baby, doesn't she? Young girls look pretty. Actually, they are all graceful and beautiful. However, once they have babies, they become so strong that they are not at all daunted even if they are hit with a hammer. Fathers do not devote themselves to their children as mothers do. I think mothers forget themselves to protect their children, and include their children in what they consider as their "self." This is not a thought, this is life-force. When mothers forget themselves for the sake of their children, their attitude may be a continuation of ego. However, when we forget ourselves in the Buddha Way, we forget ourselves because everything is the contents of the "self" and whatever we encounter is part of ourselves. This is not a continuation of egoism. To work as an all-interpenetrating self (*jinissai-jiko*) is not merely a thought. Therefore, in Buddhism it is a mistake to say that we have an idea of all-interpenetrating self. It cannot be the Buddha Way as long as we consider the word "all-interpenetrating self" a thought.

Without thinking that they are mothers, actually mothers forget themselves as mothers. This is not a thought anymore; rather they are mothers in reality. In the same way, when Shakyamuni Buddha says in the chapter of the *Lotus Sutra* entitled "A Parable," "Now, this triple world is my dwelling. All living beings within the world are my children," the Buddha is not talking about his "thoughts." Rather this is awakening to the self as the reality of life that is the interpenetration of all beings.

Again, I would like to bring up the example of driving a car. Driving is not done by thinking. It is awkward and dangerous if we drive thinking about what we should do each moment. When we actually drive, the scenery, which is always changing, is the content of ourselves. We forget ourselves and operate various devices with our hands and feet in response to the changing scenery. Our life-driving is the same. This is "to forget the self is to be verified by all things." Like car-driving, we act as one with the scenery, which is always changing.

Therefore it is a mistake to consider the self and all beings as two separate things. It is off the mark to translate *banpo* into modern

Japanese as *mono* (thing) or *sonzai* (existence). In *Buddha dharma* self and all things (*banpo*) are not two. Otherwise, we cannot see *Buddha dharma*. Self is living through the experience of all beings. All beings exist as life, as experiences by the self. Precisely because of this, both self and all beings are the vivid reality of life. This is expressed by Dogen Zenji as "One-mind is all beings. All beings are one-mind" (*Shobo genzo Sokushin-zebutsu*; *Mind Is Itself Buddha*).

All beings are the mind of the self, and the mind of the self is all beings. The reality of life is that the mind of the self and all beings are not two. On the contrary, in Western thought, subject and object are divided from the beginning. Then the subject and object interact with each other and cause cognition. If we think in that way, all beings lose life and our way of thinking also becomes lifeless. Then even if we try to put subject and object together again, it is not possible to put life back into them.

One example is the human body. In Western anatomy, we dissect the body into various parts such as hands, legs, trunk, and head, and then study each part. If we put all the knowledge together, it cannot make a living human body. Today, many young doctors think it is enough to collect technical knowledge from specialized studies. This is dangerous.

Although I often criticize doctors, many doctors read my books. This is strange. I think this is because many doctors try to see the reality of life. Doctors are scientists, and yet there are many doctors who encounter life when they treat actual human bodies. For these doctors, what I say makes sense. Doctor Ifuku, who died recently, often said, "Medical science for survival is not enough. It should be a science of life." Of course, knowledge from dissection or specialized study is important, but in the science of life, it is not enough to collect knowledge from separation and analysis. I wish doctors would see life itself as the study of science of life, instead of just collecting data from specialized fields.

This is the same as in the case of driving. I don't want to ride in a car driven by a person who separates himself from the changing scenery and operates the car with his thinking mind alone. It is very dangerous; such a person cannot drive a car with vitality. When we talk about *Buddha dharma* and the Buddha Way, we are talking about interpenetrating life itself as it actually is.

To be verified by all things is to let the body and mind of the self and the body and mind of others drop off.

In the case of driving, as long as we think that "I" drive a car, separating the self from other, we cannot drive a car with vitality. Only when we let go and drop off self and other can we drive freely. There is an old saying, "There is no person in the saddle and no horse under the saddle." We can apply this to car-driving: "There is no driver in the driver's seat, and no car under the driver's seat." Our driving of the reality of life in the Buddha Way is the same.

There is a trace of realization that cannot be grasped. We endlessly express this ungraspable trace of realization.

We cannot say that there is no enlightenment. And yet, we cannot say, "I have attained enlightenment." The trace of realization cannot be grasped. We must be free from the trace of realization. The Buddha Way is actually living our lives expressing the realization whose trace is ungraspable.

This is the end of the outline of *Genjo koan*. The following sections detail points about the Buddha Way.

Seeking the way with green for enlightenment cannot be *Buddha dharma*.

(7) *When a person first seeks the dharma, the person strays far from the boundary of the dharma. When the dharma is correctly transmitted to the self, the person is immediately an original person.*

If a person riding in a boat watches the coast, the person mistakenly perceives the coast as moving. If one watches the boat, then one notices that the boat is moving. Similarly, when we perceive the body and mind in a confused way and grasp all things with a discriminating mind, we mistakenly think that the self-nature of the mind is permanent. When we intimately practice and return right here, it is clear that all things have no [fixed] self.

When we seek the *Buddha dharma*, unless we are already dwelling within *Buddha dharma*, that practice is not *Buddha dharma*. For example, if I don't have any money and I want to do charitable work, if I try to cheat an old lady who has money, that is not a charitable way. My intention of doing charitable work cannot justify my action of robbing an old lady of her money.

In the same way, when I seek *Buddha dharma,* if I want to become a great person by attaining enlightenment, my practice is motivated by greed from the beginning. Seeking the Way in this manner is not in accordance with *Buddha dharma*. In many cases, when we start to practice the Buddha Way, we set forth with a greedy mind. This is why we stray far from the boundary of the dharma.

When I was ordained as a priest and started the life of zazen, I peacefully steeped myself in the life of practice with a simple determination that to practice zazen under Sawaki Roshi's guidance would be enough. But no matter how much we practice zazen, we do not change so much. Two or three years later, that became clear to me. I felt uncertain whether this practice was good enough. I began to think that I should attain so-called perfect enlightenment. However, once I set up enlightenment outside myself as a goal and wanted it, I was seeking the Way with greed. And while seeking the Way, I ended up endlessly running 'round and 'round. Consequently, I suffered for many years.

The practice of the Buddha Way is not at all simple. It is related to the whole of our lives, such as the troubles and agony of our youth, middle age, and final days when we face death. We can never say that we are always free from troubles. If we think that we are all right, sooner or later we will be thrown off. This is because we are already far from the boundary of dharma.

> *When the dharma is correctly transmitted to the self, the person is immediately an original person.*

Here, the most important thing is the *Buddha dharma*. I always focus on the *Buddha dharma*. The criterion of the *Buddha dharma* is that "*Buddha dharma* should be studied by giving up the view of self and others" (*Shobo genzo Bendowa*).

Buddha dharma is prior to the separation of self and others, of subject and object, of the self, which sees, and the object, which is seen, or of the self and the world. This is what is meant by expressions such as "mind and dharma are one reality," and "one mind is all dharmas; all dharmas are one mind." The self experiences all dharmas and all dharmas exist being experienced by the self.

In *Shobogenzo Shoji* (*Life-and-Death*), Dogen Zenji says, "Life-and-death is the 'Life of Buddha' (*hotoke no on-inochi*)." After all, life is prior to the separation between life and death, and simultaneously includes life and death. My expression, "the reality of life," refers to this "Life of Buddha." Without any exception, each and every one of us is living this life right now, right here.

We always breathe. I don't know how many times we breathe from birth to death. I have had pulmonary consumption for more than fifty years. When I see my X-ray, the parts that have vesticular emphysema look black, and the parts that have tuberculosis have white patches. My right lung is a mixture of black and white. This is quite something. I'm not proud of it, but I cannot help admiring that I have been breathing since my birth. I am not sure how many times I breathe a minute, but I have been breathing for more than seventy years! I breathe even while I sleep! For sure, this is not accomplished by this "I." However, "I" am actually breathing, the force that makes me breathe is the "Buddha's Life."

In Christianity "Buddha's Life" is called the power of God. If we use an expression from *Kanmuryojukyo* (*The Meditation on the Buddha of Infinite Life Sutra*, one of the three most important sutras in Pure Land Buddhism), we are in the light of Amitabha Tathagata, who embraces all living beings without discarding any. We are, from the beginning, living within the light of Amitabha Buddha. When you read this talk, you may think, "It is true," or "I don't believe it." We know that all such thoughts welling up from our brain are actually from the "Buddha's Life" that penetrates heaven and earth. They don't come up because "I" want them to come up. Somehow, they appear from the "Buddha's Life" that is the reality of life (one mind is all dharmas; all dharmas are one mind.

Without exception, we are all living completely interpenetrating life. However, the contents of our thoughts are not universal at all, but are very individual and even egocentric. Isn't it interesting? We often think,

"How can I get a good deal that no one else can get?" From the universal interpenetrating Life, very non-universal, un-interpenetrating thoughts come out.

Even now when I seek after *Buddha dharma*, "I" seek the *Buddha dharma*, "I" want to attain enlightenment, and "I" want to be a great person. Thus we are far from the boundary of *Buddha dharma*.

From the beginning, we are soaked in *Buddha dharma* and we cannot seek the dharma outside ourselves. We are actually living out "Buddha's Life." When this reality is correctly transmitted to the self, the person is immediately an original person.

In this age of science, we think we view all things objectively, and yet the problem is that the self, which is subjective, does not cease to be.

> *If a person riding in a boat watches the coast, the person mistakenly perceives the coast as moving. If one watches the boat, then one notices that the boat is moving. Similarly, when we perceive the body and mind in a confused way and grasp all things with a discriminating mind, we mistakenly think that the self-nature of the mind is permanent. When we intimately practice and return right here, it is clear that all things have no [fixed] self.*

When we are on a boat, from the point of view of a person, it seems the coast is moving. But when we return to the true self, we see that the boat is moving. It is a mistake to use ourselves as a yardstick. These days, the boat is becoming bigger and bigger. It is a luxury ship called the age of science. We cannot see that we are moving. This is a hallucination.

In the luxury ship called the age of scientific technology, we believe that we can see and deal with things objectively. Although objective observation is important, we cannot eliminate the subjective. We are human beings living here. If we don't include ourselves, we will view things simply in an objective manner. We will start to feel that we are objective beings. We will have an illusion that we are, like God, eternal and perfect beings who observe things completely objectively. I think there are scientists today who think this way.

For example, when an astronomer talks about the vastness of several million light years or the condition of the universe several hundred million years ago, he is talking about such a long period of time that he might forget his life is only eighty or ninety years. If he is already forty or fifty years old, he can only live for thirty or forty years more. I suppose such an astronomer might believe he will live forever.

It seems that doctors have a tendency to put themselves in a higher position than their patients. They get used to dealing with their patients' sickness objectively. Some of them might have the illusion that they themselves will never be sick. I know a doctor who guessed from his symptoms that he might have cancer. When he was finally informed about this cancer from another doctor, he didn't know what to do. He dealt with other people's cancer objectively, but he could not be objective about his own. He was frightened and upset. He said, "I never expected that I would get cancer."

Another example is schoolteachers. Of course, not all teachers are the same, but in this age of scientific technology, there are teachers who carelessly think that they can deal with students objectively, as scientists deal with their data, instead of dealing with them as human beings who are connected to their teachers and need to be nourished. I don't think teachers should deal with their students coldly and divide them into groups based only on their grades. This results in many students who are left behind and cannot complete their schooling.

I hear in a certain prefecture it was found that the highest percentage of juvenile delinquents had parents who were schoolteachers. If this is true, it means schoolteachers today deal with their children using schoolroom techniques. Many elementary and middle school teachers marry each other, and thus they both work. Their children feel lonely because they stay home alone after school. Their loneliness is dealt with by giving them lots of pocket money. Unfortunately, their children do not check their desires and they easily misbehave. This is why the police arrest many children of teachers.

These examples result "when we perceive the body and mind in a confused way and grasp all things with discriminating mind, [so] we mistakenly think that the self-nature of our own mind is permanent." We believe our mind-nature is eternal and deal with things as if they are outside ourselves. When we intimately practice and return right here, it is clear that all things have no fixed self. If we return to the reality of our life, it is clear that things do not exist as separate entities outside ourselves.

Dogen said in the second section, when all "dharmas are not [fixed] self, there are no (, no (, no (." In contrast to our usual thinking, all things do not exist outside ourselves in a fixed way. This is because the mind, which assumes that things are outside of ourselves, is the mind that is moving and changing.

> *(8) Firewood becomes ash. Ash cannot return to firewood again. However, we should not view ash as after and firewood as before. We should know that firewood dwells in the dharma position of firewood and has its own before and after. Although before and after exist, past and future are cut off. Ash stays in the position of ash, with its own before and after. As firewood never becomes firewood again after it has burned to ash, there is no return to living after a person dies. However, in* Buddha dharma, *it is an unchanged tradition not to say that life becomes death. Therefore we call it no-arising. It is the established way of Buddha's turning the dharma wheel not to say that death becomes life. Therefore, we call it no-perishing. Life is a position in time; death is also a position in time. This is like winter and spring. We don't think that winter becomes spring, and we don't say that spring becomes summer.*

On the surface, it looks like the preceding paragraphs have no connection with one another. Each section seems to go this way and that way without logical coherence. This seems similar to a typical Zen dialogue. Because of this, many masters think it is not appropriate to read Zen texts as a whole and trace a thread of connection in each paragraph. Neither commentaries made before the Meiji era (1868–1912) nor those published in modern times make an effort to grasp what Dogen Zenji says as a whole. They just interpret words and sentences and make commentaries on each paragraph disconnectedly. Furthermore, they don't investigate the meaning of important words such as *Buddha dharma* or Buddha Way. Naturally readers are confused when they read these commentaries. And yet, for the people who wrote those commentaries, this is the authentic way to understand Zen texts.

I don't agree with such an attitude. Since Dogen Zenji wrote this work and entitled it *Genjo koan,* I believe that he wrote about *Genjo koan* as a whole, not merely as a collection of short paragraphs like aphorisms about scattered, miscellaneous topics. Therefore, I am trying to follow the thread of connection and understand the meaning of *Genjo koan* as one whole piece.

Even though I am reading *Genjo koan* with such an intention, this section, which begins, "Firewood becomes ash. Ash cannot return to firewood again," seems inserted in an abrupt way. Why did Dogen Zenji bring up the analogy of firewood becoming ash? It is written like a bullet shot from a gun in the dark without warning. And yet, because Dogen Zenji purposely put it in this order, I wish to catch the meaning of this analogy. When we read between the lines, we can understand the deep meaning of what Dogen Zenji points to in this section.

I have been trying to understand this point for many years. After repeatedly reading *Genjo koan,* I have come to understand it as follows: In the seventh section, Dogen Zenji says, "When a person first seeks the dharma, the person strays far from the boundary of the dharma. When the dharma is correctly transmitted to the self, the person is immediately an original person."

What he says is that *Buddha dharma* is not something we can gain even if we want to do so, and yet when the dharma is transmitted to the self, the person is immediately an original person.

In the beginning of the ninth section, Dogen Zenji says, "When a person attains realization, it is like the moon's reflection in water." So in the ninth section, the person has already attained enlightenment. If so, then the eighth section should be about attaining enlightenment. With this expectation, we begin to read this section with our hearts aflutter. Finally, we can stop wasting time in preliminaries and get to the heart of the text.

> *Firewood becomes ash. Ash cannot return to firewood again. However, we should not view ash as after and firewood as before.*

Firewood becomes ash. This is, at first glance, a matter of course. However, our rational minds have concepts of each thing, of firewood as "firewood," ash as "ash." At the same time, we link these two concepts together and think of transformation, as in "firewood" "becomes" "ash." The ability to link two or more ideas together is called apperception. This apperception points to the order, which is first and which is second; so firewood is first, ash is second. Further apperception links a causal relationship, for example: Because I made a fire and burned the firewood, the firewood became ash. Our human mind thinks about two or more things in relationship to each other.

> *We should know that firewood dwells in the dharma position of firewood and has its own before and after. Although before and after exist, past and future are cut off. Ash stays in the position of ash, with its own before and after.*

Here, Dogen Zenji talks about firewood becoming ash. If we replace these terms with *delusion* and *enlightenment*, this is about how delusion turns into enlightenment. We want to know how to make delusion into enlightenment. And yet, here Dogen Zenji says there is no such transformation.

What does this mean? At this point, we must pay attention to the "dharma position (*hoi*)," as in "firewood dwells in the dharma position of firewood" and "ash stays at the dharma position of ash." "Dharma position" means the Way dharmas are independent prior to separation between subject and object or self and others; that is, the way things are. This reality of life is beyond subject/object, self/other. Firewood is not a step to becoming ash, and ash is not a continuation of firewood. Firewood is just firewood; ash is just ash.

And yet, we cannot say there is no before and after. For firewood to be firewood, for example, a tree is cut down and becomes firewood. Later if we put it in a fireplace, it will become ash. This is after. However, including both before and after, past and future, firewood is just firewood in the dharma position of this present moment. "Although before and after exist, past and future are cut off." In the dharma position of firewood, firewood is not firewood in relationship to ash. It is firewood as the reality of life prior to ash. In this sense, firewood is only firewood.

Ash has a "before" that was produced by burning firewood and an "after" that returns to the soil. Including connections such as "before" and "after," firewood is "just" firewood. At the dharma position of ash, ash is not ash in relationship to firewood. It is the reality of life prior to the relationship to firewood. Thus, it is also true that although ash has "before" and "after" as its own being, past and future are cut off. We cannot say firewood becomes ash.

When we say firewood becomes ash with the human rational mind, we apperceive both of them and relate "before" and "after" to one another, making a causal order. That is because we burn firewood and it becomes ash. The reality of life before such thoughts come from our brain is that firewood is only firewood; ash is only ash.

I have never seen potassium cyanide, so I don't know what color it is. But suppose that potassium cyanide were in this glass of water. Putting this glass with potassium cyanide in front of me, I am thinking of committing suicide by drinking it. I think about "before," that because I made such a stupid mistake then, I have to drink this now. And also I think about "after," that when I drink it in one gulp, I will immediately die.

In such a case, as the reality of life, such a stupid mistake is cut off and finished as a stupid mistake. Potassium cyanide is potassium cyanide. That is all. Dying is dying. They are all cut off. A problem is that potassium cyanide has a chemical property that has strong virulence, which can kill a human being who drinks it. However, we think that because I made such a mistake I have to drink potassium cyanide and when I drink it I will die. With such a causal sequence, we put ourselves into a straitjacket. This is because we put everything into a sequence in time and based on such thinking throw ourselves into it.

However, as the reality of life, "before" and "after" are cut off. Such a mistake is such a mistake. Potassium cyanide is potassium cyanide. That's it. Each thing is cut off. Because of this, actually, at any point in time, it is possible to make a fresh start.

While I was practicing under Sawaki Roshi, I often made foolish mistakes in front of the Roshi. Sawaki Roshi never overlooked even a small fault, and scolded me in a loud voice. Because I had no choice, I just listened silently. While I was listening silently, when Sawaki Roshi had nothing more to say, he finally became silent. Then I thought, "That's over now." To think, "That's over now" is salvation. If I make a mistake, there is no way to escape from the fact. Since I made a mistake, if I fall into hell due to my mistake, I will have to work diligently in hell. And yet, when I finish working in hell, I can just think, "That's over."

In this sense, the fact that "past and future are cut off" is perfect salvation for us. Although I continuously make mistakes, when I say, "Oh, no! I made a mistake," actually it has already gone. Therefore, I can make a fresh start. Even though "before" and "after" are cut off, "before" and "after" exist. I can learn lessons from the experiences of previous mistakes, and start fresh, using them as wisdom to do a better job.

To make a fresh start is to arouse bodhi-mind. Then, I arouse bodhi-mind again and again, repeatedly millions of times. After all, to live means to have continuous aspiration to make a fresh start each moment. Because we have to live breathing one breath in each moment, the present breath is only for the present moment. The next moment we have to breathe a fresh breath.

I had a chance to become acquainted with Reverend Doyu Ozawa when he visited me while I lived in Ogaki. Reverend Ozawa was taken prisoner at the end of World War II. While being taken to Siberia on a freight train, both of his legs were frostbitten, because he was wearing summer clothing. He was sent back to Japan because he couldn't walk. At a hospital, he was told that both his legs should be amputated at the knee. When he had the operation, he only said to his army surgeon, "Please cut both legs evenly." I can sympathize with his words. After he had his legs amputated, he had to wear artificial legs. Since he put his whole weight on the artificial legs to walk, he had to be really patient until the wounds healed where it touched the artificial legs. He had to practice walking with the artificial legs. He experienced extreme pain and agony. Yet, he always had a warm smile and walked only with a walking stick. He never used a pair of crutches.

The pivotal point for him was that he chose to think: "Today, at this moment, I am born." One could think, "I was born with both legs, then I was drafted and forced to go to war. Because we lost the war, I was sent to Siberia as a prisoner. On the way, my legs got frostbitten and I had to have both of them amputated." If we think of this sequence of events, it's too painful even to cry. We will be infinitely vexed and miserable. However, Reverend Ozawa chose to think that he was born today, this moment, without legs. That was the turning point for him, to live with a bright and cheerful attitude. This is not an idealistic story but his own actual experience. Reverend Ozawa's saying, "Today, this moment, I am born," carries infinite weight.

Each and every one of us without exception can experience such misery at any moment. We want always to be ready to thoroughly accept such conditions. Fundamentally, if our parents had an abortion before we were born, we could not have done anything about it. No parent asks their baby's permission for an abortion. It's a completely one-sided decision. We cannot even make a complaint.

We should know this about the origin of our lives. And yet, since we are actually born and a living self, we need to live arousing bodhi-mind millions of times: "I am born today, at this moment." This is the reality of life; although "before" and "after" exist, past and future are cut off.

We live and die with the power of the reality of life prior to any separation between life and death.

> *As firewood never becomes firewood again after it has burned to ash,* there is no return to living after a person dies. However, in Buddha dharma, *it is an unchanged tradition not to say that life becomes death. Therefore we call it no-arising. It is the established way of Buddha's turning the dharma wheel not to say that death becomes life. Therefore, we call it no-perishing.*

Recently I received a letter from Reverend Toru Imagawa, who is a Pure Land Buddhist temple priest in Komatsu-shi, Ishikawa Prefecture. Last year, Reverend Imagawa was informed that he had cancer. While in the hospital for treatment, he thought seriously about life and death. As he was thinking, something came to mind. The last stroke of the Chinese character for life and the first stroke of the Chinese character for death are one, so that we can create a new character.

And if we have a character like this, how should we read it? Since he is a Pure Land Buddhist, he asked many Pure Land priests. Finally, he wrote a letter to me asking how I would read it. He said that since he was at the border of life and death, the one stroke at the center would be most significant and he read the character as "here/now."

When I read the letter from Reverend Imagawa, I thought that what he said fit with the subject of my next lecture on *Genjo koan*. So I wrote back to get his permission to use his thought about the character he created.

I also wrote to him about the character. The character refers to the matter of life/death prior to separation into life and death as two different things. Here life has not yet formed into "life," and death has not yet formed into "death." Therefore, I would like to read this character as "the formless Life before any separation between life and death." My way of reading this character and Reverend Imagawa's "here/now" are precisely what I want to address here as a matter of *Genjo koan*.

Returning to the text, in the case of firewood as the reality of life, firewood is just firewood. It is not firewood relative to ash, or a step to becoming ash. In the same way, our life as the reality of life is just life. It is neither life as a step to becoming death, nor life that is relative and opposite death. That is why Dogen Zenji says, "As firewood never becomes firewood again after it has burned to ash, there is no return to living after a person dies."

If there is a substantial entity called "life" that dies, it might be possible that "life" becomes "life" again after death. However, this is not the case. Life is just living, going beyond any dichotomy. Then what can we call such a reality of life? The only possible name is "the formless Life prior to any separation between life and death" or "no-life." Therefore, Dogen Zenji said, "However, in *Buddha dharma*, it is an unchanged tradition not to say that life becomes death. Therefore we call it no-arising."

It is the established way of Buddha's turning the dharma wheel not to say that death becomes life. Therefore, we call it no-perishing.

Just as in the reality of life ash is just ash, death is just death. It is not the next stage after life, but it is formless life prior to any separation between life and death, that is, no-perishing. Without any exception, whether we think so or not, whether we believe it or not, accept it or reject it, all of us live and die such a formless life.

Buddha dharma is about the reality of life. The reality of life is, as described in the *Heart Sutra*, "no-arising, no-perishing, not-tainted, not-pure, not-increasing, not-decreasing." It is not-going and not-coming. However, when we see it with the discriminating eyes of a karmic, individual human being, we see coming and going. And yet, even such a discriminating mind is animated by the reality of life. In conclusion, we have to say, "the coming and going of not-coming and not-going."

Arising/perishing and coming/going are included in not-arising and not-perishing, not-coming and not-going. That is why the Buddha is called Tathagata (like-coming, like-going).

Therefore, the *Daichidoron*, Nagarjuna's commentary on the *Mahaprajnaparamita Sutra*, says, "Life and death are only names. They are not substantial. Within the conventional dharma, life and death really exist, but in the true reality of dharma, there is no life and death." The chapter of the *Lotus Sutra* called "Life Span of the Tathagata" says, "The Tathagata knows and sees the character of the triple world as it really is: [to the Tathagata] there is neither birth nor death, neither going away nor coming forth, neither living nor dying, neither reality nor unreality, neither thus nor otherwise. Unlike [the Way] the triple world beholds the triple world, the Tathagata clearly sees such things as they are." This is the fundamental philosophy of life and death in Buddhism.

This is the reality of life. Whether we are alive or dead, we are just formless "Life of Buddha" itself. We are always fresh, yet ordinary. The reality of life is nothing special(just right now, right here. This is what Reverend Imagawa said, "right now, right here."

> *Life is a position in time; death is also a position in time. This is like winter and spring. We don't think that winter becomes spring, and we don't say that spring becomes summer.*

Life is just life. It is only a formless position at one moment. Death is just death. It is only a formless position at one moment. In Japan, we don't say that winter becomes spring and spring becomes summer. Winter is just winter beyond any dichotomy. Spring is just spring beyond any dichotomy.

Therefore, even though we say a person attains enlightenment, there is no such transition as delusion becoming enlightenment. This is the essential point in this section. Delusion is formless in itself. Enlightenment is the formless life prior to any separation between delusion and enlightenment. All of us are living and dying such formless life. We are deluded or enlightened within formless life. Dogen Zenji is going to discuss this point in the next section.

(9) When a person attains realization, it is like the moon's reflection in water. The moon never becomes wet; the water is never disturbed. Although the moon is a vast and great light, it is reflected in a drop of water. The whole moon and even the whole sky are reflected in a drop of dew on a blade of grass. Realization does not destroy the person, as the moon does not make a hole in the water. The person does not obstruct realization, as a drop of dew does not obstruct the moon in the sky. The depth is the same as the height. [To investigate the significance of] the length and brevity of time, we should consider whether the water is great or small, and understand the size of the moon in the sky.

Commonly we think that we are deluded human beings who wish to make ourselves into buddhas by using some technique to attain enlightenment. As I said regarding the eighth section, we assume there must be a transition from delusion to enlightenment. However, Dogen Zenji wrote that there is no such transition, but all of us, whether we are deluded human beings or not, are living the reality of life prior to any separation between delusion and enlightenment and life and death.

According to Zen tradition, when Shakyamuni Buddha attained enlightenment, he said, "I, the great earth, and sentient beings simultaneously attained the Way; mountains, rivers, grass, and trees have all become Buddha." In the *Lotus Sutra* there is an expression, "Ten directions are all within Buddha's land." The *Kanmuryoju-kyo* (*Sutra of Seeing Infinite Life*, one of the three major sutras of Pure Land Buddhism) says, "The light of the Tathagata of Infinite Life (Amitabha) embraces all living beings without rejecting any." We have already been enlightened by Shakyamuni Buddha, and are from the beginning in the hands of Amitabha Buddha, who saves all living beings without exception. This is not a matter of understanding it or not. Whether we know it or not, whether we say I don't believe in Amitabha or not, it is true. It is not a problem. The light of Amitabha embraces all living beings whether we believe in it or not.

The reality of life or the "Life of Buddha" is thus. And yet, all of us think and measure and say, "I don't believe it." Don't say such cheeky things! The force which makes us think that our minds are great and makes us say such cheeky things itself wells up from the power of

Amitabha or the "Life of Buddha." We must deeply understand that whether we think so or not, believe it or not, understand it or not, venerate it or not, accept it or reject it, in whatever conditions, we are living out the formless reality of life prior to its division into dichotomies.

Because life/death prior to the separation between life and death, and delusion and enlightenment are formless, we must say they are an empty circle. We are actually living out this empty circle, and this is going to die. This empty circle is deluded or enlightened. All myriad things without any exceptions reflect this empty circle. This is like the moon reflecting upon the water.

Therefore, it is not right to determine that "I" am a deluded human being. Such a judgment is possible because the power of the formless reality of life is working. Whatever we may think, this present moment is the time that the dharma is correctly transmitted to the self and the time a person attains enlightenment. This is what is said in the *Lotus Sutra* as "*kuon-jitsujo* (the eternal manifestation of reality)." From the beginningless beginning, we are living at the time when "a person attains enlightenment." It is not a matter of putting our self-power to work and seriously practicing in order to attain enlightenment. Instead of that, whether we think so or not, whether we believe it or not, whether we accept or reject it, we are completely living out the reality of life. We are reflecting the formless moon. The formless moon dwells in us.

Even though the formless moon is reflected in us, the moon does not get wet and the water is not destroyed. These days, since human beings have been to the moon, we think the moon is just a branch of the earth. But, we must read this section of *Genjo koan* with the feeling of the ancient people who called the moon *nonosama* and worshiped it. The moon is a symbol of the absolute that is beyond human discriminating thoughts. It is a vast and great light.

The absolute vast light of reality, like the moonlight, is the light of Amitabha. It seems far apart from us, but actually it is always reflected in us. Even though it is reflected in us, Amitabha does not become tainted. Even though Amitabha is reflected in us, we do not become something else. "I" am "I" and Amitabha is Amitabha. Therefore:

> *Although the moon is a vast and great light, it is reflected in a drop of water. The whole moon and even the whole sky are reflected in a drop of dew on a blade of grass.*

The moonlight is reflected in a drop of dew on the leaf of a tree and in water in a mountain stream. While I am talking and you are listening, you may think what I am saying is true, or you may think what I am saying is nonsense. You may have various thoughts. The power of the interpenetrating formless life is functioning in such thoughts.

In the spring, violets bloom violet flowers. Dandelions bloom dandelion flowers. When violets bloom, the whole universe blooms in the violets' way. When dandelions bloom, the whole universe blooms in the dandelions' way.

> *Realization does not destroy the person, as the moon does not make a hole in the water.*

Although we are animated by the power of interpenetrating formless life, it is not an entity to be possessed. It does not make a hole of enlightenment in us. Enlightenment does not eliminate us as an individual.

The person does not obstruct realization, as a drop of dew does not obstruct the moon in the sky. Even though we are deeply deluded human beings, there is no reason we cannot be enlightened. Even in a dirty pool of water, the heavenly moon is reflected.

The reality of life cannot be discussed in general for all people. It is a matter of how a particular person lives.

> *The depth is the same as the height. [To investigate the significance of] the length and brevity of time, we should consider whether the water is great or small, and understand the size of the moon in the sky.*

Dogen Zenji's writing is beautiful and sophisticated. Without explanation, he says that the depth is the same as the height. Dogen Zenji has been discussing the general principle of *Buddha dharma*, but from now on, he talks about the particular person who is living the reality of life.

All of us without exception are living out the reality of life. We don't need to worry about it. Whether we think so or not, whether we believe it or not, whether we practice it or not, each and every one is living within the power of Amitabha, which embraces all and rejects none. This is really true. However, if we only understand the principle, that is the same as the fallacious view of Senika, which Dogen Zenji criticized in *Shobogenzo Bendowa* (*Talk on Wholehearted Practice of the Way*).

We should not mix up karmic self with original self as Senika did. Our karmic individual self is not the original self. As a karmic self, the human mind discriminates. Using this mind, we think about many things. This discriminating mind is animated by the original reality of life, which is also universal. And yet, various thoughts that well up from this mind are clearly non-universal. Therefore, the karmic self who always takes action based on discriminating mind often lives a non-universal way of life.

As the original self, each and every one of us lives the universal life without any question. However, we should clearly understand that we are merely karmic selves as long as we take action based on such non-universal thoughts.

The important matter for us is how we wave the fan and actualize the wind of life, which is boundless and infinite. How can we actualize universal life right here and right now? This is what Reverend Imagawa expressed as "here/now." Whatever the conditions, we are always living within the "Life of Buddha." But, at the same time, it is really crucial to see that this reality is the "Life of Buddha." Our problem is how to actualize the reality of the "Life of Buddha" right here and right now. This is what Dogen Zenji meant when he said that water has its own depth and the moon has its own height.

This is not a matter of whether we can succeed or fail by measuring how high or how deep. We cannot say, "You succeed because you have such a height." Or, "You failed because you are so shallow." As I often say, we cannot measure the height of dharma or judge the depth of a person even with a computer.

Whatever the conditions, we are living the "Life of Buddha." Whatever the conditions, we are always successfully living Buddha. Even so, whatever the conditions, we have to actualize with our own body and mind that we are living out the "Life of Buddha." Here lies the infinite profundity of depth and height. This is what I meant by rendering *Genjo koan* as "the ordinary profundity of the present moment becoming the present moment." Beginning with this section, Dogen Zenji talks about the particular person who is living out the universal "Life of Buddha." Here he simply says that the depth is the same as the height.

[To investigate the significance of] the length and brevity of time,
we should consider whether the water is great or small, and under-
stand the size of the moon in the sky.

Neither water nor moon exists as a fixed entity. It is a matter of the
length and shortness of time. Within moment-by-moment practice,
the greatness and smallness of water or the profundity of the person is
investigated, and the reality of life is understood in the infinite moon.

We cannot measure success or failure by how deep a person is. Height
and depth of dharma is immeasurable. We cannot judge whether a person is enlightened or deluded, whether he or she gains or loses. *Buddha
dharma* is really profound. Since it is infinitely profound, it is called
radiant light.

Although religion can be used to discriminate among people, spiritual light cannot be analyzed and compared between individuals. It is
holistic brightness. I think about this brightness of light when I take
a walk in the evening twilight. The evening sky in February, the early
spring in Kyoto, is different from the evening sky in the fall and winter. I have been thinking what the difference is between them. In the
evening sky in the fall and winter, although the light remains in the
west after sunset, the eastern part of the sky is already completely dark.
However, after *risshun* [February third], not only the western part but
also the eastern part of the sky is bright after sunset—the whole sky is
equally bright. This is a characteristic of twilight in early spring. At this
time of year, if the cold wind stops blowing, we feel the warmth of an
early spring. Within the brightness of the whole sky, though we cannot
measure the unit of light, there is clearly a different feeling in spring,
fall, and winter.

The light of Amitabha is like this. The religious light is an ungraspable holistic brightness. Within that brightness, there is an individual
difference that reflects the universal brightness. There is length and
shortness, vastness and narrowness in the feelings of each person, of
each condition. This is the profundity of the "Life of Buddha."

(10) When the dharma has not yet fully penetrated body and mind,
one thinks one is already filled with it. When the dharma fills
body and mind, one thinks something is [still] lacking. For

example, when we sail a boat into the ocean beyond sight of land and our eyes scan [the horizon in] the four directions, it simply looks like a circle. No other shape appears. This great ocean, however, is neither round nor square. It has inexhaustible characteristics. [To a fish,] it looks like a palace; [to a heavenly being,] a jeweled necklace. [To us] as far as our eyes can see, it looks like a circle. All the myriad things are like this. Within the dusty world and beyond, there are innumerable aspects and characteristics; we only see or grasp as far as the power of our eye of study and practice can see. When we listen to the reality of myriad things, we must know that there are inexhaustible characteristics in both ocean and mountains, and there are many other worlds in the four directions. This is true not only in the external world, but also right under our feet or within a single drop of water.

We have a finite body and mind. These days we modern Japanese don't think that our bodies and minds are finite. We think we understand the infinite "Life of Buddha," but we don't. It is precisely like our youth, when we don't know much about the world, but we feel we know everything. We call such teenagers "cheeky kids." In the twentieth century, all human beings are like "cheeky kids" in a phase of contrariness. Japanese people are cheeky when they proudly declare that they have no religion. They are completely ignorant about what religion is. Many of them spend their whole lives without any spiritual growth. This is a problem. This period of contrariness does not continue forever. When cheeky kids grow up they eventually realize that they used to be foolish children. However, today Japanese are pitiful because they spend their whole lives not knowing the "Life of Buddha." They do not grow spiritually. People in later generations will think the Japanese in the twentieth century were foolish. Many people living in this age will die without knowing this. This is truly pathetic.

It is important to know that no matter how developed we are in terms of science and technology, if we lose the mind of veneration and prayer, we are living in a most pitiful situation. Since we are living the infinite "Life of Buddha" whether we think so or not, whether we accept it or not, it is natural that we should value this "Life of Buddha."

When the dharma fills body and mind, one thinks something is [still] lacking.

When we are filled with the universal "Life of Buddha," we can see how small, foolish, and ignorant we are. This is great wisdom.

When I was a student I read that in ancient Greece someone asked the god at the temple of Delphi who was the wisest person in Athens. The Delphi oracle said that Socrates was the wisest. When Socrates heard this, he was surprised and thought that he could not be the wisest person, and yet the Delphi oracle could not be false. He concluded that he knew that he was ignorant. Others didn't know that they were ignorant, which was why he was the wisest. To know that we are ignorant is the foundation of wisdom.

However, today no one knows they are ignorant. In this way, after World War II, Japanese education made people foolish. Schools emphasized democracy and forced children who didn't know anything to express their opinions. Since the children don't understand, teachers should teach them. But teachers let children speak their opinions, thinking that is democracy. This produced cheeky, half-baked people.

Such cheeky, half-baked kids grow only physically and give birth to the next generation, whose standard of spirituality falls lower and lower. People become more and more childish. Foolishness becomes deeper and deeper, growing exponentially. Even in this foolishness, we can see that the depth is the same as the height.

The immeasurable and boundless "Life of Buddha" cannot be grasped by our finite mind. Even an elementary-school child understands this.

When I was in trouble in my practice, Sawaki Roshi said, "*Buddha dharma* is immeasurable and boundless; it cannot be something which fulfills your desire for satisfaction." With this saying, I was truly turned around. This was not some special enlightenment experience. If our understanding is as easy as elementary mathematics, we can understand that the immeasurable and boundless *Buddha dharma* cannot be something that fulfills our personal desire for satisfaction. Thus, naturally, we feel dissatisfied.

For example, when we sail a boat into the ocean beyond sight of land and our eyes scan [the horizon in] the four directions, it simply looks like a circle. No other shape appears.

Dogen Zenji went to China by boat. It must have been scary to cross the ocean in a small boat like a leaf. Once at sea, he could only see the horizon. Actually, there were islands and ports on the other side of the ocean, but they could not be seen. As far as he could see, no other shape appeared.

This great ocean, however, is neither round nor square. It has inexhaustible characteristics.

Since it has inexhaustible characteristics, the ocean is infinite.

[To a fish,] it looks like a palace; [to a heavenly being,] a jeweled necklace. [To us] as far as our eyes can see, it looks like a circle. All the myriad things are like this.

In Buddhist tradition, an analogy called "the four views of water" has been used since ancient times. In seeing the water, fish think it is their house or palace. Heavenly beings view it as a jewel. Human beings see it as water. Hungry ghosts see it as fire. This is "the four views of water." After all, whatever we see, we see it in our own way. However, myriad dharmas (things) include both what we see and what we don't see. Myriad dharmas are not only what we can see.

Within the dusty world and beyond, there are innumerable aspects and characteristics; we only see or grasp as far as the power of our eye of study and practice can see.

The dusty world refers to the mundane society, while "beyond" refers to the world of *Buddha dharma*. There are many things in the secular world and the world of dharma. The very person who is the finite self, upon whom vast, boundless light is reflected, sees and understands as much as he encounters right now.

When we listen to the reality of myriad things, we must know that there are inexhaustible characteristics in both ocean and mountains, and there are many other worlds in the four directions.

There are innumerable characteristics in the "Life of Buddha" beyond the boundaries that we can conceive. There are many worlds in the four directions.

This is true not only in the external world, but it is the same right under our feet or within a single drop of water.

This is not only true about the things we see outside ourselves. Our body and mind, which is right here, is also like this. Each and every thing taking place in our body—circulation, breathing, and thought— is animated by the reality of life, the "Life of Buddha" that is vast, boundless, and interpenetrating.

Next, Dogen Zenji discusses in detail this very person who is living the vast and boundless "Life of Buddha" right now and right here.

In car-driving, you are in the principal role—in life-driving, this is even more true.

> *When a fish swims, no matter how far it swims, it doesn't reach the end of the water. When a bird flies, no matter how high it flies, it cannot reach the end of the sky. When the bird's need or the fish's need is great, the range is large. When the need is small, the range is small. In this way, each fish and each bird uses the whole of space and vigorously acts in every place. However, if a bird departs from the sky, or a fish leaves the water, it immediately dies. We should know that [for a fish] water is life, [for a bird] sky is life. A bird is life; a fish is life. Life is a bird; life is a fish. And we should go beyond this. There is practice-enlightenment—this is the Way of living beings.*

Beginning in this section, Dogen Zenji discusses the concrete way of life in which this very person must walk day by day. It has become clear that in *Genjo koan* Dogen Zenji is talking about the Buddha Way, in which one should practice *Buddha dharma* for the sake of *Buddha dharma* [Dogen's expression in *Gakudo-yojinshu*] on the ground of *Buddha dharma*; that is the reality of "Life of Buddha."

Buddha dharma is "one mind is all things; all things are one mind." That means all things without exception. Therefore, regardless of whether we think so or not, whether we believe it or not, whatever conditions we are in, we are living as *Buddha dharma*, the reality of life. As Dogen Zenji said in the ninth section, all beings reflect *Buddha dharma* as the moon is reflected in each drop of water.

"Attaining enlightenment" means that we realize interpenetrating reality. Because such enlightenment lies in unconditional reality, we cannot say that "I" get enlightenment or "I" fail to get it. All are living in the interpenetrating reality. And yet, there is depth and height.

> *The depth is the same as the height. [To investigate the significance of] the length and brevity of time, we should consider whether the water is great or small, and understand the size of the moon in the sky.*

There is a depth to the self that is just the self. This cannot be measured. This is the general principle of *Buddha dharma*. In section ten, regarding this very person who is living out such *Buddha dharma*, Dogen Zenji said, "When the dharma has not yet fully penetrated body and mind, one thinks one is already filled with it. When the dharma fills body and mind, one thinks something is [still] lacking."

As I said in the commentary on section three, Dogen's definition of the "Way" is "to practice the dharma for the sake of the dharma." This "Way" is not something that people commonly talk about. People commonly talk about a pathway outside themselves by which people come and go. Rather, this "Way" is one's own attitude toward life: to practice *Buddha dharma* for the sake of *Buddha dharma*, or to live the reality of life for the sake of the reality of life.

Therefore, *Buddha dharma* is the Way of life—life-driving in which we live out the reality of life. We cannot escape from *Buddha dharma*. Such life-driving or way of life is a matter of this very person. It cannot be a matter of general principle.

Regarding this very person, within the immeasurable and boundless "Life of Buddha," we must know that there are inexhaustible characteristics in either oceans or mountains, and there are many other worlds in the four directions. This is true not only in the external world, but is the same right under our feet or within a single drop of water. This is what he said in the end of the last section. In this section, as an example of the Way of this very person, he says, "When a fish swims, no matter how far it swims, it doesn't reach the end of the water. When a bird flies, no matter how high it flies, it cannot reach the end of the sky."

When we read *Genjo koan* in this way, we see how precise and logical Dogen Zenji is in discussing the essential points of the Buddha Way. By reading the original text of *Genjo koan* repeatedly and respectfully, we will appreciate it deeply.

A fish is swimming in the water. Water is the "field of activity" for the fish. For the fish, as for this very person, the field of activity is completely boundless. The sky is the same for the bird.

> *When the bird's need or the fish's need is great, the range is large.*
> *When the need is small, the range is small.*

Fish and birds are finite beings. In the same way, we are finite beings in human form. When this finite being is carrying out the life-driving, which is immeasurable and boundless, the driver and the ground of driving are not two. When a bird flies great distances in the sky, the bird uses the large space as its field of activity. Also, when a fish swims a short distance in the water, the fish uses only a small space in the water as its field of activity.

In this way, each fish and each bird uses the whole space and vigorously acts in every place. Even though a goldfish is swimming in a small goldfish bowl, the goldfish is penetrating the whole universe. A sparrow flies from twig to twig traversing the whole sky.

However, if a bird leaves the air, or a fish leaves the water, they will immediately die. Even though a sparrow flies only a short distance, if we take this space, the place of life-driving, from the sparrow, it will die. If we throw even the tiny bit of water in the bowl away, the goldfish will die.

If the place is taken away, this very person who is carrying out life-driving cannot function at all. One-mind is all beings; all beings are one-mind. We are experiencing all things in our life and all things exist being experienced by us. The person who is life-driving and the place of life-driving are not two; they are without separation. This is the way *Buddha dharma* is.

> *We should know that [for a fish] water is life, [for a bird] sky*
> *is life.*

For this very person who is life-driving, the water is life and the sky is life. After all, whatever we encounter is our life.

The expression, "Whatever I encounter is my life" is one I have been using since 1967 when I wrote *Refining Your Life*. In the *Tenzo-kyokun* (*Instructions for the Cook*), Dogen gives very concrete and practical teaching on the practice of the Buddha Way. If you aspire to practice the Buddha Way, please read the *Tenzo-kyokun* and illuminate your mind with the ancient teachings that apply directly to your life.

A bird is life; a fish is life.

This expression means that for a fish, to be a fish is life, and for a bird, to be a bird is life. For me, to be myself is life. Because I am living with my karmic nature, I cannot do anything but live these karmic conditions by refining my life.

Until the Meiji era, people from lower-class families could not join the elite class even if they were talented, capable people, because family status was crucial in that society. In the age of feudalism, people from the common class thought that was ridiculous and wished to change the social system so that one could achieve high status regardless of which class they were from. As long as people were capable and responsible, they should be equal members of society.

Now we are living in such a society. I think this is very fortunate. Yet, people want to be elite regardless of their capability or talent. Everybody wants to go to a first-class university to join the elite. Consequently, schoolchildren are put under great duress and forced to compete with each other in order to pass entrance examinations. I think it is a bizarre situation because, in order to select a small number of elite people, a large number of people must fail.

First of all, the whole Japanese population cannot become the elite. Society is like a play in a theater. Not all the actors can play the role of a prince or a princess. If we only have princes or princesses, we cannot make a play. A prince or a princess is not even necessarily the starring role. A chief retainer can be the star of a drama. A low-class official can create a great performance as the leading character in a drama. The important point is, even if I am a low-class official, I can give a masterly performance. Even if I play the role of a servant of a low-class official, that role is my life. Actors and actresses should have this attitude when they perform.

Wherever we are, the important thing to which we aspire is to perform masterfully with our karmic conditions in the present moment. This is the deep meaning of the *koan* I talked about, the title of *Genjo koan*. A violet blooms a violet flower. A rose blooms a rose flower. It is a mistake for a violet to think that a violet flower is too small and should have plastic and reconstructive surgery and bloom into a big flower like a rose. I heard that some people want to have surgery on their faces to make them into beautiful pop singers. I don't think such an attitude is healthy.

When I was in Nagano Prefecture during the summer, I saw a traffic admonition that said, "In driving, you are in the principal role." This is true not only for car-driving, but it is even more so in life-driving. When we are living our lives, we ourselves are in the principal role. We wholeheartedly give a masterly performance with our own faces, with our own personality, with our karmic attributes, within our present role in the present situation. When all people live with such an attitude, aiming at our own masterly performance, our society truly becomes one of matured people. In our society, to create such maturity is our goal. I think that this society is childish because people are like hungry ghosts. They complain that they cannot be elite and they cannot satisfy their hunger for fame and profit.

Life is a bird; life is a fish.

With immeasurable and boundless Life, a servant gives a masterly performance as a servant, a low-class official gives a masterly performance as a low-class official, and a prince gives a masterly performance as a prince. A society in which each and every person gives a masterly performance with his or her karmic attributes can be called a really mature society. It is a society of buddhas. I deeply wish to create such a mature society, where people live making prostration to their own life. I believe that is living the bodhisattva vows.

And we should go beyond this. There is practice-enlightenment— this is the Way of living beings.

As for the true life, it is important that each one of us gives a masterly performance with our karmic attributes and the situation of the present moment. And yet, this does not mean that we have to be certified to offer a masterly performance. It has nothing to do with pass or fail or a license. This profundity of the self that is the self cannot be measured from outside with yardsticks. We cannot judge it. Only when we are carrying out the practice/enlightenment of infinite profundity can we give a masterly performance. Therefore, Dogen Zenji says, "We should go beyond this. There is practice-enlightenment." We have to endlessly carry out practice-enlightenment with our own concrete, practical activities. This is the way we live out our very own concrete lives.

(12) *Therefore, if there are fish that would swim or birds that would fly only after investigating the entire ocean or sky, they would find neither path nor place. When we make this very place our own, our practice becomes the manifestation of reality* (Genjo koan). *When we make this path our own, our activity naturally becomes actualized reality* (Genjo koan). *This path, this place, is neither big nor small, neither self nor others. It has not existed before this moment nor has it come into existence now. Therefore, [the reality of all things] is thus. In the same way, when a person engages in practice-enlightenment in the Buddha Way, as the person realizes one dharma, the person permeates that dharma; as the person encounters one practice, the person [fully] practices that practice. [For this] there is a place and a path. The boundary of the known is not clear; this is because the known [which appears limited] is born and practiced simultaneously with the complete penetration of the* Buddha *dharma. We should not think that what we have attained is conceived by ourselves and known by our discriminating mind. Although complete enlightenment is immediately actualized, its intimacy is such that it does not necessarily form as a view. [In fact] viewing is not something fixed.*

This is a matter of course. A fish can swim even if it does not investigate the whole ocean. A bird can fly even if it does not know the entire sky. As I said before, a goldfish in a small goldfish bowl swims the totality of water. And when a small sparrow flies from a tiny twig to another twig, it is flying the whole sky. We don't need to discuss this.

However, though this is true of a fish or a bird, I wonder whether it is possible to simply apply this to our lives today. I am sure human life was not so different from the life of a fish or a bird in ancient times. But today, it seems that we cannot live without seeing the situation of the whole society.

More than ten years ago, I created a new origami, which I thought had some merit. The way of folding the paper was simple, yet sophisticated. I published it proudly as an original production. After that, an origami artist told me that it was interesting but seemed similar to origami that someone else had published earlier. He said this in such a way that I could not tell whether he praised it or criticized it. When I investigated the origami, I found the work was done before mine and with the same idea. Some people thought that I pirated the idea from the other person's origami work and published it as my own. I could not refute that the origami was published earlier.

In a small field such as origami, it is not strange that two people have the same or a similar idea. As a matter of fact, lately there are some origami artists who have copied the works I made and published in 1955 and 1962, grandly publishing them in their own books as original works. I have never complained about them. However, since my pride as an origami master wouldn't allow me to do the same, I immediately wrote a letter of apology to the person who had published the same work before me. Although many origami books are sent to me, I don't have time to examine all of them. That is why I made this mistake.

So today, we need to know the overall circumstances of a subject in society. We cannot swim or fly without knowing what is happening in the world by collecting the necessary information. Housewives get information about sales through TV or newspaper ads to find a good deal.

We are living in the information age. We cannot live unless we collect lots of information. In small fields such as origami or shopping, this is not such a big problem, but in managing a big company or governing a country, people don't accept an apology like, "I am sorry. I didn't know." Big companies and governments try to collect enormous amounts of information; they even hire spies. It is precisely because they have huge amounts of, or even too much, data that people easily get confused.

Consequently, it becomes important to process and sort information, selecting only that which is useful. Therefore, we input all that data into computers and take action according to the oracle of the computers. Although, honestly speaking, I have never seen a computer, it seems that is how people act today. So, if we say, as Dogen did, "If there are fish that would swim or birds that would fly only after investigating the entire ocean or sky, they would find neither path nor place," people today may think that is anachronistic.

However, what Dogen Zenji is saying here is not that those people who are collecting information and taking action accordingly are foolish or mistaken. Rather, we are actually living in the information society in the same way a fish or a bird is swimming in the water or flying in the sky. What Dogen Zenji is saying is not that gathering information is wrong, but the important thing is our attitude toward the information that we encounter.

As I said before, fundamentally work and the place of work are one; "I" and the world in which "I" am living are not-two. However, people today do not know that reality. As people often talk about processing information, they make a separation between themselves and information about the world. The important thing for them is their own desires. According to their desires, they process and sort information existing outside of themselves. Here, self and others, subject and object are clearly separated into two.

If we live with the same view about beings and system of values as President Marcos, it is clear that our end will be similar to President Marcos's.

I would like to talk about this point in terms of our view of existence, and our system of values. In this age, people think that things exist outside themselves. They think the self is like a god who can deal with objects outside itself and manipulate them according to its desires. Desires form the basis of value.

On the contrary, the attitude of the Buddha Way based on the *Buddha dharma* is different. There is nothing outside us. We and the things that we encounter are one. Work and the place of work are not two.

One mind is all things and all things are one mind. This is the view of existence in the *Buddha dharma*.

We aim at actualizing the reality of life as the reality of life, that is, how we can practice the *Buddha dharma* for the sake of the *Buddha dharma*. This is the Way. What is the difference between the two attitudes? The first deals with everything outside us in relation to our desires. The other is actualizing life through including everything we encounter. President Marcos is a very good example.

When he lost popularity and support among the people in his country, he escaped, taking his country's property illegally. For Mr. Marcos, the Philippine people's existence was outside, with no relationship to himself, so he used them to satisfy his desires. When the Philippine people became something he could not exploit to satisfy his desires, he escaped from his country with its wealth.

Contrary to Mr. Marcos, when Japan lost World War II, the emperor submitted a list of his property to General MacArthur and said, "I give it up. Use it in any way. But please save the Japanese people from starvation." For the Emperor, the Japanese people were his life. Therefore, he didn't think about how he alone could be saved. For the emperor, the actualization of his life includes the Japanese people. This was the most important thing.

When I compare Mr. Marcos with the emperor, it seems like one is a bad guy and the other is a good guy. I don't like such a stereotyped way of judging people. But I feel that Mr. Marcos was a good example. I pity him. He was laughed at by people all over the world and he could not find a place to settle down. Since he escaped with the stolen wealth in secret, he might think that he owns it now. However, sooner or later that wealth will be taken away, and finally he will die by the roadside in despair.

Actually, Mr. Marcos represents the people of today. The view of existence and system of values hidden in the way of life of people today is the same as Mr. Marcos's. Our way of doing things is the same as Mr. Marcos's. We have to know that we will die by the roadside in despair. We must be ready for it.

This morning, I read an article in the newspaper. The article quoted a father and mother who told their grandfather, "The way you eat your meals is messy. You should eat in a separate room by yourself." So, the grandfather started to eat meals in his room by himself. Then the children told their father, "When we grow up, we will do the same thing to you." It is clear that what we do now will lead to consequences in the future.

Not only common people's actions bring about karmic results. I think that which we human beings have been doing to the earth is precisely the same as what Mr. Marcos did to the Philippine people.

Human beings think they can do anything to the earth to satisfy their desires. Desire is the standard of their actions. If we continue to deal with the earth on that basis, nature will rebel against human beings. This has been cautioned against already. When the earth is destroyed and human beings cannot live anymore, some people think we should move to another planet with our plundered wealth, as Mr. Marcos did. They are looking for a planet where human beings can live when the earth is destroyed. However, unless human beings change their view of beings and system of values from that of Mr. Marcos, they will have the same problems on another planet. The secret wealth will be taken away and we will have to die by the roadside in despair.

> *Therefore, if there are fish that would swim or birds that would fly only after investigating the entire ocean or sky, they would find neither path nor place.*

Therefore, Dogen Zenji is saying not that we should avoid gathering information but that the information society is where we are living right now, and we should live the "Life of Buddha," which includes the information that we encounter.

What does this mean? We put things outside ourselves as separate and collect information about them. We deal with everything according to our purpose, which is nothing other than our desires. That is a kind of value judgment—from such an attitude, we cannot find our own non-dualistic way of life. This is simply because we cannot collect all the information about everything. Unless we are the creator of the world (God), no matter how widely and in what detail we collect information, there will be something missing. This is just a matter of course. This is what Dogen Zenji meant when he said in section ten, "When we listen to the reality of myriad things, we must know that there are inexhaustible characteristics in either an ocean or mountains and there are many other worlds in the four directions."

Even though we are living in the age of science and we think that we have enough knowledge about everything, still we should know that there are inexhaustible characteristics in either an ocean or mountains. We should not think that the information that we have collected and the scientific knowledge that we have obtained is enough. Even if we had all the information and knowledge about things, we still could not live the true way of life.

Rather, if we had all the information we have now, including the inexhaustible characteristics in either an ocean or mountains, everything would be the "Life of Buddha." Whether we have information or not, we should encounter everything with the attitude that everything we encounter is our lives. This is the ultimate way of life.

I value and try to collect as much information as possible. Yet, since I am a priest, it is a matter of course that I am an uninformed person. It is amazing that such an uninformed person as I can live. However, even a goldfish swimming in a small goldfish bowl is swimming in the whole water. Even a sparrow that flies from twig to twig is flying in the whole sky. I believe even an uninformed person like myself, who doesn't know anything about the trend of current society, is living the all-pervading universal life. It is precisely the attitude that encounters everything in my life as the "Life of Buddha," which penetrates heaven and earth.

In other words, "I" and "the things I encounter" are not two. This is the Buddhist view of existence. However, in this case existence is not our usual concept of "existence." We should value this reality of life that is not-two. This is what Dogen Zenji meant when he said, "We should practice the *Buddha dharma* for the sake of the *Buddha dharma*. This is the Way." How deep can we actualize this not-two "Life of Buddha" right now, right here? This is the Buddhist view and system of values.

To work to actualize "Life" as the "Life" that is not-two is as follows:

> *When we make this very place our own, our practice becomes the manifestation of reality* (Genjo koan). *When we make this path*

our own, our activity naturally becomes actualized reality (Genjo koan). *This path, this place, is neither big nor small, neither self nor others. It has not existed before this moment, nor has it come into existence now. Therefore, [the reality of all things] is thus.*

This path and this place refer to actually living out real thus-ness before the separation between self-mind and myriad things. This driving of the reality of life is the very path and place. The path in terms of the Buddha Way is not some road fabricated outside ourselves. Rather, the path is our own attitude living right now, right here.

To live out this reality of life for the sake of this reality of life is the not-two of self/others and subject/object that is this path and this place. Since this path and this place are the not-two reality of life, they are before the separation between things. Since this path and this place are before the separation between self and others, they are neither self nor others. They are before the separation of past and present: "It has not existed before this moment, nor has it come into existence now." It is just as it is.

Therefore, [the reality of all things] is thus.

Here Dogen Zenji first uses the word *Genjo koan.* After a long discussion about *Buddha dharma* and Buddha Way, he finally uses the word *Genjo koan.*

Then what is *Genjo koan? Genjo koan* is to continue life-driving. It is the not-two of self/others, of subject/object *as* the reality of life before the separation between self and others and subject and object. This life-driving is *Genjo koan.* That is the truth of life in terms of the present moment becoming the present moment. This is the absolute way of life.

In *Shobo genzo Zazenshin* (*Acupuncture Needle of Zazen*), Dogen Zenji expresses *Genjo koan,* saying, "Actualized within not-thinking. Manifested within non-interacting." Not-thinking means beyond thinking. Non-interacting means without separation with others.

For example, since it is beyond thinking and without separation, in the role of servant, to be a servant is the actualization of the reality of life as a servant. Without thinking, "The role of a servant is not good.

I want to become a king," without comparing or bargaining, we just aim to be a perfect servant. This is the ordinary profundity in which the present moment becomes the present moment. In the ordinary way, in our body, the head plays the role of head, hands play the role of hands, and legs play the role of legs. This is the profundity of how our body can work in a healthy way.

In living out myself, I play the primary role. This is obvious. Therefore, the most important thing to aim at is how we can play that primary role perfectly, with deepest mastery. This is a matter of course.

Aiming at this ordinary profundity of the present moment becoming the present moment is to live ourselves. We should not make a mistake in choosing the direction of our life. Like most people today, if we aim only at satisfying our own desires, we follow a fundamentally mistaken view about living life.

> *In the same way, when a person engages in practice-enlightenment in the Buddha Way, as the person realizes one dharma, the person permeates that dharma; as the person encounters one practice, the person [fully] practices that practice.*

Finally, Dogen Zenji briefly concludes what he has been discussing. That is, "as the person realizes one dharma, that person permeates that dharma; as the person encounters one practice, that person [fully] practices that practice." As a practitioner of the Buddha Way, we have to always keep this point in mind, to continuously and endlessly practice to deepen our lives. As I said, though a fish swims in the whole water, we cannot say that a fish has completely finished swimming in the whole water. There is no time that a bird has completely finished flying in the whole sky. When a bird stops flying, the bird stops being a bird. No matter how far we fly or swim, we encounter everything as our own life, right now and right here. We just live in the circumstances we encounter.

If we talk about enlightenment in terms of living out the reality of life, we are already enlightened by the Shakyamuni Buddha. He said, "I and the great earth and all living beings attain the Way at the same time. Mountains, rivers, grasses, and trees, all have become Buddha." Therefore, we are living within the light of enlightenment, as Dogen

Zenji said, "These ten-direction worlds are all Buddha's land," and as the Pure Land Buddhist sutra said, "The light of Amitabha (Infinite Life) Tathagata embraces all living beings without rejecting anyone." However, unless we carry out practice/enlightenment right now and right here, the light of enlightenment is not actualized. Continuously actualizing "as the person realizes one dharma, that person permeates that dharma; as the person encounters one practice, that person [fully] practices that practice" is living out enlightenment. And within the way of actualization, there is infinite depth.

Earlier, Dogen Zenji said, "The depth is the same as the height. [To investigate the significance of] the length and brevity of time, we should consider whether the water is great or small, and understand the size of the moon in the sky." Therefore, within the ordinariness of "the present moment becomes the present moment," there is also infinite profundity. It is never a matter of using some tool of mystical intuition to obtain an entity outside ourselves called enlightenment. This is a common, mistaken idea of enlightenment.

> *[For this] there is a place and a path. The boundary of the known is not clear; this is because the known [which appears limited] is born and practices simultaneously with the complete penetration of the* Buddha dharma.

Within the attitude of realizing one dharma, permeating that dharma, and encountering one practice, practicing that practice, therein lays the "path" and "place" to live out the "not-two" reality of life. The path is not a way outside of us to reach somewhere else. Rather, this path is an attitude with which the reality of life awakens to the reality of life itself and actualizes it endlessly. In this case, the boundary of life actualization cannot be known. This is because the attitude of practice in which the reality of life awakens to the reality of life itself right now, right here, is born together and is practiced together with the complete penetration of the reality of life.

In the reality of life awakening to the reality of life, there is no dichotomy of the subject that awakens and the object of awakening. We can understand this when we think of driving: driving without sleeping, without being involved in illusory thinking, without too much tension or being drunk is important. And yet, while we are driving a car, if we are *thinking* of whether we are driving safely without thinking, without sleeping, without too much tension or being drunk or not, then that is dangerous. Without thinking such things, just to be awake while we drive moment by moment is important.

> *We should not think that what we have attained is conceived by ourselves and known by our discriminating mind. Although complete enlightenment is immediately actualized, its intimacy is such that is does not necessarily form as a view. [In fact] viewing is not something fixed.*

When we live the reality of life, the reality of life is immediately actualized. The reality of life is before the separation between being and non-being. It is not necessarily seen. It is not formed as a view (*kenjo*). Here, Dogen Zenji contrasts the similar words "*genjo*" and "*kenjo* (view forming). I think Dogen Zenji uses the word *kenjo* in order to point out that we should simply see reality before seer and seen separate into subject and object.

Intimacy (*mitsu-u*) means being prior to separation between being (*u*) and non-being (*mu*). The reality prior to separation between being and non-being cannot be divided into subject, which is seeing, and object, which is seen. This is the same point as my eyes cannot see my eyes. The expression "not-necessarily (*ka-hitsu*)" refers to the reality before separation between any dichotomies such as seeing/seen, grasping/grasped. This is the same as the common Zen expression, "thusness," "suchness," "as-it-is-ness."

Fan the wind of life that penetrates heaven and earth right now, right here, breathing a breath for each moment.

> *(13) Zen Master Hotetsu of Mount Mayoku was waving a fan. A monk approached him and asked, "The nature of wind is ever present and permeates everywhere. Why are you waving a fan?"*
>
> *The master said, "You know only that wind's nature is ever present—you do not know how it permeates everywhere."*
>
> *The monk said, "How does wind permeate everywhere?"*

The master just continued waving the fan.

The monk bowed deeply.

The genuine experience of Buddha dharma *and the vital path that has been correctly transmitted are like this. To say we should not wave a fan because the nature of wind is ever present, and that we should feel the wind even when we don't wave a fan, is to know neither ever-presence nor the wind's nature. Since the wind's nature is ever present, the wind of the Buddha's family enables us to realize the gold of the great Earth and to transform the [water of the] long river into cream.*

In this final section Dogen Zenji introduces an appropriate example of what he has been discussing. This is a very simple story that we can understand without much explanation. Although the wind-nature is ever present in heaven and earth, if we don't use a fan, the wind is not actualized. If we don't use a fan, we don't have wind.

I would like to use another example. We human beings can be physically alive precisely because we breathe a breath each moment, right now, right here. If we think that because we breathed a lot in the past, we don't need to breathe right now, we will die. In the same way, if we think that because we practiced a lot and attained enlightenment in the past, we don't need to practice anymore, such enlightenment is already dead.

Living enlightenment is the same as breathing each moment; we arouse bodhi-mind, moment by moment, billions of times, and practice right now and right here. This is called *shusho-ichinyo* (practice and verification are one) or *shojo-no-shu* (practice/enlightenment). This is the way life is.

Since the wind's nature is ever present, the wind of the Buddha's family enables us to realize the gold of the great Earth and to transform the [water of the] long river into cream.

The wind-nature is ever present. Life is enlightened from the beginningless beginning. It is not that wind-nature is ever present only after we attain personal, mystical, and intuitive enlightenment. The reality of the ever-presence of the wind-nature is not something we have to create through practice. Rather, we fan this beginningless realization with endless practice. This is the wind of the Buddha's family. And such wind enables us to realize the gold of the great earth and to transform the [water of the] long river into cream.

Here, the great earth and the long river refer to all beings. Gold means absolute. Transform the water into cream means to make milk into delicious cream, butter, or cheese. The wind of Buddha's family, the wind of the practice of the reality of life as the reality of life, enables everything to actualize its absolute form and mature our way of life so that we reach the other shore. This is nirvana.

When we read the *Genjo koan* in this way, we can understand that from the title to the end, Dogen Zenji focuses on one topic, *Genjo koan*, and step by step shows its infinite profundity. I hope we read this chapter many times and illuminate our own minds with this old teaching, continually deepening our life.

Finally, I would like to offer my humble poem about *Genjo koan*.

GENJO KOAN
*Ordinary profundity of the present moment becoming
the present moment*

All of us are always living the "present moment"
the profundity of the present moment
Even when we don't know it and are blind to it
the profundity of the present moment is embracing us
 as the present moment
All of us are living out the self-interpenetrating whole world
the profundity of the self-interpenetrating whole world
Whether we know it or not
even when we doubt it and reject it
Still we are the self-interpenetrating whole world
Including delusions and doubts
Thus is the present moment of the self-interpenetrating
 whole world
Fanning the wind of the profundity of life
right now and right here—
is *Genjo koan*
the ordinary profundity of
the present moment becoming the present moment